ADVANCED PROJECTS FOR
Microsoft® Access 2000
MICROSOFT® CERTIFIED EDITION

Philip A. Koneman
Colorado Christian University

Prentice
Hall

Upper Saddle River, NJ 07458

Acquisitions Editor: Lucinda Gatch
Assistant Editor: Jennifer Stagman
Managing Editor: Monica Stipanov
Editorial Assistant: Mary Toepfer
Senior Marketing Manager: Kris King
AVP/Director of Production and Manufacturing: Michael Weinstein
Associate Director Manufacturing: Vincent Scelta
Manager, Production: Gail Steier de Acevedo
Project Manager: Lynne Breitfeller
Design Manager: Pat Smythe
Manufacturing Buyer: Lynne Breitfeller

ISBN 0-13-088541-X

Microsoft and the Microsoft Office User Specialist Logo are registered trademarks of Microsoft Corporation in the United States and other countries. Prentice Hall is an independent entity from Microsoft Corporation and not affiliated with Microsoft Corporation in any manner. This publication may be used in assisting students to prepare for a Microsoft Office User Specialist Exam. Neither Microsoft Corporation, its designated review company, nor Prentice Hall warrants that use of this publication will ensure passing the relevant Exam.

Use of the Microsoft Office User Specialist Approved Courseware Logo on this product signifies that it has been independently reviewed and approved in complying with the following standards:

> *Acceptable coverage of all content related to the expert level Microsoft Office Exam entitled "Access 2000"; and sufficient performance-based exercises that relate closely to all required content, based on sampling of text.*

Prentice-Hall International (UK) Limited, London
Prentice-Hall of Australia Ptry. Limited Sydney
Prentice-Hall Hispanoamericana, S.A., Mexico
Prentice-Hall of India Private Limited. New Dehli
Prentice-Hall of Japan, Inc. Tokyo
Editora Prentice-Hall do Brasil, Ltda., Rio de Janerio

Printed in the United States of America
www.prenhall.com/selectadvanced

10 9 8 7 6 5 4 3 2 1

Dedication

I dedicate this work to my wife, Tanya, and our children, Megan, Jonathan, and Andrew. As always, they have supported me during this project.

Acknowledgements

I wish to thank Marlen Wells and Kevin Miller, two colleagues who provide invaluable encouragement to me.

I also wish to thank the administration at Colorado Christian University for granting me a sabbatical, which afforded me the time to complete this project.

To Lucinda Gatch, Monica Stipanov, Jennifer Stagman and Lynne Breitfeller at Prentice Hall: Thank you all for working with me under extreme deadlines and tight schedules to bring this work forth. Each of you went beyond the call of duty to make this work possible. It is a joy to work with such dedicated professionals.

Contents

Preface

The SELECT Lab Series uses a class-tested, highly visual, project-based approach that teaches students through tasks that use step-by-step instructions. You will find extensive 4-color figures that guide learners through the basic skills and procedures necessary to demonstrate proficiency using each software application.

SELECT Lab Series: Advanced Projects for Microsoft® Access 2000 introduces an all-new design with ample space for note taking. The easy-to-follow, clean presentation uses bold color and a unique design program that helps reduce distraction and keeps students focused and interested as they work. We have developed additional instructional features to further enhance the students' learning experience as well as provide the opportunity for those who want to go beyond the scope of the book to explore the features of Access 2000 on the Web. Each project concludes with a review section that includes a Summary, Key Terms and Operations, Study Questions (multiple choice, short answer, fill-in, and discussion), and two Hands-On Exercises. In addition, two to six On Your Own Exercises provide students the opportunity to practice and gain further experience with the material covered in the projects.

Microsoft Certification

The content of this text is driven by the Microsoft Office User Specialist (MOUS) guidelines, and the author has developed the material from the ground up to reflect these objectives. Everyone who masters the projects in this text will be prepared to take the expert level exam in Microsoft® Office 2000. It is becoming more and more important in today's competitive job market to have the skills necessary to be productive with today's most widely used applications software. SELECT Lab Series: Advanced Projects for Microsoft® Access 2000 is designed with this purpose in mind.

Access 2000

The new Microsoft® Access 2000 features improved tools that simplify traditional Access-processing tasks and adds an expanded menu of Web-related capabilities and e-mail integration. Ten new SELECT: Advanced Projects for Microsoft® Access 2000 introduce students to features of Access, focusing on the MOUS objectives needed to prepare students for the expert certification exam.

Features

Running Case

The Selections, Inc. Department store is an all-new case for SELECT Lab Series: Projects for Microsoft® Access 2000. As a Running Case, Selections, Inc. puts students in an environment they can relate to, both as students and as future professionals. Each project begins with a scenario that puts students in the department store where they perform tasks that relate to a particular area or division of the store. For example, this Advanced Access module has students create product information for Ritchey Bicyles. Using Access 2000's powerful tools, the students integrate various graphics into company brochures for printing or publishing on the web.

Students relate what they're doing in Access 2000 to a real-world situation that helps prepare them for what they may encounter in the business world as professionals.

Challenge/Solution/Setup

Once the student is familiar with the Running Case scenario for the project, the Challenge explains what they are actually going to do as they work through the tasks, and the Solution summarizes a plan for achieving that goal. The Setup provides the settings necessary to ensure that the screen the student sees will match what is shown in the book.

Web Tip

This all-new feature provides the student with links to helpful Web sites and tips for locating additional information about specific topics on the World Wide Web. Web Tips often relate to Access 2000, but include tips students can use in their everyday lives. Each project contains numerous Web Tips that encourage students to explore Web sites that relate to the tasks they are performing in the application, highlight professional organizations that enhance the material, or direct them to topics of interest on their own. Because the Web is constantly changing, some links referenced in Web Tips may become inactive during the course.

Check Point

Check Points are placed at intervals throughout each project and provide review questions that seek to assess a student's conceptual or procedural understanding of the current task.

Break Point

Each project in SELECT: Advanced Projects for Microsoft® Access 2000 has been designed to take approximately one hour in the lab. Because students learn at different paces or may not have a full hour to complete a project, the Break Point feature appears at about the midpoint in each project and alerts students of a good stopping point if they need a break but want to continue the project later. Break Points take the guess work out of having to decide whether or not it's appropriate to stop, and make it easier for students to start working on a project that they may not have time to complete.

Tips and Troubleshooting Boxes

These feature boxes, popular with both instructors and students, appear throughout the text and have been revised and updated for SELECT: Advanced Projects for Microsoft® Access 2000.

TIP Tip boxes include material that may be useful but that is not required in the step-by-step task instructions.

TROUBLESHOOTING Troubleshooting boxes alert students to problems they may encounter while using the applications and suggest possible causes for the problems along with potential solutions.

Modifying Table Design and Setting Table Properties

Now that you have created tables and established relationships in your database, you are almost ready to begin designing queries, which you will do in Project 4. Before you combine data from the tables in your solution, however, you will want to modify the table design to improve the accuracy of the information in your database.

Objectives

After completing this project, you will be able to:

➤ Rename the primary key field in a table

➤ Change the field size property of text fields in the Customers and Products tables

➤ Define data validation criteria

➤ Set data validation text

➤ Test validation criteria

➤ Create and modify input masks

➤ Create and modify Lookup fields

Running Case

As you learned in Project 2, once you have designed the table structure for your database, you are ready to begin designing other database objects that pull information together, such as queries, forms, and reports. However, you want your database to be as efficient as possible to preserve the integrity of data. Therefore, it is important to consider ways in which you might modify the table specifications to produce the most accurate information possible.

The **Introduction** sets the stage for the project and explains its purpose.

Clearly defined and measurable **Objectives** outline the skills covered.

The **Running Case** puts the student in the real-life environment of the Selections, Inc. department store.

The Challenge states the reasoning for the project.

The Solution describes the plan for completing the project, which consists of tasks leading to the final product.

The Setup

To create the three tables and establish the relationships described in the previous section, launch Microsoft Access, open the *Selections.mdb* database you modified in Project 1, and make sure that you select the settings listed in Table 2.1. If you need additional assistance setting these options, refer to Figure 1.1 through 1.3 of Project 1. This will ensure that your screen matches the illustrations and the tasks in this project function as described.

Table 2.1   Access Settings

Location	Make these settings:
Office Shortcut Bar	If the Office Shortcut bar is visible, close it by right-clicking the Office icon on the shortcut bar and choosing Exit.
Office Assistant	Hide the Office Assistant.
Tools, Customize	Click the Toolbars tab and display the Database toolbar and the Menu Bar, as shown in Figure 1.1 of Project 1, if they are not currently visible.
Tools, Customize	Click the Options tab, and make sure the check box to display recently used menu commands first is deselected, as shown in Figure 1.2 of Project 1.
Tools, Options	Click the View tab and display Status bar, Startup dialog box, New object shortcuts, and Windows in Taskbar, as shown in Figure 1.3 of Project 1.

Understanding Relationships

As you learned in Project 1, a relational database management system (RDBMS) often establishes relationships between relations. Entities and their relationships are often graphically represented using E-R diagrams. Figure 2.3 shows a high-level E-R diagram of the four tables your database will contain.

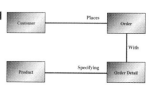

FIGURE 2.3

PROJECT 5

The Challenge

Mr. Traylor wants you to design an attractive and functional user interface for the Selections, Inc. database. He has asked you to create the following screen forms.

First, he wants you to design a form for entering and editing customer records. As with any e-commerce database, there will most likely be thousands of customer transactions each week, so you need to design a customer form that allows data entry personnel to add new customers to the database as well as search for existing customer records.

Mr. Traylor anticipates that the online product offering will expand greatly, thus he wants you to design a form displaying the products in the database. This form should allow users to locate current products as well as add new product records to the database.

Finally, Mr. Traylor needs you to create a form for entering customer orders. This form should display customer, product, order, and order detail information. In addition, it should also list the extended price for each item on a customer's order, and display the order total.

The Solution

Access has the tools and capabilities that will enable you to meet each of Mr. Traylor's interface design objectives. The easiest way to create a form displaying customer information is to create an AutoForm based upon the Customers table. Once you have created the AutoForm, you can use Form Design view to make any necessary modifications. Figure 5.1 displays the Customers form you will create.

FIGURE 5.1

The Setup tells the students exactly which settings should be chosen so their computer screens match the illustrations in the book.

Each topic begins with a brief introductory paragraph that explains the concepts and operations students will learn.

An illustration shows the typical screen the student will see.

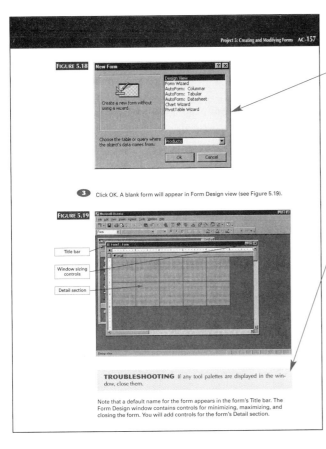

Appropriate, full-color **illustrations** move the emphasis away from text and toward the visual-based application.

Tip and **Troubleshooting** boxes appear at appropriate places throughout each project to highlight important, helpful information pertinent to the topic being discussed.

New **Check Points** reinforce a concept.

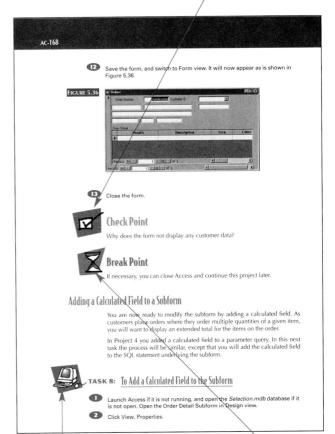

Clearly defined **Tasks** guide students step-by-step through each process, providing reassurance and increasing confidence for independent or group work.

New **Break Points** show where students can pause within a project.

Web Tip boxes refer students to Internet sites and offer helpful information about using the World Wide Web.

Project 3: Modifying Table Design and Setting Table Properties AC-95

Using Lookup Fields

A database with data stored in multiple tables is efficient because you can table data when it is needed. For example, by adding a lookup field to the Orders table, you can look up a specific customer by Customer ID and associate this data with each time card record. From an end user perspective, this means that by simply selecting a customer number in a drop-down list, the name and address information will appear in a form, as you will see in Project 5. A *lookup field* displays values looked up from a related table and displays them in a list. The data can be looked up because the foreign key in the table displaying the looked up list corresponds to the primary key in the table that contains the values. A lookup list is based upon existing data in a table or query, or upon a value list that you create.

 Web Tip

For more information on lookup fields, visit
http://msdn.microsoft.com/library/officedev/off2000/acdecWorkingWith
LookupFieldsS.htm

Why use lookup fields? In a database containing relationships, a related (child) table must have a value as the foreign key that matches a primary key value in the parent table. If you have enforced referential integrity, an error message will occur if an invalid value is entered into the foreign key field of the child table because there is no associated primary key. To prevent an error such as this from occurring, you can look up a corresponding value in the parent table. Because the user can select the values from a list instead of typing it into the field, you will always have a valid entry in the foreign key field.

> **TIP** A lookup field requires a relationship between tables. If one does not exist, Access will create it.

You will also add a lookup field to the Order Detail table. What data will you look up? As a customer places an order, each order detail record specifies a single item that will appear in the customer's invoice. Therefore, by looking up a product using its product number, a customer can specify each item appearing on the order. In the task that follows, you will create and modify a lookup field in the Orders table.

 TASK 7: To Create and Modify a Lookup Field in the Orders Table

1 Open the Orders table in Design view.

2 Click the CustID field in the upper pane of the Table Design grid to select it.

Summary and Exercises

Summary

- Once you have created a table structure, you can modify the properties of specific fields in the table using the Table Design grid in Table Design view.
- To validate data as it is entered into fields, set the DataValidation property of one or more fields in a table.
- When you add data validation specifications to a field, it is a good idea to set the ValidationText property of the field as well, so that a descriptive message is displayed when the validation criterion is violated.
- An input mask provides a preset format for entering data into a field.
- You can use a lookup field to assist data entry by looking up corresponding records in a related table.

Key Terms and Operations

Key Terms

display control	validation rule
input mask	validation text
InputMask property	ValidationRule property
lookup field	ValidationText property
row source	

Operations

change the field size property of text fields	create an input mask
change the ValidationText property of fields	modify a lookup field
create a lookup field	rename a primary key field
	specify validation rules
	test a validation rule

Study Questions

Multiple Choice

1. You should always change the validation text property of a field when you enter a(n):
   a. input mask.
   b. lookup field.
   c. relationship.
   d. validation rule.
   e. row Source.

A **Summary** in bulleted-list format further reinforces the Objectives and the material presented in the project.

Key terms are boldface and italicized throughout each project, and then listed for handy review in the summary section at the end of the project.

Study questions bring the content of the project into focus again and allow for independent or group review of the material learned.

Web Tip

If you do not have a copy of this file, you can download it from the Select Web site at http://www.prenhall.com/selectadvanced.

Complete the following:

1. Click Tools, Relationships.
2. Add both the Employees and the PayrollData tables to the Relationships window.
3. Create a one-to-one relationship using the EmpID field. Enforce referential integrity. The relationship will appear as shown in Figure 2.32.

FIGURE 2.32

4. Save your changes, close the Relationships window, and close the database.

On Your Own Exercises

1. Compacting a Database

Whenever you modify your database objects, the database file grows in size. If you open your database from a floppy disk, it is a good idea to periodically compact it. By keeping the file size as small as possible, you can locate and manipulate records more quickly.

To compact the Selections database:

1. Open the *Selections* database file on your floppy disk.
2. Select Database Utilities from the Tools menu.
3. Select Compact and Repair Database from the cascading menu.
4. Close the database when you are finished.

---

2. A query returning records that meet one condition or another is called a(n) _____ query.

3. Queries are modified in _____ view.

4. A _____ _____ uses an expression to return data in a query.

5. Fields appearing in a query are displayed in the _____ pane of the Query Design window.

6. You can prompt the user for a specific value for returning records by creating a _____ query.

7. When you run a query, the results are displayed in a _____.

8. The _____ property of a field determines whether currency data is displayed as such.

9. Queries can be based on one or more _____ or _____.

10. A query returning records meeting two conditions simultaneously is called a(n) _____ query.

For Discussion

1. How does a query datasheet differ from a table datasheet?
2. What is a calculated field and where does it store data?
3. How do you create a parameter query?
4. How does an AND condition differ from an OR condition?
5. How do you create a query based on more than one table?

Hands-On Exercises

1. Filtering Records in a Query

There might be times when you need to quickly filter records returned by an Access query. When you filter a query datasheet, the procedure is identical to filtering a table's datasheet. You have two options: filter by form, and filter by selection. In this exercise you will filter a query's datasheet using these two methods.

To Filter a Query Using Filter By Selection and Filter By Form.

1. Open the *Products.mdb* database.

Web Tip

If you do not have a copy of this file, you can download it from the Select Web site at http://www.prenhall.com/selectadvanced.

2. Open the Inventory query in Datasheet view.

In-depth **Hands-On Exercises** present tasks for building on the skills acquired in the project.

Two to Six **On Your Own Exercises** are provided to invoke critical thinking and integration of project skills.

Appendix

The SELECT: Advanced Projects for Microsoft® Access 2000 book contains a useful appendix, Working with Access. It reviews the basic database objects you will create in Access, how to use the different objects views, and using the Office Assistant to get help. The goal is to provide a review of Access for students who need to brush up on their skills.

Student Supplements

Student Assessment Software SkillCheck Professional Plus for Microsoft® Office 2000 features fully interactive test items that allow students to answer questions by performing complete tasks in virtually any correct way the software allows. All of the essential software features are fully simulated, so no additional software is required. In addition to independently validated tests that cover beginning, intermediate, and advanced skills, each SkillCheck Professional Plus system includes a database of more than 100 interactive questions for each Office application. The instructor has complete control over every important aspect of testing and reporting, allowing users to customize or create tests with ease and speed.

Companion Web site SELECT: Advanced Projects for Microsoft® Access 2000 is accompanied by a Companion Web site. Interactive online study guides offer interactive quizzes, chat rooms, and much more to help students with the material covered in the text.

Instructor Supplements

Instructor's Resource CD-ROM Instructors get extra support for this text from supplemental materials, including the Instructor's Resource CD-ROM. The CD-ROM includes the entire Instructor's Manual in Microsoft Access format, and Test Manager™, a computerized test bank designed to create printed tests, network tests, and self-assessment quizzes. Student data files and completed data files for Study Questions, Hands-On Exercises, and On Your Own Exercises are clearly organized on the Instructor's Resource CD-ROM. PowerPoint slides, which include keywords, objectives, running case, and solutions, are also included on the Instructor's Resource CD-ROM.

The Instructor's Manual This manual includes a test bank, with multiple choice and fill-in-the-blank questions, as well as some screen captures that illustrate the solutions. The Instructor's Manual also includes expanded Student Objectives, Answers to Study Questions, and Additional Assessment Techniques. The Instructor's Manual is available on the Instructor's Resource CD-ROM and on the Companion Web site at www.prenhall.com/selectadvanced.

Companion Web site www.prenhall.com/selectadvanced Instructors can download the Instructor's Manual and PowerPoint slides from the Web site, as well as obtain the student data files and solutions files. Additional test questions will be available for each project, and an automatic assessment will be made after each test is taken. Each test question refers to the section to review in the text.

Introducing Access 2000

Introduction to Access 2000

Microsoft Access is the database management tool included with Microsoft Office 2000 Professional and Office 2000 Premium. As part of these Office packages, Access offers features that appeal to a variety of users. For those new to database management, Access includes numerous **wizards** that can help complete a variety of database tasks. For experienced database developers, Access provides powerful features for manipulating data in tables and legacy systems, as well as data residing on Web servers. Because Access and Visual Basic share features and capabilities, seasoned programmers can develop sophisticated stand-alone applications that utilize Access data, or custom front-ends that meet a variety of business needs in a client-server environment. In short, Access 2000 is a versatile database development tool suited for both new and seasoned developers.

Because Access is based on the relational database model, it offers powerful applications that can be implemented in a variety of ways. This overview will introduce you to basic database concepts and the Microsoft Access user interface.

Objectives

After completing this introduction, you will be able to:

➤ Define basic database concepts

➤ Identify Access database objects

➤ Identify the steps required to design a database

➤ Launch Microsoft Access and create a new database

➤ Identify Microsoft Access screen elements

➤ Close a database and exit Access

Basic Database Concepts

A **database** is a collection of information related to a particular subject or purpose. For example, most people keep a list of the names, addresses, and phone numbers of the people they contact frequently. The categories of information that you keep on each individual are most likely consistent. In database terms, each individual item of information in the list, such as first name or last name, is called a **field**. The field information for one person in the list is a **record**. Therefore, a database contains fields and records. Figure 0.1 refers to five fields and one record in a sample phone list.

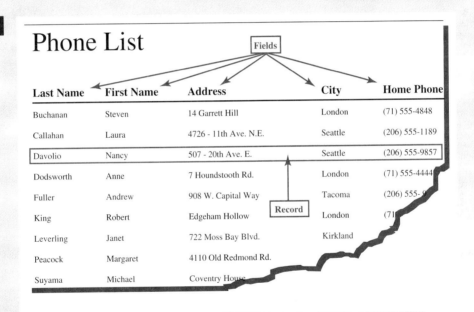

FIGURE 0.1

Phone List

Last Name	First Name	Address	City	Home Phone
Buchanan	Steven	14 Garrett Hill	London	(71) 555-4848
Callahan	Laura	4726 - 11th Ave. N.E.	Seattle	(206) 555-1189
Davolio	Nancy	507 - 20th Ave. E.	Seattle	(206) 555-9857
Dodsworth	Anne	7 Houndstooth Rd.	London	(71) 555-4444
Fuller	Andrew	908 W. Capital Way	Tacoma	(206) 555-9
King	Robert	Edgeham Hollow	London	(71
Leverling	Janet	722 Moss Bay Blvd.	Kirkland	
Peacock	Margaret	4110 Old Redmond Rd.		
Suyama	Michael	Coventry House		

Fields and a Record

> **TIP** Some sources will refer to a field as a column and a record as a row. Although these are not technical database terms, they are useful when you are viewing an Access datasheet that lists data in this row and column format.

When using Microsoft Access to store information, field and record information is contained in a database object called a **table**, or a two-dimensional grid containing field data. Figure 0.2 displays phone list data in a Microsoft Access table.

FIGURE 0.2

	Last Name	First Name	Address	City	Home Phone
▶	Buchanan	Steven	14 Garrett Hill	London	(71) 555-4848
	Callahan	Laura	4726 - 11th Ave. N.E.	Seattle	(206) 555-1189
	Davolio	Nancy	507 - 20th Ave. E.	Seattle	(206) 555-9857
	Dodsworth	Anne	7 Houndstooth Rd.	London	(71) 555-4444
	Fuller	Andrew	908 W. Capital Way	Tacoma	(206) 555-9482
	King	Robert	Edgeham Hollow	London	(71) 555-5598
	Leverling	Janet	722 Moss Bay Blvd.	Kirkland	(206) 555-3412
	Peacock	Margaret	4110 Old Redmond Rd.	Redmond	(206) 555-8122
	Suyama	Michael	Coventry House	London	(71) 555-7773

Record: 1 of 9

Table data

A computer application that you use to create and maintain databases is a **database management system (DBMS)**. Access enables you to store information in separate tables and use the data from one or more tables through relationships. A database management system that enables you to establish relationships among tables is a **relational database management system (RDBMS)**. Relational database management systems are the most powerful kinds of database applications available for microcomputers because an RDBMS supports the storage of field data in separate tables, and then links these tables to share information. Thus, the same data is not duplicated unnecessarily, which improves the overall accuracy of the information.

Microsoft Database Objects

In addition to tables, Microsoft Access databases contain other components, each of which is called an object. A **database object** is a component of the database that gives it functionality. Each database object belongs to a category of objects known as a **class**. For example a table for storing phone list information is a specific instance of a table object. Microsoft Access has seven classes of database objects. The type and purpose of each object is listed in Table 0.1.

In Microsoft Access, the database objects you create are stored in a single database file with an *.mdb* file extension.

Table 0.1   Seven Classes of Database Objects

Object Class	Purpose
Table	An organized collection of rows and columns used to store field data
Query	An object that is used to view, change, or organize data
Form	A graphical object that displays data from a table or a query in an easy to use format
Report	An object used to present your data in a printed format
Pages	Data access pages are HTML files designed in Access and formatted to display in a Web browser
Macro	A set of one or more actions that are used to automate common tasks such as opening a form or printing a report
Module	A collection of Visual Basic for Applications programming components that are stored together as a unit

Before you design a database, you need to understand how Access database objects relate to one another. Since tables are used to store field and record information, you must create at least one table before you create any other object. For this reason, tables are the primary objects in an Access database. Because queries allow you to organize and view data in different ways, a query is always based upon one or more tables. Queries can also display data from other queries.

Working with records in a row and column format is often tedious. For this reason, forms are used to make a table or query more accessible. In a well-designed database, users work with record and field data via forms, and not at the table level. While tables are required to store field data, forms based upon tables and queries are the objects users interact with directly. Forms are designed to make data access and maintenance easy, and are also usually designed to prevent users from inadvertently making destructive changes to table data. While forms and data access pages are appropriate for viewing data on the screen, reports are used to format table or query data for printed output.

Designing a Database

Creating an efficient and easy to use database requires careful planning. The time you spend planning a database prior to designing it will greatly benefit you! In general, you will complete five steps when designing a database. Database planning includes determining the overall specifications and requirements. Database design includes implementing these specifications using a software application such as Microsoft Access. Figure 0.3 displays the steps required to implement a database.

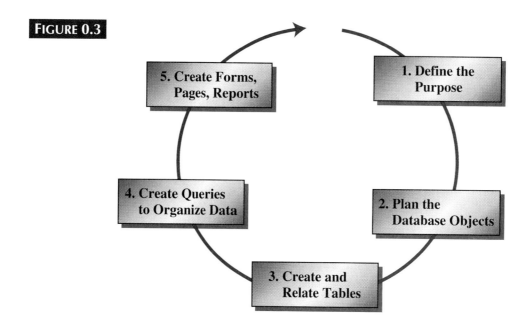

FIGURE 0.3

1. Defining the purpose

Define the overall purpose of the database, including a list of user specifications for input and output. Input and output specifications include tasks such as entering data from a common source (employment applications, or printing a report of payroll data for the current pay period). This data is often gathered by interviewing end users.

2. Planning the database objects

The objects contained in your database must be carefully planned. During this step in the design process you determine how data will be input into the database, and what kind of data outputs your solution must support. You will also need to determine the appropriate number of tables, the ways in which the records will be reorganized using queries, and the kinds of forms and reports your database will contain.

3. Creating and relating tables

You already know that tables are the primary objects. As you will see in Project 1, when designing a table you must first specify the kind of data each field will contain. You might decide to add some of the fields to additional tables. If your database contains more than one table, you will need to establish relationships among the tables.

4. Creating queries to reorganize data

You rarely need to see all of the field data in a database for all records at the same time. For this reason, queries are used to determine how data is reorganized to fulfill a specific request. You might need a listing of all customers from California, or a calculation of a member's outstanding balance. Queries are often used for this purpose.

5. Creating forms, pages, and reports

Because forms and reports are used by end users to work with records on the screen and in printed form, they are essential to a database. To share database information with other users, you can create data access pages to list records in HTML format that can be viewed with a Web browser. Forms, data access pages, and reports get their data from tables and queries.

Designing a full-fledged database is a complex and time-consuming process that requires careful planning and documentation. For the databases you will design in this module, use a word processor such as Microsoft Word to document your intended design.

In the projects in this module, you will complete the stages of database design for a database where the data is stored in four related tables, and then use the advanced features of Access to customize your database solution. In this Introduction you will launch Microsoft Access, and explore the user interface that has been designed to assist you in creating and maintaining relational databases.

Launching Microsoft Access and Creating a New Database

As with each of the Office applications, you can launch Microsoft Access in a variety of ways from the Windows desktop. In the steps that follow, you will use the Start button to launch Access and create a new database.

TASK 1:   To Launch Microsoft Access and Create a New Database

1   Click the Start button on the Windows taskbar.

2   Select Programs from the Start menu, and then choose Access, as shown in Figure 0.4.
The Microsoft Access dialog box shown in Figure 0.5 will appear. You have three options: opening an existing database using the list of recently used databases, creating a new database using the Database Wizard, or creating a blank database.

FIGURE 0.4

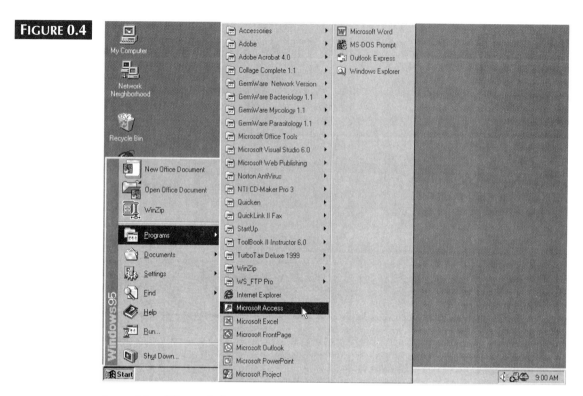

Launching Microsoft Access

FIGURE 0.5

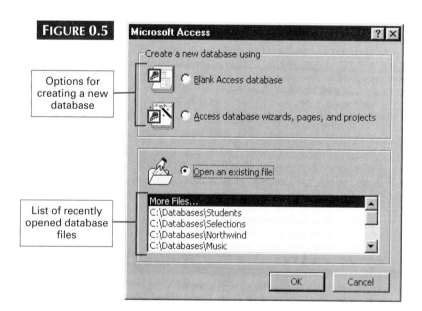

Options for creating a new database

List of recently opened database files

TROUBLESHOOTING The files you see displayed in the file list will be different on your computer. This list displays the databases that were most recently opened.

3 Select the Blank Database option and click OK.

The File New Database dialog box shown in Figure 0.6 will appear. Notice that the dialog box specifies a default location and database name.

FIGURE 0.6

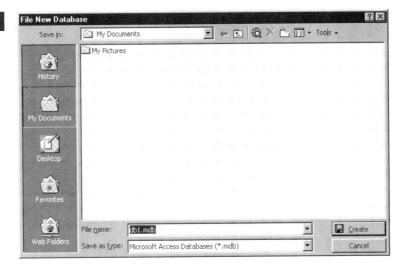

4 Select your floppy disk or network folder as the storage location, and type **Selections** as the database name, as shown in Figure 0.7.

FIGURE 0.7

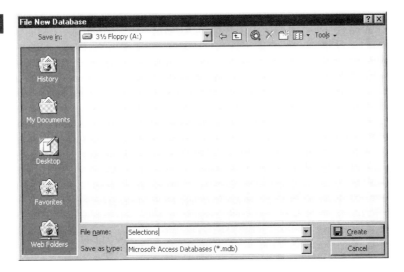

TIP When you name your database file, Access will automatically add the .mdb extension to the filename.

5 Click the Create button. Access creates a new database and displays the Database window shown in Figure 0.8.

FIGURE 0.8

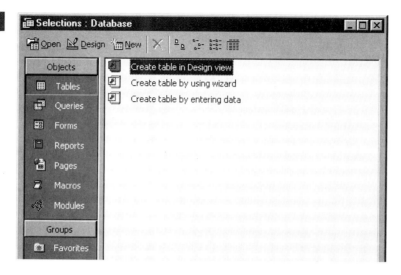

The Database window

> **TIP** Unlike other applications in the Office suite, only one database file can be open at a time.

Identifying Microsoft Access Screen Elements

You will notice three things about the database file you have just created. First, the Database window appears in a restored state within the Application window. Second, the name of the database appears in the title bar of the Database window. Third, the Database window contains object buttons that display the database objects you will create, and the uppermost Tables object button is active.

> **TIP** Notice that the object buttons in the Database window appear in the same order as the seven classes of database objects listed in steps for designing a database. Since tables are the primary repositories for the data in a database, the Tables object button is listed first.

You will notice that the Microsoft Access screen shown in Figure 0.9 has unique elements that are not seen in other Office applications.

The most striking feature of the Access interface is the Database window. As you create database objects, they will be displayed in the appropriate page for that particular object type. You will also notice that the Application window contains only one toolbar. You will use this toolbar in the same manner as the other toolbars in the Windows environment. Table 0.2 identifies the purpose of each interface element you see.

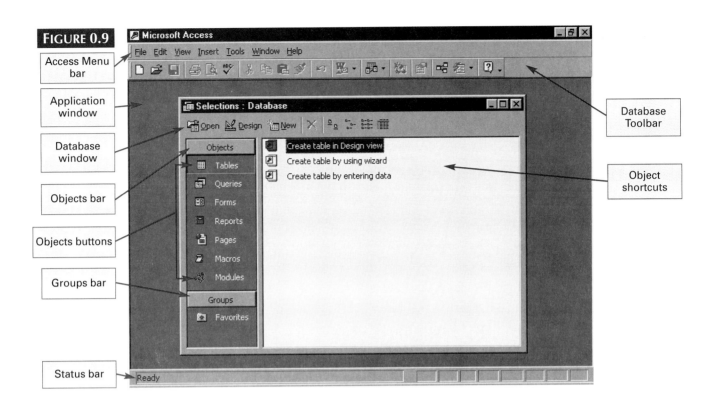

FIGURE 0.9

Table 0.2   Access Interface Elements

Screen Element	Purpose
Access menu bar	Provides access to the commands used to perform tasks.
Application title bar	Identifies the current application and contains Control Menu items for minimizing the Application window, restoring the Application window, and exiting the application.
Database toolbar	Provides shortcuts to the most common database tasks.
Database Window	Displays Object buttons for the seven kinds of database objects you can create.
Objects bar	Displays the database objects you create in the Objects bar. The Objects bar has an easy to use vertical orientation.
Groups bar	View your groups, which can contain shortcuts to database objects of different types.
Object Wizards and shortcuts	Create a new database object by using a wizard, or by opening a new database object in Design view. Once you create an object, open it using its Object shortcut.
Status bar	Displays program status, instructions, and information for performing specific tasks.

Closing Your Database File and Exiting Microsoft Access

Since you are finished with your database for the time being, you can close it and exit Microsoft Access. As you have not yet created any database objects, there is nothing to update in the file. Any time you close a database that you have modified, it is updated automatically.

TASK 2: <u>To Close Your Database File and Exit Microsoft Access</u>

1 Click the Close button of the Database window to close the database file.

2 Select Exit from the File menu, or click the Close button in the Application window to exit Microsoft Access.

Beyond the Basics: Exploring the Power of Microsoft Access 2000

In this Introduction we have reviewed basic database concepts that apply to Access 2000. You should be able to create a database file, and identify each Access interface element.

In the projects that follow you will be challenged to master the advanced tools and features available in Access 2000. Although no prior database experience is assumed, you will master the custom solutions more easily if you have used Access 2000 before. If you need to review additional database concepts and procedures in Access, please refer to the Appendix. Here is a summary of what you will learn in the next ten projects.

In *Part I* of this module you will learn how to design and develop a database solution that you can implement in Access 2000. The emphasis in this section is upon table design and table relationships.

Project 1 explains the database design process, how to diagram the entities and relationships in a database solution, and how to create a data dictionary. You will conclude this project by importing structured data into an Access table.

In **Project 2** you will design an additional database table, and establish the necessary relationships. You will update your entity-relationship diagram to include these changes to the database solution, and learn more about how cardinality affects relationships.

In **Project 3** you will learn how to make data entry in a database more efficient and accurate by validating data by using lookup fields to assist data entry, and using input masks to define data as it is entered.

In *Part II* of this module you will learn how to manipulate and report database records using queries, forms, and reports.

In **Project 4** you will learn how to create queries, modify queries, and perform calculations in queries. You will learn how to create Select and Append queries, and add multiple criteria to the query design.

In **Project 5** you will learn how to create and use forms for data entry and display. In addition to using Design view to customize form controls, you will learn how to create a form that contains a subform, add calculated controls to forms, and use a form to enter records into the database.

In **Project 6** you will learn how to create Access reports for printing and distributing database information. You will learn how to sort and group records in reports, use the main form/sub form control, and add parameter specifications to the SQL query underlying a report.

Part III of this module introduces you to maintaining and customizing Access databases.

In **Project 7** you will learn how to specify table join properties, analyze a database using the Performance Analyzer, set password and security options, and create a database switchboard and set startup options.

In **Project 8** you will learn how to create both static and dynamic Web resources. You will use the data object new to Access 2000, the data access page. You will also learn how to add hyperlinks to database forms.

In **Project 9** you will learn how to customize your Access solutions using macros and Visual Basic for Applications. Here you will learn the basics of Visual Basic for Applications (VBA).

Project 10 explains how to integrate Access with Excel 2000 and Visual Basic 6. You will learn how to link an access database to an Excel data source, add a chart to a report using MS Graph, how to convert an Access 2000 database to an Access 97 version, and how to create a Visual Basic front end to an Access database.

This module also includes an **Appendix** that reviews basic Access concepts, the Access interface, and getting help using the Office Assistant.

These projects will help you to extend your basic knowledge of Microsoft Word so you can create a variety of sophisticated and professional documents. After completing Project 10, you will have learned all of the tasks assessed on the Microsoft Office User Specialist Expert examination.

Summary and Exercises

Summary

- Microsoft Access is a relational database management system (RDBMS).
- A database is a collection of information related to a common purpose.
- When launching Access, you must specify whether you want to open an existing
- database or create a new one.
- Access includes two methods for creating a new database.
- An Access database file can contain multiple objects, including tables, queries, forms, reports, access pages, macros, and modules.
- Tables are the primary kind of database object in Access.
- Only one database can be open at a time.
- The Database window provides a graphical method for designing and using database objects.

Key Terms

Key Terms

Access menu bar
Application title bar
class
data access page
database
database management system (DBMS)
database object
Database toolbar
Database window
field
form
Groups bar
macro
module
object shortcut
Objects bar
query
record
relational database management system (RDBMS)
report
status bar
table
wizard

Study Questions

Multiple Choice

1. Which Access object is considered primary?
   a. Table
   b. Query
   c. Form
   d. Report

2. Which screen element is used to easily design or open the objects within a database?
   a. Close button
   b. Status bar
   c. Database toolbar
   d. Database window

3. A database contains the first name, last name, and phone number for a group of students. The first name entries are what kind of data?
   a. Field
   b. Record
   c. Query
   d. Table

4. During which phase of the database design are the output specifications identified?
   a. Defining the purpose
   b. Planning the objects
   c. Creating and relating tables
   d. Creating queries

5. How many database files can be open simultaneously?
   a. One
   b. Two
   c. Thee
   d. Four

Short Answer

1. What is the Database window?

2. How many object classes are there in Access?

3. All database objects are displayed in which screen element?

4. Which database object is used to create and format printed output?

5. Microsoft Access is based upon which model?

Fill in the Blank

1. Database users typically interact with field data by using a(n) _____.

2. A(n) _____ is used to display fields in a Web browser.

3. A table is an instance of an object _____.

4. You can use a(n) _____ to open a database object quickly.

5. A(n) _____ is the primary object in Access.

For Discussion

1. How do fields and records differ?

2. What steps are required to design a database?

Part I: Database Design

Microsoft Access 2000 is one of the most powerful relational microcomputer database management system (DBMS) applications on the market today. You can use its features and functions to create simple databases, or complex data management solutions.

As you know from Introducing Access 2000, it is a good idea to follow a design process when planning a database. In this section you will learn how to plan and model database solutions, how to implement a solution in Access by crating tables, and how to establish relationships among tables. Once you have defined the basic structure of a database, you will learn how to modify table design to optimize database performance.

This section focuses on database design. In the sections that follow, you will learn how to manipulate data using queries, forms, and reports (Part II), how to maintain and customize databases, and share Access databases with other applications (Part III).

If you are new to Access or need to review database objects, data types, or object views, consult the Appendix. We have designed this text to accommodate users with limited experience in Access. If you are an intermediate user, these projects will extend your knowledge of relational database design.

Designing a Relational Database

In Introducing Access 2000, you learned that Microsoft Access is a relational database management system (RDBMS). The database objects you will create—tables, queries, forms, data access pages, and reports—are the basic tools for managing data using an RDBMS. Microsoft Access includes all the tools you need to create, modify, and manage these objects. In this project you will learn how to design a relational database solution that minimizes data redundancy, and is easily implemented.

Objectives

After completing this project, you will be able to:

➤ Describe the database design process

➤ Explain the role of an entity-relationship diagram in database design

➤ Design a simple data dictionary

➤ Open a Microsoft Access database

➤ Import an ASCII-delimited file into a Microsoft Access database as a table object

➤ View records in a table

Running Case

Selections, Inc. is a national department store chain with retail outlets throughout the United States. The stores have been so successful that upper management is considering launching a Web-based e-commerce initiative to market products directly. As a part of the overall Information Systems (IS) planning process, Travis Traylor, Manager of Accounting and Finance, wants you to design a prototype database for processing sales transactions.

The Challenge

The current computer system used for tracking mail order transactions is not capable of handling the number of daily sales transactions generated by the e-commerce initiative. Mr. Traylor has asked you to work in conjunction with the IS department to plan a sales transaction database that works in conjunction with the existing Selections, Inc. computer systems. He wants you to design a prototype database in Microsoft Access for processing and fulfilling orders. This database will store customer, product, and order information.

The Solution

To design the sales transaction database, you will need to follow a database design process. During the analysis and design phases, the overall needs and structure of a database will be determined. You will conclude these phases by creating a simple entity-relationship diagram showing the overall database structure, and a data dictionary that lists the characteristics of all relations. Finally, you will **migrate** (convert) a sample of the current customer data from the old database to the prototype you design.

Before creating your database, it is important to understand the characteristics of relational database management systems. The relational database model was designed to address specific problems associated with storing information on computers. By understanding the strengths of the relational model, you will be equipped to design more efficient databases.

The Setup

To design the database and create the table specified above, launch Microsoft Access, and make sure that you select the Access settings listed in Table 1.1. This will ensure that your screen matches the illustrations and the tasks in this project function as described.

Table 1.1   Access Settings

Location	Make these settings:
Office Shortcut Bar	If the Office Shortcut bar is visible, close it by right-clicking the Office icon on the shortcut bar and choosing Exit. 
Office Assistant	Hide the Office Assistant.
Tools, Customize	Click the Toolbars tab and display the Database toolbar and the Menu Bar, as Shown in Figure 1.1, if they are not currently visible.
Tools, Customize	Click the Options tab, and make sure the check box to display recently used menu commands first is deselected, as shown in Figure 1.2.
Tools, Options	After you have opened or created a database, click the View tab and display Status bar, Startup dialog box, New object shortcuts, and Windows in Taskbar, as shown in Figure 1.3. This is the default setting in Access.
Tools, Options	After you have opened or created a database, click the General tab and deselect the setting for displaying dates in four-digit format, as shown in Figure 1.4. This is the default setting in Access.

FIGURE 1.1

FIGURE 1.2

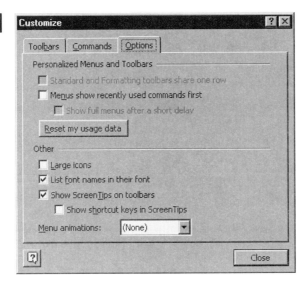

FIGURE 1.3

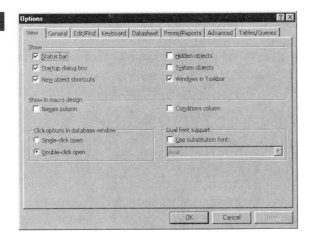

FIGURE 1.4

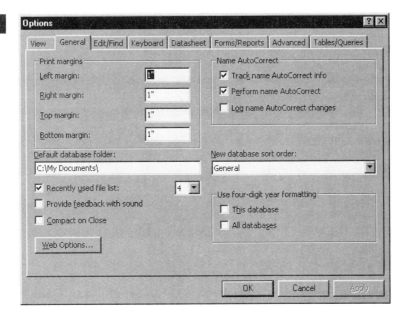

Most of the figures in this project will display the Database window and other Access dialog boxes in a restored state. You can resize any dialog boxes by clicking the Restore button in each dialog box.

File Processing Systems

In many organizations, the traditional approach to designing information systems focuses on the data processing needs of individual departments within the organization. A **file processing system** is an application or program designed for individual use, often without regard to the information resources that exist throughout an organization. Although file-processing systems automate certain procedures, they have serious limitations. Many companies use databases or other information processing applications such as electronic spreadsheets to automate and organize redundant tasks, but these applications lack a coherent method for tying together all of an organization's data resources. Therefore, the computerized systems are merely duplicating the manual file systems on which they are based. The proliferation of file processing systems within an organization has serious limitations. Uncontrolled data redundancy leads to inconsistent data, and inflexible programs with private files limit data sharing. There are also problems with poor enforcement standards such as using two different terms for the same data item. All of these problems characterize file-processing systems. The database approach seeks to eliminate these problems.[1]

The Database Approach

It is important to understand databases in the broader context of how and why an organization values data and information. There are different ways of describing the relationship between data and information, but in general, **data** is unevaluated facts and figures, and **information** is data that makes sense in a specific context and for a specific purpose. Data is a valuable commodity that a company must carefully acquire, manage, and protect.

[1] F. R. McFadden, A. Hoffer, & M.B. Prescott (1999), *Modern Database Management*, 5th ed. (Reading, MA: Addison Wesley), pp. 8-10.

As you learned in Introducing Access 2000, a **database management system (DBMS)** is a software application that manages databases stored on a computer. Many businesses use databases designed according to the relational database model to conduct daily business. As more and more organizations convert their databases to microcomputers or to client-server systems on micro-, mini-, and mainframe computers, the relational model has become a popular logical model. A DBMS that manages a relational database is a **relational database management system (RDBMS)**. Most DBMSs for microcomputers are RDBMSs.

As you know from Introducing Access 2000, Microsoft Access is a software tool for creating databases in which the information can easily be shared among users to fulfill a variety of business functions. Based on E. F. Codd's **relational model**, Access enables database designers to create efficient databases that minimize data redundancy, which is information stored in more than one location and therefore increase data integrity, or the accuracy of information. You will now learn how efficient databases are designed, created, and maintained.

 **Web Tip**

Are you interested in learning more about Codd's relational model? Visit http://www.iemagazine.com/9810/feat4.shtml.

The Database Design Process

The database approach emphasizes data integration and data sharing throughout an enterprise. Conceptually, the database approach is easy to understand—in the Overview, you read about a simple database design process. In the real world, however, organizations are sometimes slow to implement databases that truly integrate and share data. This might be due to the complexity (and therefore the cost) of designing a relational database. At a minimum, the database design process for organizations developing a database for the entire enterprise involves the phases shown in Figure 1.5.

FIGURE 1.5

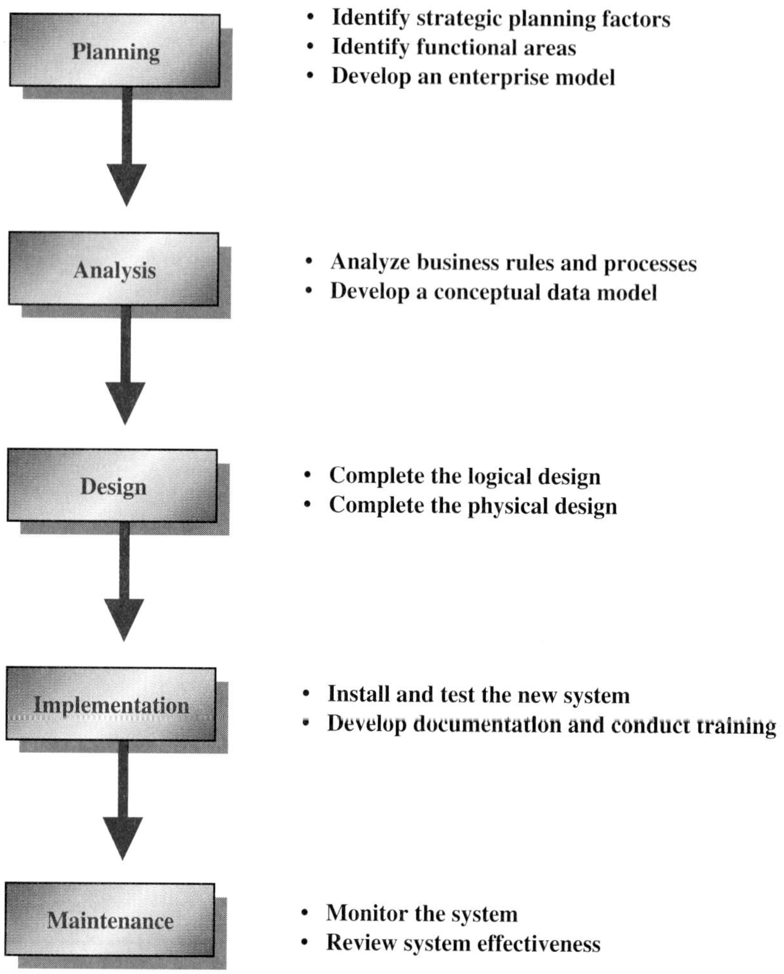

Planning	• Identify strategic planning factors • Identify functional areas • Develop an enterprise model
Analysis	• Analyze business rules and processes • Develop a conceptual data model
Design	• Complete the logical design • Complete the physical design
Implementation	• Install and test the new system • Develop documentation and conduct training
Maintenance	• Monitor the system • Review system effectiveness

Although these phases appear simple, the stages they represent are actually rather complex.

The Planning Phase

The planning phase focuses on understanding the information needs of the organization. This includes the factors contributing to the organizations' success, as well as the organizational units and functions of the enterprise. During this phase, analysts develop the *enterprise data model*, which is a high-level model displaying the relationships among the entities in an enterprise. The enterprise data model emphasizes data, not processes.

The Analysis Phase

In the analysis phase, database developers examine the flow of information within an organization and the business rules that govern information processes in order to develop an overall structure for the organization's data. This **conceptual data model** is independent of any specific DBMS and includes a description of the attributes defining each entity. The analysis phase also involves identifying the processes affecting the flow of information. The result of this phase is often a detailed entity-relationship (E-R) diagram.

The Design Phase

It is during the design phase that database developers design the database according to a specific RDBMS. There are two specific steps to this phase. First, database designers translate the conceptual data model to specific structures in the database system. This includes normalizing the database, which is a process of designing the most efficient combination of relations (database tables). In the second step, database designers complete the physical design of the database using a specific application. This includes understanding the logic for each process and building the user interface elements (such as forms and reports) that support use of the database.

The Implementation Phase

During the implementation phase, programmers install the database on the computer system. This includes creating database definitions and writing program code for the database system. It is necessary to migrate the data from the old system to the new, and develop training materials and documentation before the database application can be used.

The Maintenance Phase

During the maintenance phase, the database is evaluated and monitored, and changes are made to the database design. These changes can include reworking the structure of the database, creating additional database objects, and correcting errors in the original design. If the system is determined to be ineffective, a new development process might be initiated.

Merely reading about the database design process might tempt you to give up on database management and revert to the file processing approach! A description of this process has been included here to give you an appreciation for its complexity as a field. Designing a relational database is a costly and time-consuming task. However, organizations adopting the RDBMS approach know that the time and cost are worthwhile because the database will be serviceable and operational for a longer period of time than a non-relational database. As with other things in life, you get what you pay for, and careful planning and analysis will yield better results.

In this project, you will focus on the enterprise model and a simple data dictionary. A **data dictionary** is a set of specifications for how to design the database tables. The data dictionary is designed according to the detailed E-R diagram.

Using the Entity-Relationship Model in Database Design

In 1976 Peter P. Chen introduced the entity-relationship approach to systems analysis and design.[2] His approach is well suited to database design because it enables developers to more easily convert the enterprise data model into a specific database design during the design phase.

Entities and Relations

The entity-relationship approach develops a data model concerning an organization's **entities**, the persons, places, things, and activities it desires to keep data about. An example of an entity for a retail sales organization is the customer. Assuming that a business services more than one customer, the company needs a way of distinguishing each **instance** of the customer entity, in this case, distinguishing one customer from another. A database with address information for 500 customers thus contains 500 instances of the customer entity.

Entities often relate to other entities within an enterprise. The relational database model stores the data describing entities in **relations,** which are two-dimensional, named tables containing data. Microsoft Access stores data this way (see Table O.2 of the Overview).

> **TIP** All relations are tables, but not all tables are relations. A table is a relation only if each cell contains exactly one value, and each row of data is unique. This is accomplished through the process of database normalization, which we will cover in more detail in Project 8.

From this point on, "table" and "relation" will be used interchangeably.

---

[2] P. P. Chen, (1976), The entity-relationship model: Toward a unified view of data. *ACM Trans. on Database Systems* 1, 1 (March 1976): 9–37.

Attributes

Entities are identified by their attributes. An **attribute** is a characteristic that helps to distinguish one instance of an entity from another. For example, Last Name, First Name, and Address are three attributes that help distinguish one customer from another in a customer relation. Most likely, no two customers will be represented in the database by exactly the same values of all three attributes, so this combination of attributes will adequately identify each customer in most databases. In Microsoft Access, attributes such as Last Name and First Name are the field data that describe each instance of an entity. For example, Mary Smith is one instance of a customer entity in the organization's database.

Keys

In a relational database, each entity must have a **candidate key** to be able to establish relationships among tables. A single attribute or combination of attributes that uniquely identifies each instance of an entity is a candidate key. A **simple key** is based on only one attribute, a **compound key** on two or more. In some situations, more than one candidate key can exist. For example, a database containing Last Name, First Name, Address, Phone Number, and Social Security Number will include more than one candidate key. The database designer could use the combination of Last Name, First Name, Address, and Phone Number to uniquely identify each customer. Or, the designer could use the Social Security Number attribute as the key. In general, a simple key is preferred to a compound key (this is why many schools use a Social Security Number as a Student Number). A **primary key** is the candidate key selected to be the unique identifier for an entity. Database developers usually determine the keys of a database when creating its structure during the design phase. When selecting a candidate key for a relation, certain considerations are important: The values of the key should (1) not change over time, (2) never include the null (empty) value, and (3) be simple, as opposed to compound, for the sake of simplicity. As noted above, a student's Social Security Number is often selected as a primary key because it fulfills each consideration listed here.

The Entity-Relationship Diagram

In an RDBMS, you create relationships between entities to make the database efficient, or to reduce it to the minimum number of relations required to minimize redundant data. An **entity-relationship (E-R) diagram** represents these relationships. For example, when customers place an order with Selections, Inc., you will need to store information about at least four things: the customer, the fact that he or she is placing an order, the available products, and the specific products ordered. Figure 1.6 displays an E-R diagram for these entities.

FIGURE 1.6

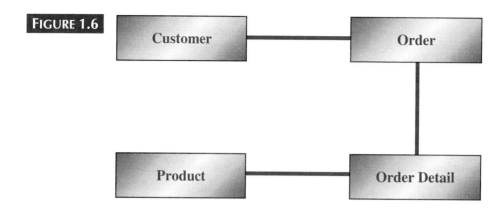

The rectangular boxes identify the entities, while the lines between the entities indicate that some relationship exists between them.[3] This E-R diagram is high-level, because it does not specify any information about entity attributes or exactly how the entities interrelate. You will develop a more detailed E-R diagram in Project 2.

What information is usually required to identify customers? Recall that the term *attribute* refers to the field data in a Microsoft Access data table. Customers are uniquely identified by name and address attributes. The E-R diagram shows attributes as ellipses, with the primary key attribute underlined. Figure 1.7 displays the updated E-R diagram with the attributes for the Customer entity.

FIGURE 1.7

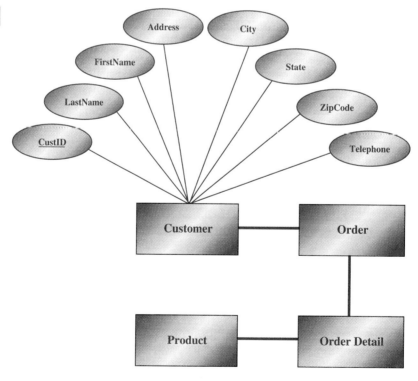

[3] Some E-R diagrams represent relationships with a diamond symbol. Lines simplify the concept of entities and their associated attributes.

Designing a Simple Data Dictionary

When designing relational databases, you will find it useful to create a simple data dictionary for documenting your design, should you or someone else modify the database at a later date. The data dictionary is a paper document that lists all the database entities and their attributes. Figure 1.8 shows the data dictionary for some of the information documenting the database you will create—in particular, for the Customer entity.

FIGURE 1.8

Field Name	Field Size	Data Type	Field Description
CustID	Auto	AutoNumber	Primary key
LastName	25	Text	Last name of customer
FirstName	20	Text	First name of customer
Address	35	Text	Street address or post office box
City	20	Text	Customer's city of residence
State	2	Text	Customer's State of residence
ZipCode	10	Text	Zip code with optional extension
HomePhone	14	Text	Customer's home telephone number

Later, the Customers data table will be filled in with the name and address information for each customer who orders products from Selections, Inc. We will update this dictionary to display information about each table, as additional tables are added to the database.

Break Point

If necessary, you can finish this project later.

Opening a Microsoft Access Database

Some of the data your database will need to contain already exists in computer format, so you can import it into a Microsoft Access table object. You can import this data into the blank database you created in Introducing Microsoft Access 2000.

TASK 1: To Open a Microsoft Access Database

1 Launch Microsoft Access. The Microsoft Access dialog box shown in Figure 1.9 will appear. From this dialog box you can either create a new database or open an existing one. A list of recently opened databases appears in the lower pane of the Microsoft Access dialog box.

FIGURE 1.9

② With the Open an existing file option selected, click OK.

TROUBLESHOOTING If Access is already running, click File, Open.

③ The Open dialog box will appear. Select your floppy disk drive in the Look in: drop-down list.

④ Click *Selections.mdb* in the file list, and click Open, as shown in Figure 1.10.

 Web Tip

If you do not have a copy of the files needed for this project, you may download them from the Select Web site at http://www.prenhall.com/selectadvanced.

FIGURE 1.10

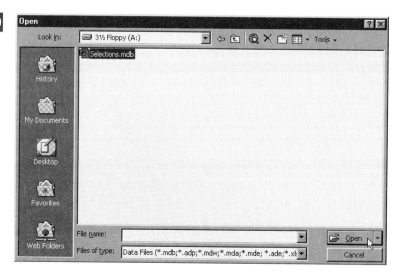

Access opens the database file, as shown in Figure 1.11.

FIGURE 1.11

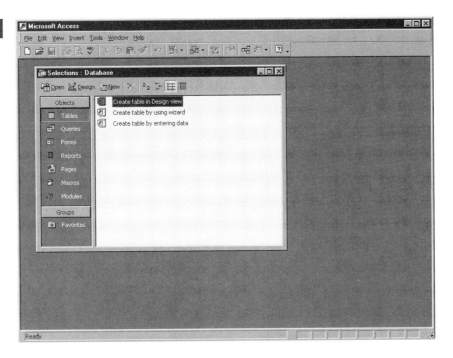

Check Point

How many objects does this database contain?

Creating a Table Object by Importing Data

Most microcomputer database systems support importing and exporting text data to and from a variety of sources. This is because microcomputer database systems are often used in client/server environments where data is stored in different formats. Data about the Selections, Inc. customers has been exported from another application as ASCII text. Data stored in **ASCII text** format contains only letters, numbers, and symbols, and is not formatted in any way. ASCII text files enable sharing data among computers with differing operating systems. In addition, virtually all microcomputer applications can read ASCII data.

ASCII text files imported into database applications often store data in a specific format. Each row of data in an ASCII file usually constitutes one database record. Recall that a **record** is all the information about an instance of an entity, such as a customer, that is kept in the database, while **field** data (or attributes of an entity) are the categories of information defining each entity.

ASCII files are often **delimited** to separate the attributes included in the file. To delimit means to fix the limits of or specify a boundary for something. ASCII-delimited files delimit field data with one or more characters. The **delimiting character,** or **delimiter,** is the specific ASCII character used to separate field data. Figure 1.12 displays an ASCII-delimited text file opened with the Windows Notepad text editor.

FIGURE 1.12

This file uses both the comma character as a delimiter, and the double quote character as a text qualifier. The text qualifier encloses each data attribute. ASCII-delimited files can easily be imported into Microsoft Access. The delimiter and text qualifier will differentiate the field data as Access builds a table from the file.

TASK 2: <u>To Create a Table from an ASCII File</u>

1 Click File, Get External Data, and choose Import, as shown in Figure 1.13.

FIGURE 1.13

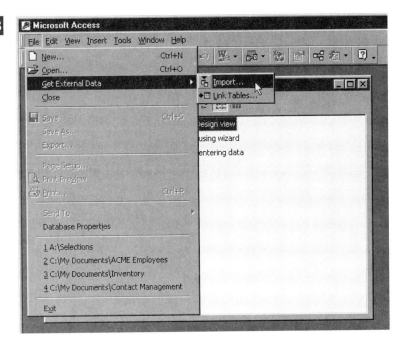

2 In the Import dialog box, select the 3½ inch floppy disk, and Text Files in the Files of Type list, as shown in Figure 1.14.

FIGURE 1.14

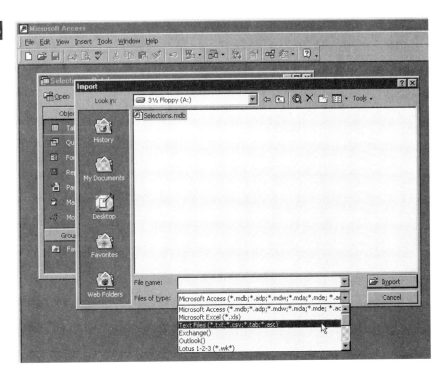

TROUBLESHOOTING If you do not see the Text Files option, then not all import filters have been installed. Inform your instructor, and open the *Selections.mdb* file your instructor gives you.

3 Select the *Customers.txt* file and click the Import button. Access now opens the Import Text Wizard.

4 In the Import Text Wizard, select the Delimited option button, which should appear as the default. Click the Next button, as shown in Figure 1.15.

FIGURE 1.15

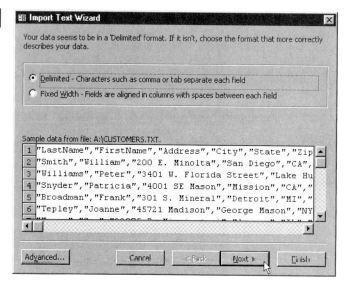

5 The Comma delimiter option button should be selected by default. Check the check box for First Row Contains Field Names. When the dialog box settings match those in Figure 1.16, click Next.

FIGURE 1.16

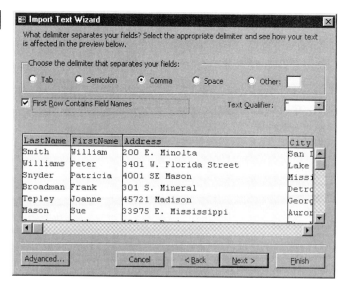

6 Select In a New Table, the default option to store the data in a new table, as shown in Figure 1.17. Click Next.

FIGURE 1.17

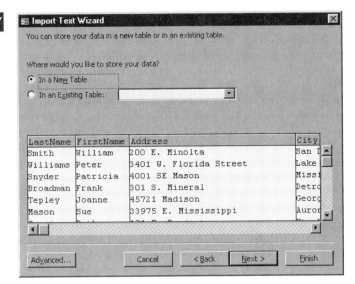

7 Access will now verify the field name and data type for the first attribute, and will automatically name the field LastName, since this in included in the first row of data. Retain the default field name LastName, and the default data type Text . Click Next, as shown in Figure 1.18.

FIGURE 1.18

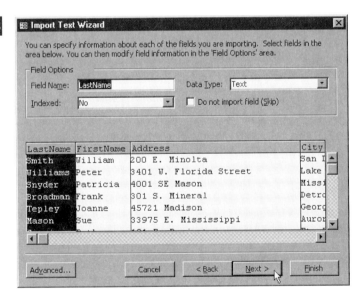

TIP Although Microsoft Access table objects can contain spaces in the field names, it is a good idea to name the fields without spaces or special characters, in the event that the database will be used in conjunction with other applications that do not support spaces in the field names.

8 The Access Import Text Wizard will recommend that you add a primary field to the table. Select the option button for Access to add a primary key. When your settings match those in Figure 1.19, click Next.

FIGURE 1.19

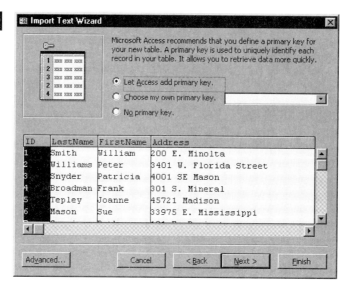

9 The final step of the Import Text Wizard enables you to name the database table object. By default, Access uses the name of the text file as the table name. Select the default name for the table as shown in Figure 1.20, and click the Finish button.

FIGURE 1.20

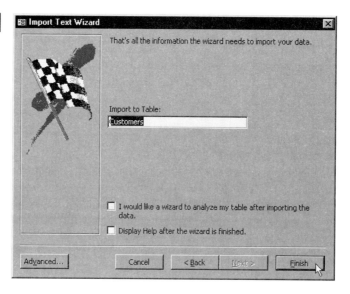

10 The Text Import Wizard will indicate that the file has been successfully imported, as shown in Figure 1.21.

FIGURE 1.21

11 Click the OK button. Notice the Table Object icon that now appears in the Database window, along with the table name, as shown in Figure 1.22.

FIGURE 1.22

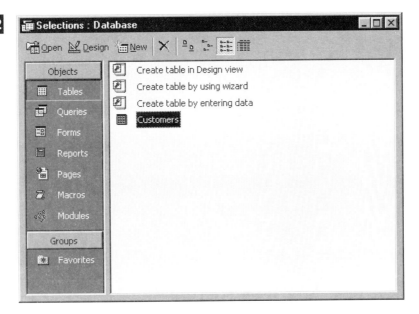

 Check Point

How many objects does the database now contain?

Viewing Records in a Table

Now that you have created a table by importing data, you can open the table and view the records it contains. Remember that the Database window contains an icon representing each database object contained in the database. In the next task you will open the table to view its records, and then exit Access.

TASK 3: To View Records in a Table and Exit Access

1 Double-click the Customers icon in the Tables page of the Database window. Access opens the table in Datasheet view, as shown in Figure 1.23.

FIGURE 1.23

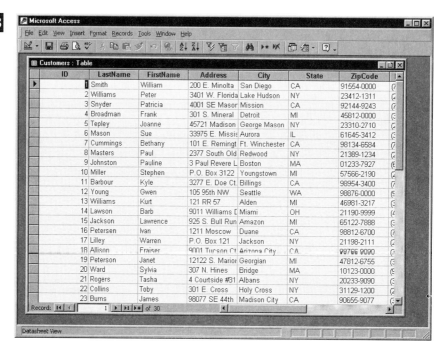

Note that this table contains 30 records, and the ID numbers are sequential.

TIP In Project 2 you will learn more about Datasheet view and Design view.

2 Click the Close button in the Application title bar. This will close the table, and close Access.

TIP You do not need to save the table before closing the database, since you did not change any record data.

You are finished working with the Customers table for now. After you create additional tables in Project 2 and establish relationships between tables, you will modify the Customers table in Project 3 to make data entry and record editing more efficient.

Summary and Exercises

Summary

- Relational database management systems (RDBMSs) can minimize redundant and inaccurate data.
- File processing systems have inherent weaknesses that the database approach can correct.
- Efficient databases are built according to a specific design process.
- During the planning phase, database designers construct an enterprise data model.
- The analysis phase usually produces a high level entity-relationship (E-R) diagram.
- A database is normalized during the design phase.
- A database is fully constructed during the implementation phase.
- A data dictionary contains documentation about the database design.
- A relation is a two-dimensional, named table containing data.
- An entity is a person, place, thing, or event about which an organization desires to keep data, for example, customers.
- An instance of an entity is one representation of it in the database; for example, a particular customer could be an instance of the entity Customers.
- An attribute is a characteristic of an entity.
- Keys are used to identify instances of an entity.
- ASCII text is a common format for storing data.

Key Terms and Operations

Key Terms

ASCII text	entity-relationship (E-R) diagram
attribute	field
candidate key	information
compound key	file processing systems
conceptual data model	instance
data	migrate data
database management	primary key
system (DBMS)	record
data dictionary	relation
delimited text	relational database management
delimiting character	system (RDBMS)
(delimiter)	relational model
enterprise data model	simple key
entity	

Operations

create a database
create a table by importing ASCII data
design a data dictionary
interpret an entity-relationship diagram
open a table in Datasheet view

Study Questions

Multiple Choice

1. Which Microsoft Access object can you create from ASCII data?
   a. Table
   b. Query
   c. Form
   d. Report
   e. Module

2. Which database design phase includes designing the user interface?
   a. Planning
   b. Analysis
   c. Design
   d. Implementation
   e. Maintenance

3. What term is used to describe unevaluated facts and figures?
   a. Table
   b. Information
   c. Data
   d. Entity
   e. Relation

4. What term best describes the process of designing an efficient relational database?
   a. Entity
   b. Attribute
   c. Relation
   d. Input mask
   e. Normalization

5. Which of the following is the formal name for a table?
   a. Entity
   b. Instance
   c. Attribute
   d. Relation
   e. Normalization

6. Which term is the formal name for a field?
   a. Entity
   b. Instance
   c. Attribute
   d. Relation
   e. Normalization

7. Which of the following describes a combination of fields that uniquely identifies each record in a table?
   a. Instance
   b. Compound key
   c. Primary key
   d. Candidate key
   e. Attribute

8. What is used to differentiate field data in an ASCII data file?
   a. Compound key
   b. E-R diagram
   c. Instance
   d. Input mask
   e. Delimiter

9. Which Access data type is a good candidate for the primary key?
   a. AutoNumber
   b. Text
   c. Number
   d. Date/Time
   e. Yes/No

10. At the conclusion of this project, how many database objects does your Selections database file contain?
    a. One
    b. Two
    c. Three
    d. Four
    e. Five

Short Answer

1. What does a detailed E-R diagram include that a high level E-R diagram does not?

2. What information is included in a data dictionary?

3. What character is commonly used to delimit ASCII data?

4. Which phase of the database design process results in a detailed E-R diagram?

5. Microsoft Access is based upon which logical database model?

6. What is used to differentiate instances of an entity?

7. What is a more common term for a relation?

8. What is the name of a field that uniquely identifies each instance of a relation?

9. What is the more common term for an attribute?

10. What Access tool do you use to import ASCII-delimited data into a table?

Fill In the Blank

1. A(n) _____ is a row of data appearing in an Access table.

2. In an E-R diagram, tables are depicted using one or more _____.

3. A(n) _____ _____ file contains text in a structured format that you can import into Access.

4. You create a detailed E-R diagram during the _____ phase.

5. Microsoft Access is based upon the _____ model.

6. A(n) _____ _____ contains information documenting the database design.

7. To open an Access table, double-click the table's icon in the _____ _____.

8. In Access, you view table data using _____ view.

9. A table's _____ _____ uniquely identifies each record.

10. A(n) _____ separates field data in an ASCII-delimited file.

For Discussion

1. What are the limitations of file processing systems? Why is the database approach deemed superior?

2. What steps are included in the database design process?

3. Explain the difference between entities, relations, instances, and attributes.

4. How are ASCII files delimited?

5. What is the procedure for creating an Access table from existing data?

Hands-On Exercises

1. Creating an Employees Database

Mr. Traylor wants you to create an Access database table for storing employee records. He has given you a list of specifications for the Employee table design. Complete the following steps:

1. Create a blank database named *Employees.mdb* on your floppy disk.

2. Select Get External Data from the File menu.

3. Select Import. When the Import Text wizard appears, import the employees.txt ASCII file into the database.

4. Accept the default specifying that the file is delimited.

5. Indicate that the delimiting character is a comma and that the first row contains field names.

6. Change the data type of the DateHired field to Date/Time.

7. Change the data type of the PayRate field to Currency.

8. Do not set a primary key.

9. Name the table *Employees*. Your table should appear similar to the one shown in Figure 1.24.

FIGURE 1.24

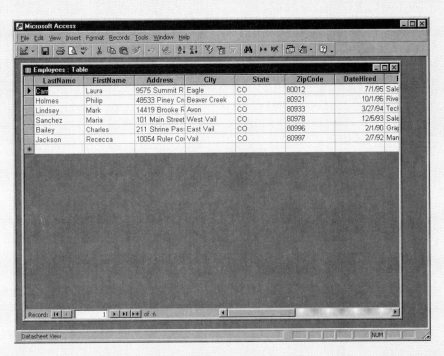

10. Close the table and the database.

2. Exporting Data from Access to Excel

It is common in many professional environments to integrate data among Office applications. For example, you might need to export data from Access into Excel for analysis, or simply distribute data to individuals who do not have Access installed on their computers. In this task you will learn how to export data from an Access table to an Excel worksheet. Complete the following steps:

1. Open the *Employee* table you created in the previous exercise.

2. Click File, Export.

3. Choose your floppy disk as the destination, and select Excel 97-2000 as the data type, as shown in Figure 1.25.

FIGURE 1.25

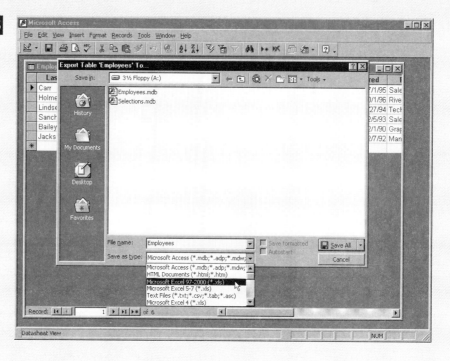

4. Click Save. Access will export the data to Excel.

5. Close the database.

6. Using the Windows Explorer or My Computer, open the *Employees.xls* file from your floppy disk. The Excel worksheet will appear as shown in Figure 1.26.

FIGURE 1.26

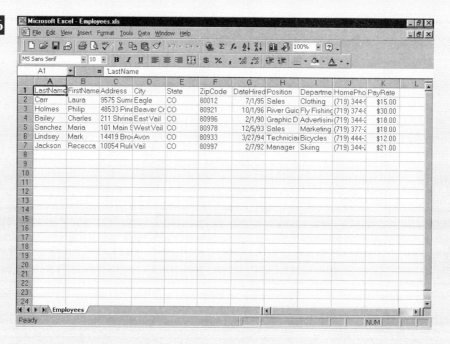

7. Close the workbook and exit Excel.

8. Close Access.

On Your Own Exercises

1. Creating a Student File

Create a blank database named *Students*. Using the Text Import wizard, create a table from the *Students.txt* file that is available on your data disk. Set the StudentID field as the primary key. Name the table *Students*. Close the table and the database when you are finished.

2. Creating a Database Using an Access Database Wizard

Access includes wizards to assist you in creating entire databases. Launch Access if it is not currently running and create a Contact Management database by using a database wizard. Save your database to a blank floppy diskette using *Contact management.mdb* as the database name. Close the database and exit Access when you are finished.

3. Creating a Database Using the Hyperlink Data Type

The HyperLink data type was first introduced in Access 97. In this assignment you will create a new database that incorporates this data type. Create a new database with the name *Web sites.mdb*. Create a table named *Sites* with the following structure:

Field Name	Data Type	Size
Company	Text	50
Primary Product	Text	50
Company URL	HyperLink	N/A

When you save the table, allow Access to create a primary key. Close the database when you are finished.

4. Adding Records to a Table

In this assignment you will modify the database you created in the previous exercise by adding records to the table. Open the database and add the following three records to the table:

Company	Primary Product	Company URL
Microsoft	Software	http://www.microsoft.com
Adobe	Graphics Software	http://www.adobe.com
Fidelity	Financial Services	http://www.fidelity.com

After you have added these records, use the navigation controls on the form to move to the first record. If you can access the World Wide Web from your lab or computer, click the company URL field for Microsoft. When you are finished, close your web browser and the database.

Planning and Creating Tables and Establishing Relationships

In Project 1 you began constructing a relational database using Microsoft Access. At this point your database contains only one object, the Customers table. A database needs two or more tables (relations) to be relational, yet should not contain more tables than necessary to minimize redundant data. How do you determine the optimum number of relations? You can use a process known as normalization to determine the optimum number of relations in a database, and the kinds of relationships that are required to optimize data integrity. The goal of normalization is to convert complex data structures into a simple form. This is done by considering the attributes necessary to identify each instance of an entity and the kinds of relationships that must exist between entities. In this project you will create two additional tables in your database, learn about cardinality, and optimize the database.

Objectives

After completing this project, you will be able to:

➤ Define cardinality in relationships

➤ Read cardinalities in a detailed entity-relationship (E-R) diagram

➤ Create an updated data dictionary

➤ Describe database normalization

➤ Create a table by importing data from an Excel workbook

➤ Create two tables using Table Design View

➤ Add tables to the Relationships window, and create one-to-many relationships

➤ Establish a many-to-many relationship

Running Case

You are well on your way in designing the prototype database Mr. Traylor has requested. Now that you have created the table required to keep track of customers, you need to plan the additional tables and establish the required relationships.

The Challenge

In Project 1, you completed the first step in planning and creating your database by identifying each customer with a customer identification number. This is a critical characteristic of the Customer table (remember that a table is also called a relation). You are now ready to design the remaining tables in the database. Since the database will track e-commerce orders, you will need to represent product and order information as well. At this point in the design process you need to carefully consider the number of tables required to store sales transactions. You also need to consider the relationships the database must support to optimize how this information is stored, accessed, and maintained. As with your initial design, it is best to plan your database on paper before implementing a solution in Access.

The Solution

To complete the database design you will need to plan and create three additional tables. One table will list product information. Another will contain information about the customer as well as the date and time of each order. The final table will list the specific products and quantities listed on each order that a customer places with Selections, Inc. Once you have created these tables, you can establish relationships among all the tables in the database. As was the case in Project 1, this project introduces concepts and procedures that are important to consider as you design a relational database. You will begin by planning your database using an Entity-Relationship (E-R) diagram. Figure 2.1 shows the detailed E-R diagram that represents your database.

FIGURE 2.1

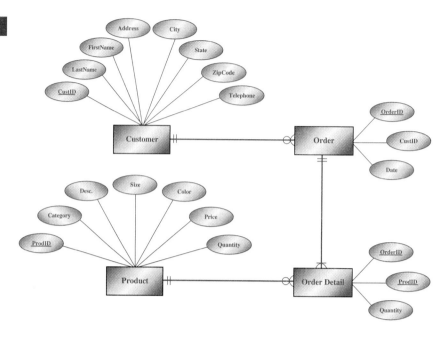

In Microsoft Access, you create relationships using the Relationships window. Figure 2.2 shows how the relationships in the E-R diagram above appear in Access.

FIGURE 2.2

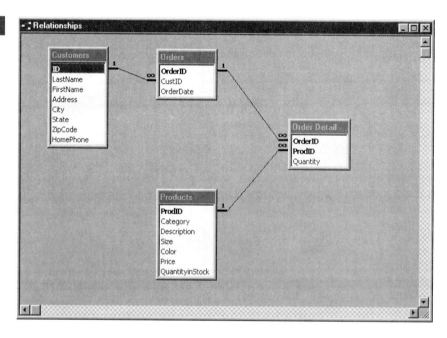

The Setup

To create the three tables and establish the relationships described in the previous section, launch Microsoft Access, open the *Selections.mdb* database you modified in Project 1, and make sure that you select the settings listed in Table 2.1. If you need additional assistance setting these options, refer to Figure 1.1 through 1.3 of Project 1. This will ensure that your screen matches the illustrations and the tasks in this project function as described.

Table 2.1   Access Settings

Location	Make these settings:
Office Shortcut Bar	If the Office Shortcut bar is visible, close it by right-clicking the Office icon on the shortcut bar and choosing Exit.
Office Assistant	Hide the Office Assistant.
Tools, Customize	Click the Toolbars tab and display the Database toolbar and the Menu Bar, as shown in Figure 1.1 of Project 1, if they are not currently visible.
Tools, Customize	Click the Options tab, and make sure the check box to display recently used menu commands first is deselected, as shown in Figure 1.2 of Project 1.
Tools, Options	Click the View tab and display Status bar, Startup dialog box, New object shortcuts, and Windows in Taskbar, as shown in Figure 1.3 of Project 1.

Understanding Relationships

As you learned in Project 1, a relational database management system (RDBMS) often establishes relationships between relations. Entities and their relationships are often graphically represented using E-R diagrams. Figure 2.3 shows a high-level E-R diagram of the four tables your database will contain.

FIGURE 2.3

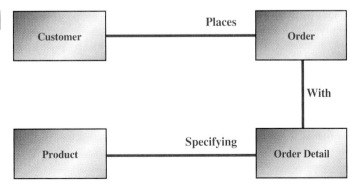

Read this diagram as follows: A customer places an order with details specifying one or more products.

Cardinality in Relationships

What happens when a customer places multiple orders? In a relational database, not only are the relationships between tables important to consider, but you must consider the cardinality between relationships as well. The **cardinality** of a relationship is the number of instances of one entity that can or must be associated with instances of a second entity. The first entity in a relationship is called the **parent** entity (or table), and the second is the **child** entity (or table).

Cardinality in relationships can be mandatory or optional. **Mandatory cardinality** occurs when each instance of the parent entity *must* relate to one or more instances of a child entity, while **optional cardinality** occurs when one or more instances of the parent entity may relate to *no* instances of the child entity. You will see examples of both kinds of cardinality shortly.

Another characteristic of cardinality is the minimum and maximum number of related entities in a relationship. The three types of relationships are one-to-one, one-to-many, and many-to-many. In a **one-to-one relationship** each record in Table A can have only one matching record in Table B, and each record in Table B can have only one matching record in Table A. This type of relationship is not common, because most information related in this way would be in one table. You might use a one-to-one relationship to divide a table with many fields, to isolate part of a table for security reasons, or to store information that applies only to a subset of the main table.

A **one-to-many relationship** specifies that each record in the parent table can have one or more associated records in the related child table, but each record in the child table will relate to one and only one record in the parent table. An example would be the individual timecard records in a child table that relate to employee records in a parent table. For each employee, there will be multiple time card records, but each time card record is related to one and only one employee in the parent table. It is also possible to conceive of a situation where there is a zero to many cardinality expressed in a one-to-many relationship. How can this be true? If a business purchases a mailing list with information about potential customers, the database will most likely contain records in a customer table that have not placed an order with the company. Thus, records in the Customer table relate to zero or many records in the Orders table. Each order, however, will relate to one and only one customer.

In a ***many-to-many relationship***, a record in Table A can have many matching records in Table B, and a record in Table B can have many matching records in Table A. This type of relationship is only possible by defining a third table (called a ***junction table***) whose primary key consists of two fields: the foreign keys from both Tables A and B. Although it is an acceptable practice to create a new primary key and use the foreign keys in the junction table, a compound key consisting of the two foreign key fields works equally well. A many-to-many relationship is really two one-to-many relationships with a third table. For example, in the database you are currently designing, the Orders table and the Products table have a many-to-many relationship that is defined by creating two one-to-many relationships to the Order Details table. This is represented in Figures 2.1 and 2.2.

Reading Cardinalities in E-R Diagrams

Cardinalities are represented in E-R diagrams using specific notation. Figure 2.4 displays four common ways to represent E-R cardinalities.

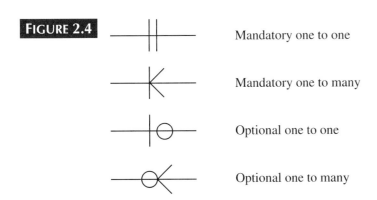

FIGURE 2.4

Mandatory one to one

Mandatory one to many

Optional one to one

Optional one to many

TIP There is no consistent standard for representing cardinalities in E-R diagrams. Some diagrams use the symbolic approach shown here, while others use text representations such as (1:1) for one-to-one and (1:n) for one-to-many.

Cardinalities are sometimes difficult to read in E-R diagrams. Look at the expanded E-R diagram shown in Figure 2.5.

FIGURE 2.5

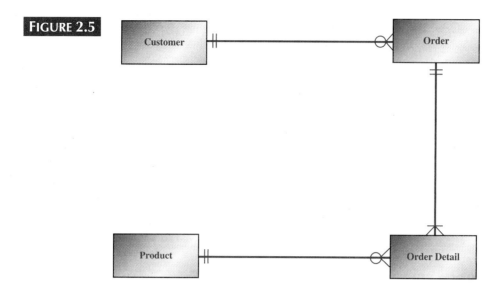

You read an E-R diagram such as this in two directions to determine the cardinality between any two entities. The symbol closest to an entity indicates its cardinality when it is the child table in the relationship. For example, notice the "optional one-to-many" symbol to the left of the Order entity. The cardinality between the parent Customer table and the child Order table is one-to-many because some customers may have placed one or more orders. In addition, the cardinality is optional because there may be a customer instance with no corresponding order instance. This could happen if the name of a customer was added to the database by referral or from a purchased mailing list, but they have never (or not yet) placed an order.

Now let's consider the relationship in the reverse direction, reading from the Order entity to the Customer entity. The mandatory one-to-one symbol next to the Customers entity in Figure 2.5 means that whenever a customer places an order, the cardinality between the order and that customer is one-to-one, because one and only one customer places any order. Because an Order entity instance must have a corresponding customer entity, the cardinality is mandatory.

In a similar fashion, consider the cardinalities for order and order detail, and product and order detail. There is a mandatory cardinality in both directions for the relationship between an order and the order detail, but an optional cardinality between a product and the order detail. Note that the relationship from an order detail to a product is mandatory. How can this be? The optional cardinality is due to the fact that a company may have an inventory item in the Product table for which no customer has placed an order. Once a customer places an order, however, there is a mandatory one to one cardinality between the Order Detail entity and the Product entity, as each order detail relates to one, and only one detail record in the database.

Figure 2.1 displays the detailed E-R diagram for the completed database table structure. This logical data model includes all the information required to complete a data dictionary for the Selections, Inc. e-commerce database.

Updating the Data Dictionary

We can now update the data dictionary according to the detailed E-R diagram shown in Figure 2.1. Recall that the purpose of the data dictionary is to assist in developing the database and to provide documentation for subsequent updates. Using the information shown in Figure 2.1, you can modify the data dictionary as shown in Figure 2.6.

FIGURE 2.6

Customers Table	Products Table	Orders Table	Order Details Table	Field Name	Field Size	Data Type	Field Description
X		X		**CustID**	Auto	AutoNumber	Primary key; format to 4 digits using \0000; non key in Orders Table
X				LastName	25	Text	Last name of customer
X				FirstName	20	Text	First name of customer
X				Address	35	Text	Street address or post office box
X				City	20	Text	Customer's city of residence
X				State	2	Text	State; input mask force to upper case, required >LL
X				ZipCode	10	Text	Zip code with optional extension; input mask
X				HomePhone	14	Text	Customer's phone; input mask
	X		X	**ProdID**	8	Text	Primary key in Product Table; part of the compound key in the Order Details junction table
	X			Category	15	Text	The product's category; used for sorting
	X			Description	45	Text	Description of the product
	X			Size	15	Text	Text field to store the size
	X			Color	20	Text	Text field to store the color description
	X			Price	Auto	Currency	The current price for the product
	X			QuantityInStock	Long	Number	Units in stock in Product Table; units ordered in Orders Table
		X	X	**OrderID**	Auto	AutoNumber	The primary key in the Orders table; part of the compound key in the Order Details junction table
		X		OrderDate	Auto	Date/Time	Stores the date each order was placed
			X	Quantity	Long	Number	Stores the number of detail items in a specific order

TIP Some of the field names in the data dictionary appear different from those shown in Figure 2.1. This is to assist in avoiding confusion when constructing queries, as you will do in Project 4. There is no limitation in Access, however, in having the same field name in two separate tables.

The data dictionary now has a total of eight columns and 18 rows. The four left-most columns indicate the four tables (relations) in the database. The rows indicate the attributes for each relation. The Field Name, Field Size, and Data Type columns are helpful for designing the table objects. The right-most column contains additional information about the fields. Later in this project you will create the three additional tables shown here, but first you will learn how the process of database normalization assists you in planning the most efficient database possible.

Database Normalization

As mentioned in Project 1, it is important to make a relational database as efficient as possible, and normalization is the process for doing this. During **normalization** you convert complex data structures into simple and stable structures to maximize the integrity of data while at the same time reducing data redundancy. Database normalization is based on the concept of functional dependency, which is a particular relationship between two attributes. For relation R, attribute B is **functionally dependent** upon attribute A if the value of A uniquely determines each valid instance of attribute B. The notation $A \rightarrow B$ is used to represent a functional dependency, and attribute A is called the **determinant,** because it uniquely determines each valid row in the relation. As you might guess, in a well-designed database, the primary key field is the determinant field.

Normalization is usually accomplished in stages, in which each stage introduces simple rules concerning dependencies between entities and their relationships. In Codd's relational model, each stage of the process corresponds to a **normal form**. There are four normal forms—first, second, third, and Boyce-Codd. Relations must be converted to each form in that order during normalization. Databases normalized to either the third normal form or the Boyce-Codd normal form are considered efficient.[1]

The First Normal Form (1NF)

The first stage of normalization is to get each relation into the first normal form, which means it contains no repeating groups. Repeating groups are also called **multi-valued attributes**. An example of a repeating group would be two sales items corresponding to a single customer and price, as shown in Figure 2.7.

FIGURE 2.7

CustName	Product	Price
Jones, Sally	Water Bottle - Clear Water Bottle - White	$4.95
Williams, Peter	Long sleeve Jersey	$39.95
Smith, Bill	T-Shirt	$19.95

Thus, to put a table into **first normal form**, you must define the attributes comprising a relation so as to avoid repeating groups. Changing the table as shown in Figure 2.8 eliminates these repeating groups, and the relation is now normalized to the first normal form.

[1] For a detailed discussion of the normal forms, see D. M. Kroenke, (1998), *Data Processing: Fundamentals, Design, and Implementation* 6th ed. (Upper Saddle River: Prentice Hall), pp. 118-121.

FIGURE 2.8

CustName	Product	Price
Jones, Sally	Water Bottle - Clear	$4.95
Jones, Sally	Water Bottle - White	$4.95
Williams, Peter	Long sleeve Jersey	$39.95
Smith, Bill	T-Shirt	$19.95

The Second Normal Form (2NF)

A relation is in the **second normal form** if it is in the first normal form and, in addition, there are no partial dependencies. A **partial dependency** occurs when one or more non-key attributes are not fully functionally dependent on the entire primary key but are dependent on only part of it. Consider the relation shown in Figure 2.9.

FIGURE 2.9

CustName	SaleDate	ProdID	Product	Price
Jones, Sally	2/1/00	A11609	Water Bottle - White	$4.95
Jones, Sally	3/2/00	B27010	Water Bottle - Clear	$4.95
Williams, Peter	2/17/00	X45661	Long sleeve T-shirt	$19.95
Smith, Bill	2/21/00	R10211	Cycling Shorts	$29.95

This relation is in the first normal form because it avoids repeating groups, but it is not in the second normal form because there are partial dependencies. Why? To uniquely identify each transaction in this table requires a compound primary key. If the key consists of customer name, sale date, and product number, then the two non-key attributes—product description and price—are not fully dependent on the primary key.

A relation with a simple primary key (a key consisting of a single attribute) is always in the second normal form. The relation shown in Figure 2.9 can be normalized to the second normal by decomposing it into two relations, one consisting of customer ID, customer name, sale date, and product number, and a second relation listing product number, product name, and price, as Figure 2.10 shows. The Product ID field can then be used to relate data between the two tables.

FIGURE 2.10

CustID	CustName	SaleDate	ProdID
0001	Jones, Sally	2/1/00	A11609
0001	Jones, Sally	3/2/00	B27010
0003	Williams, Peter	2/17/00	X45661
0004	Smith, Bill	2/21/00	R10211

ProdID	Product	Price
A11609	Water Bottle - White	$9.95
B27010	Water Bottle - Clear	$9.95
X45661	Long sleeve T-shirt	$19.95
R10211	Cycling Shorts	$29.95

The Third Normal Form (3NF)

A relation is in the *third normal form* if it is in the second normal form and no transitive dependencies exist. A *transitive dependency* is a functional dependency between two or more non-key attributes. Transitive dependencies can result in *update anomalies*, or problems with the data if the relation is changed. Consider the relation shown in Figure 2.11.

FIGURE 2.11

OrderID	CustName	SaleDate	ProdID	UnitsSold	NumInStock
1001	Jones, Sally	2/1/98	A11609	2	87
1002	Jones, Sally	3/2/98	B27010	1	121
1003	Williams, Peter	2/17/98	X45661	4	312
1004	Smith, Bill	2/21/98	R10211	2	46

This relation is in the second normal form because all non-key attributes are fully dependent on the primary key (OrderID). However there is a transitive dependency: The number in stock entity is functionally dependent on product number, and product number is functionally dependent on OrderID. If any order is deleted from the database during maintenance (such as deleting an incomplete or canceled order), information about the remaining quantity in stock will be lost. This situation can be corrected by decomposing the relation into two distinct relations: *Orders* (containing the attributes order number, customer name, sale date, and quantity) and *Products* (with the attributes product number, and number in stock).

The Boyce-Codd Normal Form (BCNF)

Conceptually, normalization is a difficult concept, and bringing a database to the third normal form is often a challenge. The *Boyce-Codd normal form (BCNF)* is a stronger version of the third normal form and easier to understand. A relation is in the Boyce-Codd normal form if and only if every determinant is a candidate key.

Review again the high-level E-R diagram (Figure 2.1) and data dictionary (Figure 2.6) for the database structure you will now complete. Each relation—Customers, Orders, and Products—is normalized to the second normal form, since each has a primary key consisting of one attribute. The Order Detail table is also normalized to the second normal form, because the non-key attribute date is fully dependent upon the compound primary key. There is, however, a transitive dependency in the Customers table: City and State are functionally dependent upon zip code.

Check Point

Have you ever ordered a product by telephone, and had the clerk ask for your zip code, and then verify your city and state? If so, you know that the database into which your order data is being entered has been designed to omit a functional dependency such as this.

The database you are designing is in a state of denormalization, which is often accepted. In fact, the wizards in Access that create databases for you often include this functional dependency. Database design is a process of refining data structures for efficiency. There are times when you will accept a degree of denormalization in your data solution.

Designing the Database

Now that you have a better theoretical understanding of database design, you are ready to map the data structure represented by the detailed E-R diagram in Figure 2.1 to an Access database. In Project 1 you created the Customers table from ASCII data. In the tasks that follow, you will create the Products table from a product list stored in Microsoft Excel. You will then use Table Design view in Access to create the Orders and Order Detail tables. Finally, you will use the Relationships window to establish both a one-to-many relationship and a many-to-many relationship using a junction table.

Creating the Products Table by Importing Data from Microsoft Excel

Before customers can place orders, data representing products must first be added to the database. Since the product data is stored in an Excel worksheet, you can import the data directly into Access.

As you might expect, Access 2000 has a number of features for importing data from a variety of formats. You used the Import Wizard in Project 1 to create the Customers table. In this project, you will learn how to use copy and paste to import Excel data into Access.

> **TROUBLESHOOTING** To complete Task 1, you must have Microsoft Excel 2000 installed on your computer. If you do not, you may use the Import Wizard and the procedures you learned in Project 1 to import the *Products.txt* file into Access.

TASK 1: <u>To Create the Products Table:</u>

1 Launch Excel and open the *Products.xls* workbook from your floppy disk.

Web Tip

If you do not have a copy of this file, you can download it from the Select Web site at http://www.prenhall.com/selectadvanced.

2 Select cells A1:G49.

3 Click the Edit menu and choose Copy.

4 Click the Microsoft Access button on the Windows taskbar to switch to Microsoft Access.

5 With the Tables button active in the Database window, click Edit, Paste.

6 Access will display a dialog box asking whether or not the Excel worksheet contains column heading names. Click Yes, as shown in Figure 2.12, because the first row of data in the Excel worksheet contains the field names.

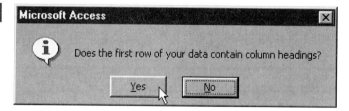

FIGURE 2.12

7 Access will import the worksheet into a table named Sheet1, and the confirmation message shown in Figure 2.13 will appear. Click OK.

FIGURE 2.13

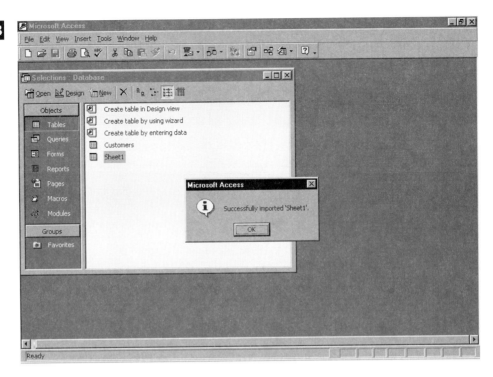

8 Right-click the Sheet1 table icon and choose Rename, as shown in Figure 2.14.

FIGURE 2.14

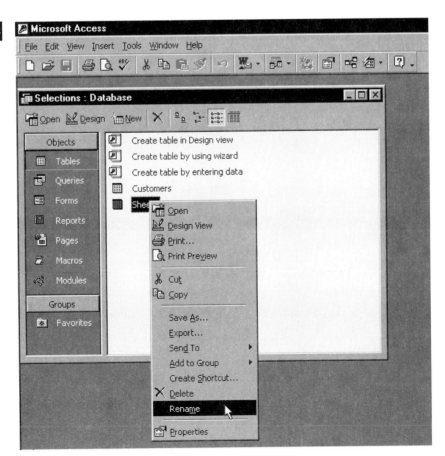

9 Type **Products**, and press (ENTER). The tables shown in Figure 2.15 will now appear in the Database window.

FIGURE 2.15

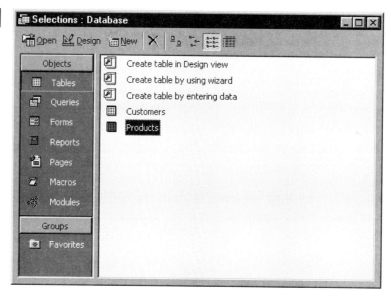

10 Close the *Products.xls* workbook and exit Excel.

There are a few modifications you will need to make to the Products table before establishing relationships. First, however, you will learn how to use Table Design view to create the two additional tables listed in the data dictionary shown in Figure 2.6.

Creating the Orders and Order Detail Tables Using Table Design View

As you know from Introducing Access 2000, you can create tables in Access using Table Design view, using the Table Wizard, or by importing data from an existing file such as a Microsoft Excel workbook. Regardless of the method you choose, you may need to modify the table in the future to accommodate updated database requirements.

Access does not place many restrictions for naming the fields in a table in Design view. A field name can be up to 64 characters in length and may include any combination of letters, numbers, spaces, and special characters except a period (.), an exclamation point (!), an accent grave (`), and brackets ([ ]).

> **TIP** If your database will include Visual Basic code or more complex expressions, consider omitting spaces from the field name.

To store your table data in the most efficient manner, Access supports different data types. A **data type** is a characteristic of the data stored in a database. Depending upon what kind of data your fields will contain, various data types are appropriate. For example, a text data type is required to store name and address information. If you need to perform calculations involving monetary units, you will need to use the currency data type. Table 2.2 summarizes the ten data types you may use for table data.

Table 2.2   Access Data Types

Data Type	Description
Text	Any combination of alphabetic and numeric characters such as names, addresses, and phone numbers. The text data type holds a maximum of 255 characters. This is the default data type.
Memo	Used for long text entries exceeding 255 characters. Holds up to 64 kilobytes of data in a random format.
Number	Numeric values such as inventory quantity or the number of items ordered. Numeric data can be used in calculations.
Date/Time	Date and time values for the years 100 through 9999.
Currency	Currency values and numeric data used in mathematical calculations involving data with one to four decimal places.
AutoNumber	A unique and sequential number is created as records are added to a table. AutoNumber data cannot be changed, edited, or deleted.
Yes/No	Single character data in a Yes/No (Boolean) format. This data type displays a check box.
OLE Object	Fields that contain embedded or linked objects such as a Microsoft Excel spreadsheet, a Microsoft Word document, graphics, or sounds.
Hyperlink	Text or combinations of text and numbers stored as text and used as a hyperlink address. This data type is used to link documents to Web pages or other documents.
Lookup Wizard	A field that enables you to choose a value from another table or from a list of values.

When you create a table using a wizard, Access may determine the data types for you. When using Table Design view, you must specify the data types. When you create a table by importing data into Access, it will determine the appropriate data type.

Creating Tables Using Table Design View

Although sales transaction data does not yet exist, you need to create the Orders and Order Detail tables before establishing the relationships. A common method for creating tables in Access is by using **Table Design view**. To create a table with this method, enter the names and properties for each field in the table. Once this process is complete, you save the table structure.

TASK 2: To Create the Orders Table:

1 Verify that the Tables button is selected in the Database window.

2 Click the New button 🖫 New.

3 Select Design View in the New Table dialog box, then click OK, as shown in Figure 2.16.

FIGURE 2.16

4 Access will open a new table in Table Design view, which consists of the two panes displayed in Figure 2.17.

FIGURE 2.17

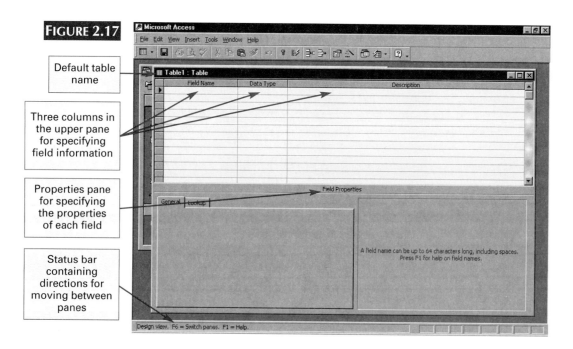

Default table name

Three columns in the upper pane for specifying field information

Properties pane for specifying the properties of each field

Status bar containing directions for moving between panes

5 The *Table Design window* is a visual workspace where you can enter information about each field in your table. Table Design view will always display this window.

6 The insertion point will be in the left column of the first row of the upper pane. Type **OrderID** in the left column of the first row and press (TAB) to move the insertion point into the Data Type column of the upper pane.

7 Click the drop-down list button in the Data Type column, and select AutoNumber as the data type for this field, as shown in Figure 2.18.

> **TIP** In Access, the AutoNumber data type is often used as a primary key, because it will always contain a unique, non-null value. In this context, a ***null value*** is missing data in a field. Since the primary key is a determinant, it must have a value.

FIGURE 2.18

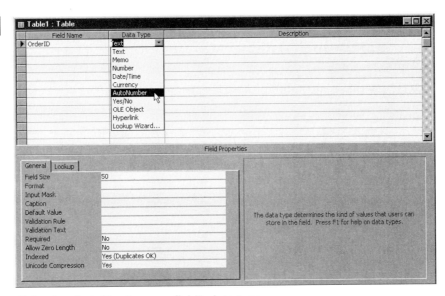

Selecting AutoNumber as a field's data type

8 Press (TAB) to move the insertion point into the Description column. Type **Primary Key.**

> **TIP** Although Access does not require anything in the Description column, you should consider documenting information about the table's structure for future reference.

9 Click the Primary Key button ![icon] on the Database toolbar to make this field the primary key.

> **TIP** An icon representing this field as the primary key appears to the left of the field name in the upper pane of the Table Design window.

10 Press (TAB) once to move the insertion point into the Field Name column for the second row. Type **CustID** as the field name.

11 Press (TAB) to move the insertion point into the Data Type column. Select Number as the data type.

> **TIP** You will need to define the CustID field in the Orders table as a Number data type because it must relate to the ID field in the Customers table. To establish a relationship that enforces referential integrity, the data types must be equal. In the case of an AutoNumber field, the required data type for a relationship is the Number type.

12 Press (TAB) once to move to the Description field. Type **Foreign key: link to the Customer's table** as the description for this field.

13 Press (TAB) once to move the insertion point into the Field Name column for the third row and type **OrderDate** as the field name.

14 Set the data type to Date/Time, and type **Date the order was placed** as the description. When you are finished, the table will appear as shown in Figure 2.19.

FIGURE 2.19

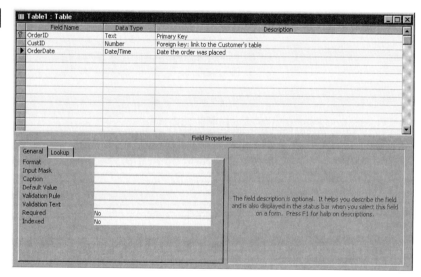

15 Click the Save button ![icon] on the Table Design toolbar to save the table structure.

16 Type **Orders** in the Save As dialog box as the table name and click OK, as shown in Figure 2.20.

FIGURE 2.20

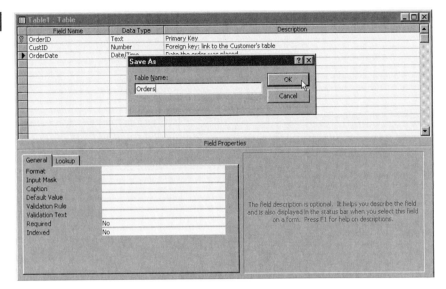

17 Click File, then click Close to close the table.

 Break Point

If necessary, you can close your database, exit Access, and continue this project later.

You are now ready to create the fourth table in your database. After you create the Order Detail table, you will be ready to establish the relationships your database will require. Remember that the Order Detail table is called a junction table, since it will be used to create a many-to-many relationship between Orders and Products.

 TASK 3: To Create the Order Detail Table:

1 Launch Access if it is not currently running, and open the *Selections* database if necessary.

2 Click the Tables button in the Database window, if it is not currently active.

3 Click the New button, select Design View in the New Table dialog box, and click OK.

4 Using the specifications shown in Table 2.3, create the Order Detail table.

Table 2.3   Specifications for the *Order Detail* table

Field Name	Data Type	Description
OrderID	Number	Compound key
ProdID	Text	Compound key
Quantity	Number	Item quantity

5   Point to the square ▶ immediately to the left of the first row of the upper pane of the Table Design grid. This is the row selector, which you can use to select the row.

6   Click the Record Selector for the first row, press and hold (SHIFT), and click the Row Selector for the second row. The selection will appear as shown in Figure 2.21.

FIGURE 2.21

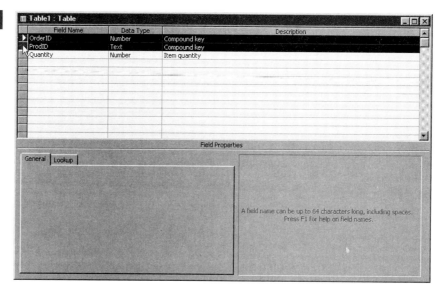

7   Click the Primary Key button on the Table Design toolbar. This will establish the primary key required for the junction table.

Check Point

How do you establish a many-to-many relationship? Remember that in Access, you can create a many-to-many relationship by defining a third table (called a junction table) whose primary key consists of two fields: the foreign keys from both Tables. A many-to-many relationship is really two one-to-many relationships with a third table.

8 Place the insertion point in the second row of the upper pane to select it. Press F6 to move to the lower pane.

9 Select the current setting for the field size, as shown in Figure 2.22. Note that your screen may display a different value, depending on how Access is configured.

FIGURE 2.22

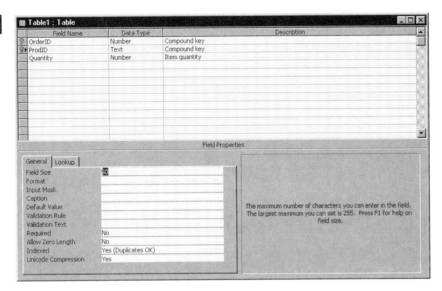

10 Type **10** as the new value for the field size. This is the maximum length of all product ID fields in the Products table, and the setting here must match that table to establish a relationship.

11 Save the table. Access will ask you to name the table.

12 Type **Order Detail** as the table name, and click OK. Close the table.

13 Select the Products table in the Database window.

14 Click the Design button [Design].

15 Set the field size property of the ProdID field to 10, and set it as the primary key.

16 Save your changes to the Products table. When the message shown in Figure 2.23 appears, click Yes, and then close the table.

FIGURE 2.23

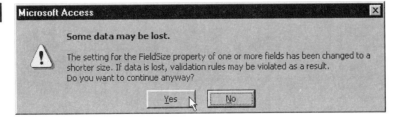

You have finished creating the tables your database requires. You will make additional modifications in Project 3, but at this point you are ready to establish relationships between tables.

Establishing Relationships

After you have determined an optimum table structure and created the tables in your database, you need a way of telling Microsoft Access how to bring that information back together again. The first step in this process is to define relationships between your tables. After you've established the appropriate relationships in your database, you can create queries, forms, and reports to display information from several tables at once.

The **Relationships window** is a visual workspace for creating and modifying relationships. Access recognizes three kinds of relationships, as summarized in Table 2.4.

Table 2.4   Three kinds of relationships

Type of Relationship	Definition
One-to-one	Each record in Table A can have only one matching record in Table B, and each record in Table B can have only one matching record in Table A. This type of relationship is not common because most information related in this way would be in one table.
One-to-many	A one-to-many relationship Is the most common type of relationship. In a one-to-many relationship, a record in Table A can have many matching records in Table B, but a record in Table B has only one matching record in Table A.
Many-to-many	In a many-to-many relationship, a record in Table A can have many matching records in Table B, and a record in Table B can have many matching records in Table A. A many-to-many relationship is really two one-to-many relationships with a third table.

Your database will contain a total of three one-to-many relationships, with two of these comprising a many-to-many relationship.

 Check Point

Why will your database contain three one-to-many relationships? A one-to-many relationship is required between the Customers and Orders tables, as any customer may place more than one order. To establish a many-to-many relationship between Orders and Products, you will need to establish two one-to-many relationships between the Orders table and the Order Details junction table, and also between the Order Details junction table and the Products table.

TASK 4: To Open the Relationships Window and Add Tables

1 Click the Relationships button ▣ on the Database toolbar to open the Relationships window. The Show Table dialog box will be displayed, as shown in Figure 2.24.

> **TROUBLESHOOTING** If the Show Table dialog box does not appear, click the Show Table ▣ button , or choose Show Table from the Relationships menu.

FIGURE 2.24

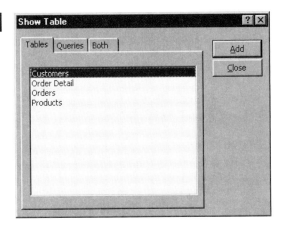

2 Select the four table names by clicking and dragging the left mouse button, and click the Add button, as shown in Figure 2.25. The tables are added to the Relationships window.

FIGURE 2.25

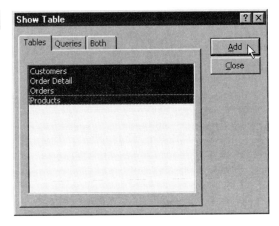

> **TROUBLESHOOTING** Make sure you only click the Add button once, as it is possible to add multiple instances of a table to the Relationships window. If you inadvertently add multiple instances, you will need to delete the extra tables from the window by selecting each table then pressing the (DELETE) key.

3 Click the Close button to close the Add Table dialog box.

4 You can move and resize the tables in the Relationships window using the title bar and the left mouse button. Click the Title bar of each table to reposition it, so your tables are arranged like those shown in Figure 2.26. Note also that the Customers and Products tables have been resized to display all field names.

FIGURE 2.26

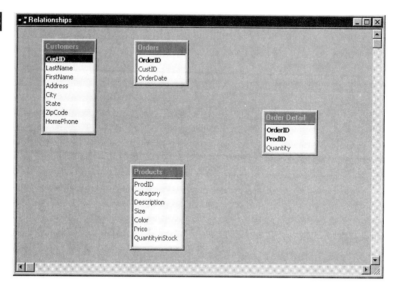

5 Click the ID field in the Customers table, and while pressing the left mouse button, drag this field to the corresponding CustID field in the Orders table, as shown in Figure 2.27. Notice the icon representing the common field.

FIGURE 2.27

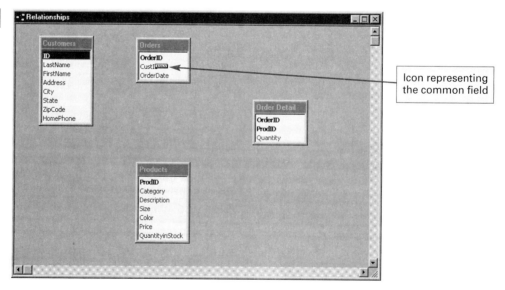

Icon representing the common field

6 Release the left mouse button. The Edit Relationships dialog box will appear.

7 Click the check box to enforce referential integrity and click the Create button, as shown in Figure 2.28.

> **TIP** *Referential integrity* is a system of rules that Access uses to ensure that relationships between records in related tables are valid, and that you don't accidentally delete or change related data. In this case, Access will not allow you to enter a value in the Orders CustID field that does not exist in the Customers table, or to delete a customer record from the Customers table if it has a related field in the Orders table.

FIGURE 2.28

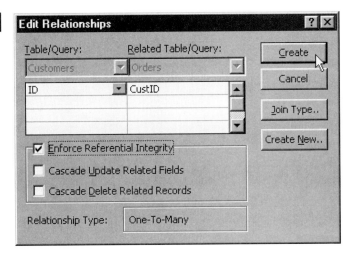

8 You have successfully created the one-to-many relationship shown in Figure 2.29.

FIGURE 2.29

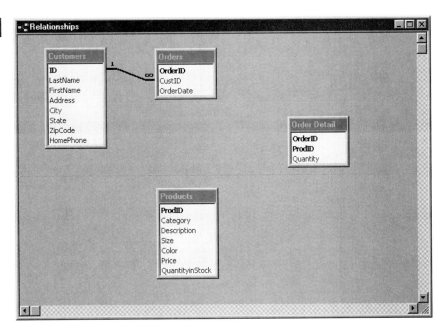

9 Repeat the procedures explained above to establish a one-to-one relationship between the Orders and Order Detail tables. Enforce referential integrity.

> **TIP** Refer to Figure 2.30 if necessary.

10 Create a one-to-many relationship between the Order Detail and Products table, with referential integrity enforced.

11 Reposition the tables in the Relationships window, if necessary.

12 Click Save. Your database will contain the relationships shown in Figure 2.30.

FIGURE 2.30

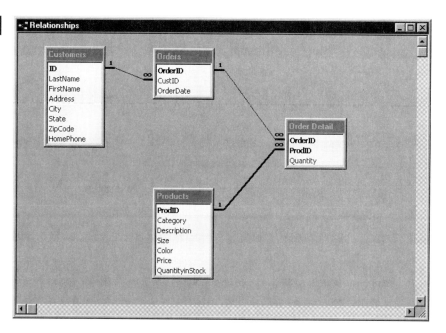

13 Close the Relationships window.

> **TIP** You may view or edit the relationships at any time by selecting Relationships from the Tools menu.

Your database is almost ready to store sales transaction data. In Project 3, you will modify the tables to make data entry more efficient, and learn how to add records to the database.

Summary and Exercises

Summary

- Cardinality determines how many records can or must be related between two tables.
- Cardinalities can be optional or mandatory.
- One-to-one cardinality relates exactly one record in the child table to each record in the other parent table.
- One-to-many cardinality relates one or more records in the child table to each record in the parent table.
- Relationships represented in an E-R diagram must be read in two directions to determine the cardinalities.
- Normalization is the process of simplifying complex data structures.
- Relations normalized to either the third normal form or the Boyce-Codd normal form are considered efficient.
- You can establish relationships using the Relationships window.
- A many-to-many relationship requires two one-to-many relationships with a junction table.

Key Terms and Operations

Key Terms

A → B	null value
Boyce-Codd normal form (BCNF)	one-to-many relationship
cardinality	one-to-one relationship
child table	optional cardinality
data type	parent table
determinant	partial functional dependency
first normal form (1NF)	referential integrity
full functional dependency	Relationships window
junction table	second normal form (2NF)
mandatory cardinality	Table Design view
many-to-many relationship	Table Design window
multi-valued attribute	third normal form (3NF)
normal form	transitive dependency
normalization	update anomalies

Operations

create a table by importing an Excel worksheet
create tables using Table Design View
enforce referential integrity
establish a one-to-many relationship
establish a many-to-many relationship

Study Questions

Multiple Choice

1. The process of converting complex data structures to a more simple form is called:
   a. cardinality.
   b. referential integrity.
   c. normalization.
   d. functional dependency.
   e. update anomaly.

2. A database in the second normal form has eliminated all:
   a. multi-valued attributes.
   b. repeating groups.
   c. partial dependencies.
   d. transitive dependencies.
   e. a and b.

3. A database in the third normal form has eliminated all:
   a. multi-valued attributes.
   b. repeating groups.
   c. partial functional dependencies.
   d. transitive dependencies.
   e. all of the above.

4. A database in the first normal form has eliminated all:
   a. multi-valued attributes.
   b. repeating groups.
   c. partial functional dependencies.
   d. transitive dependencies.
   e. a and b.

5. A Customers table is related to an Orders table. The cardinality from the Customers table to the Orders table is most likely:
   a. one-to-many.
   b. mandatory.
   c. optional.
   d. mandatory one-to-many.
   e. optional one-to-many.

6. A relation without transitive dependencies has been normalized to the:
   a. first normal form.
   b. second normal form.
   c. third normal form.
   d. Boyce-Codd normal form.
   e. None of the above

7. A relation without repeating groups has been normalized to the:
    a. first normal form.
    b. second normal form.
    c. third normal form.
    d. Boyce-Codd normal form.
    e. None of the above.

8. In Access, a many-to-many relationship consists of:
    a. two one-to-one relationships.
    b. a single many-to-many relationship.
    c. a junction table.
    d. two one-to-many relationships.
    e. c and d.

9. A high level E-R diagram contains a graphical representation of:
    a. entities, attributes, and primary keys.
    b. entities.
    c. entities, attributes, primary keys, and cardinalities.
    d. entities and attributes.
    e. attributes and data types.

10. In Microsoft Access, the many sides of a one-to-many relationship are represented in the Relationships window by which of the following?
    a. , (comma)
    b. 1
    c. 100
    d. * (the asterisk symbol)
    e. ∞ (the infinity symbol)

Short Answer

1. What is the name for the procedure required to simplify complex data structures?

2. A database is considered efficient when it is normalized to what form?

3. What term is used to describe how records in one table relate to those in another table?

4. A relation in which not all non-key attributes are dependent on the primary key attribute contains what?

5. How are entities, attributes, relations, and cardinalities graphically represented in data modeling?

6. If a database is not normalized, what can potentially occur?

7. What kind of relationship relates only one record in the parent table to many records in the child table?

8. What does normalizing a database to the third normal form eliminate?

9. A relation will always be in the second normal form if it contains what element based on a single attribute?

10. In a database containing Customers and Orders relations, what term describes the fact that a customer may never have placed an order?

Fill In the Blank

1. The relational model was developed by _____.

2. Codd's 3NF removes _____ _____ from a database.

3. A relation is in the 2NF if it does not contain _____ _____.

4. A key comprised of two or more fields is called a _____ key.

5. To establish a many-to-many relationship in Access, you need _____ one-to-many relationships.

6. A many-to-many relationship requires a _____ table.

7. A detailed E-R diagram represents entities, _____ relations, and cardinality.

8. Access uses the _____ symbol to represent the many side of a relationship.

9. In Access, _____ _____ determines when records can be added and deleted from related tables.

10. When reading E-R diagrams, you interpret the relationships by reading each cardinality in _____ direction(s).

For Discussion

1. What is database normalization? Why is it important?

2. What is referential integrity?

3. How do the second and third normal forms differ?

4. Describe the difference between mandatory and optional cardinality.

5. How do you establish a many-to-many relationship in an Access database?

Hands-On Exercises

1. Modifying the Employee Database

The *Employee* database you created in Review Exercise 1 of Project 1 needs an additional table that lists employee time card data. Follow these steps to update the database:

1. Open the *Employees.mdb* database from your floppy disk.

2. Open the Employees table in Design view, place the insertion point in the first row, and click Insert, Rows.

3. Create a field named EmpID. Set the data type to Text, and the field size to 9.

4. Save the table, and switch to Datasheet view. Enter a unique Social Security Number for each employee. Type the numbers only, with no hyphens, dashes, or spaces.

5. Switch to Design view, and set the EmpID field as the primary key. Close the table and save your changes.

6. Create a new table in Design view with the fields listed in Table 2.5. Name this table *TimeCards*, and do not set a primary key when you save it.

Table 2.5

Field Name	Data Type	Field Size or Format
EmpID	Text	9
StartDate	Date/Time	Default
EndDate	Date/Time	Default
Hours	Number	Default

7. Close the TimeCards table.

8. Select Relationships from the Tools menu.

9. Add both tables to the Relationships window.

10. Create a one-to-many relationship between the tables, using the EmpID field.

11. Enforce referential integrity. The relationship will appear as shown in Figure 2.31.

FIGURE 2.31

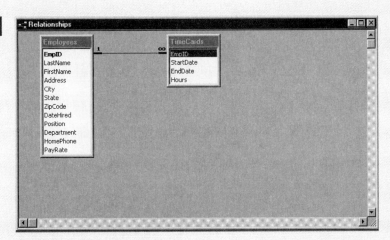

12. Close the Relationships window, save the changes you have made, and close the database.

2. Creating a One-to-One Relationship

As you learned in this Project, there are times when you may want to establish a one-to-one relationship between tables for security reasons. In a one-to-one relationship, each record in Table A can have only one matching record in Table B, and each record in Table B can have only one matching record in Table A. Open the *Secure Employees.mdb* database file from your floppy diskette.

 **Web Tip**

If you do not have a copy of this file, you can download it from the Select Web site at http://www.prenhall.com/selectadvanced.

Complete the following:

1. Click Tools, Relationships.

2. Add both the Employees and the PayrollData tables to the Relationships window.

3. Create a one-to-one relationship using the EmpID field. Enforce referential integrity. The relationship will appear as shown in Figure 2.32.

FIGURE 2.32

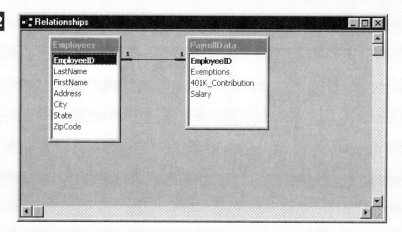

4. Save your changes, close the Relationships window, and close the database.

On Your Own Exercises

1. Compacting a Database

Whenever you modify your database objects, the database file grows in size. If you open your database from a floppy disk, it is a good idea to periodically compact it. By keeping the file size as small as possible, you can locate and manipulate records more quickly.

To compact the Selections database:

1. Open the *Selections* database file on your floppy disk.

2. Select Database Utilities from the Tools menu.

3. Select Compact and Repair Database from the cascading menu.

4. Close the database when you are finished.

2. Creating a Backup of a Database

As you work with Access, it is important to periodically back up your work. Unlike other Office 2000 applications, there is no method from within Access of backing up the entire database file. To back up the *Selections.mdb* database, do the following:

1. Using My Computer or the Windows Explorer, display the *Selections.mdb* database on your floppy disk.

2. Select the database file and click Edit, Copy.

3. Select Edit, Paste. Windows will create a copy of the file.

4. Right-click the copy of the file, and choose Rename. Use *Selections– BU* as the new filename.

5. Close My Computer or the Windows Explorer.

3. Creating a Table of Web Site Ratings

Open the *Web Sites.mdb* database you created in Project 1. Create a table with two fields that lists five ratings for Web sites. The first field will be an AutoNumber type, and the second a text data type. Save the table as *Ratings*.

4. Adding a Lookup Field to a Table

Modify the *Sites* table in the Web Sites database by adding a lookup field that looks up the Web site ratings from the Ratings table. Rate each site in the database and save your changes when you are finished.

Modifying Table Design and Setting Table Properties

Now that you have created tables and established relationships in your database, you are almost ready to begin designing queries, which you will do in Project 4. Before you combine data from the tables in your solution, however, you will want to modify the table design to improve the accuracy of the information in your database.

Objectives

After completing this project, you will be able to:

➤ Rename the primary key field in a table

➤ Change the field size property of text fields in the Customers and Products tables

➤ Define data validation criteria

➤ Set data validation text

➤ Test validation criteria

➤ Create and modify input masks

➤ Create and modify Lookup fields

Running Case

As you learned in Project 2, once you have designed the table structure for your database, you are ready to begin designing other database objects that pull information together, such as queries, forms, and reports. However, you want your database to be as efficient as possible to preserve the integrity of data. Therefore, it is important to consider ways in which you might modify the table specifications to produce the most accurate information possible.

The Challenge

Mr. Traylor is pleased with the progress you have made in designing a prototype Selections, Inc. e-commerce database. He wants to be sure, however, that the database is as easy as possible to use by the employees who will enter transaction data. Therefore, he has asked you to do the following. First, he noticed that the name of the primary key in the Customers table does not match the specifications of the data dictionary, and it needs to be changed. Second, he would like for you to find some way of limiting the data that can be entered into certain fields to avoid data entry errors. For example, for any order detail, the item quantity must be a positive, non-zero integer. Third, he wants to know if there is any method for simplifying entries like phone numbers and zip codes. Finally, he wants to know if data entry personnel can automatically access product or customer information by product or customer number.

The Solution

Now that you have designed the basic structure of the Selections, Inc. e-commerce database, you are almost ready to begin designing queries, forms, and reports. As you learned in Projects 1 and 2, good database design entails critical thinking about how best to store database information in multiple tables to make the database as efficient as possible. You know that the goal of database normalization is to arrive at stable data structures that will most effectively enable you to store information in your database. To use this information, however, you will need to create additional database objects: queries for returning data from multiple tables and for performing calculations, and screen forms based upon tables or queries. In addition, you will want to create reports for listing information such as customer invoice or shipping data.

Before you create these additional objects, however, you will need to make the modifications Mr. Traylor has requested. Fortunately, Access 2000 includes the tools and features that will enable you to easily meet each of his design objectives. First, by using Table Design view, you can rename the primary key field in the Customer table. Because you will not be changing the data type of the size of the field, Access will update all references to this table automatically. At this point, the only information that will be updated is the one-to-many relationship between the Customers and Orders tables. In addition, there are other field properties you will need to change in this table so its structure matches the data dictionary.

You can set data validation criteria to meet Mr. Traylor's second request. As you will see, a validation rule limits the data that can be entered into the field. Therefore, you can eliminate errors, such as an order for a negative quantity or zero value quantity. When you set validation rules, it is best to also specify validation text so a message will explain to the user what to do if a validation rule is violated. Figure 3.1 displays a validation text message.

FIGURE 3.1

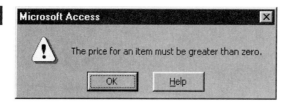

To simplify entering data such as telephone numbers and zip codes, you can add an input mask to a field. Figure 3.2 displays an input mask that makes entering telephone numbers easier in a simple screen form.

FIGURE 3.2

🔲 Customers		
CustID	31	
LastName	Samual	
FirstName	Adams	
Address	42211 E. Flint Road	
City	Boston	
State	MA	
ZipCode	02134-	
HomePhone	(617) _-___	

Record: ◄◄ ◄   31   ► ►► ►✱ of 31

Finally, to utilize existing table data when entering records such as a customer order, you can add a lookup field to a parent table. Users can select an option from a drop-down list that is bound to the related table instead of having to type a foreign key value into the field. Figure 3.3 shows how to select a specific customer when placing an order.

FIGURE 3.3

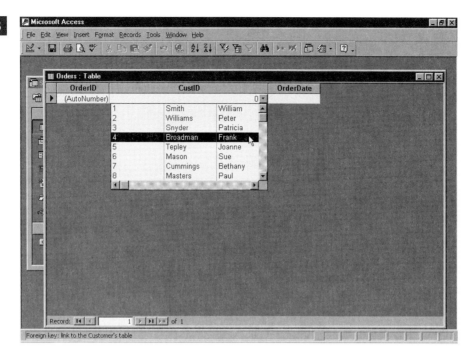

The table modifications you will complete in this project are common in Access databases. Once you have made these changes at the table level, other objects based upon the tables (notably queries and forms) can take advantage of these modifications.

The Setup

To modify the tables as specified above, launch Microsoft Access, open the *Selections.mdb* database you modified in Project 2, and make sure that you select the settings listed in Table 3.1. If you need additional assistance setting these options, refer to Figure 1.1 through 1.3 of Project 1. This will ensure that your screen matches the illustrations and the tasks in this project function as described.

Table 3.1 Access Settings

Location	Make these settings:
Office Shortcut Bar	If the Office Shortcut bar is visible, close it by right-clicking the Office icon on the shortcut bar and choosing Exit.
Office Assistant	Hide the Office Assistant.
Tools, Customize	Click the Toolbars tab and display the Database toolbar and the Menu Bar, as shown in Figure 1.1 of Project 1, if they are not currently visible.
Tools, Customize	Click the Options tab, and make sure the check box to display recently used menu commands first is deselected, as shown in Figure 1.2 of Project 1.
Tools, Options	Click the View tab and display Status bar, Startup dialog box, New object shortcuts, and Windows in Taskbar, as shown in Figure 1.3 of Project 1.

Renaming a Primary Key field

After creating tables in a database, it is not uncommon to rename one or more fields. You will recall that, in Project 1, when you imported existing customer information into Access, the Text Import Wizard assigned a primary key by creating an AutoNumber field. By default, this field is named ID. In this next task you will rename the field so it matches the specifications in your data dictionary.

TASK 1: To Rename the Primary Key Field in the Customers Table

1 Click the Relationships button to open the Relationships window.

2 Right-click over the Customers table and select Table Design, as shown in Figure 3.4.

Check Point

What other methods can you use to open the Customers table in Design view?

FIGURE 3.4

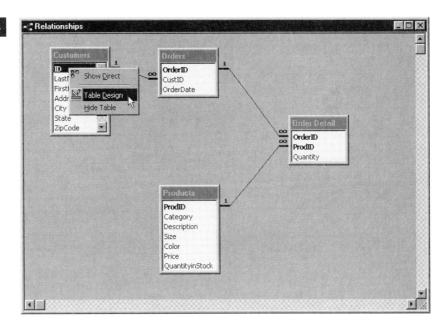

3 Place the insertion point at the beginning of the ID field name and type **Cust**. The field name will now appear as shown in Figure 3.5.

FIGURE 3.5

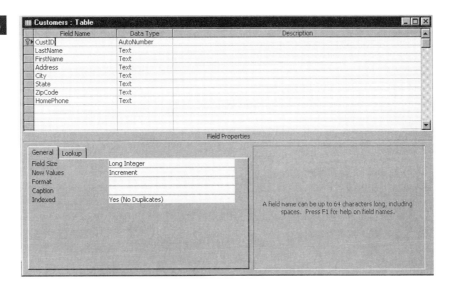

Modifying the Field Size Property of Text Fields

Now that you have renamed the primary key, you can change the field size property for other fields in the table. When you create an Access table by importing a file, the field size for all text fields is set to the default field size, up to 255 characters. Obviously, fields such as State do not need this much space reserved for each record. Figure 3.6 displays the data dictionary for this database. In the next task you will modify the field size properties for all text fields in the Customers and Products tables.

FIGURE 3.6

Customers Table	Products Table	Orders Table	Order Details Table	Field Name	Field Size	Data Type	Field Description
X		X		**CustID**	Auto	AutoNumber	Primary key; format to 4 digits using \0000; non key in Orders Table
X				LastName	25	Text	Last name of customer
X				FirstName	20	Text	First name of customer
X				Address	35	Text	Street address or post office box
X				City	20	Text	Customer's city of residence
X				State	2	Text	State; input mask force to upper case, required >LL
X				ZipCode	10	Text	Zip code with optional extension; input mask
X				HomePhone	14	Text	Customer's phone; input mask
	X		X	**ProdID**	8	Text	Primary key in Product Table; part of the compound key in the Order Details junction table
	X			Category	18	Text	The product's category; used for sorting
	X			Description	45	Text	Description of the product
	X			Size	15	Text	Text field to store the size
	X			Color	20	Text	Text field to store the color description
	X			Price	Auto	Currency	The current price for the product
	X			QuantityInStock	Long	Number	Units in stock in Product Table; units ordered in Orders Table
		X	X	**OrderID**	Auto	AutoNumber	The primary key in the Orders table; part of the compound key in the Order Details junction table
		X		OrderDate	Auto	Date/Time	Stores the date each order was placed
			X	Quantity	Long	Number	Stores the number of detail items in a specific order

TASK 2: To Modify the Field Size Property of Text Fields in the Customers Table

1 Click anywhere in the LastName field row.

> **TIP** When you are modifying field properties, the insertion point can be in any column of the field row.

2 Highlight the current field size setting.

3 Type **25** and press (TAB).

4 Using Figure 3.6 as a guide, change the field size property of the remaining text fields in the table.

5 Save your changes to the table. A message box will appear, warning you that some data may be lost when you shorten these fields. Click Yes, as shown in Figure 3.7.

FIGURE 3.7

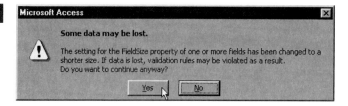

6 Close the Customers table.

7 Right-click over the Products table in the Relationships window, and choose Table Design.

8 Change the field size property of the following fields: Category, Description, Size and Color. Use Figure 3.7 as a guide as you complete this step.

9 Save your changes to the table and close it.

10 Close the Relationships window.

Defining Data Validation Criteria

Now that all the fields in the database are set to the appropriate field size, you are ready to specify validation criteria. Access supports two methods for improving the accuracy of field data as it is entered into tables or forms: input masks and validation rules. A *validation rule* is a field property that specifies requirements for data entered into a record, field, or control. If users enter data that violates the *ValidationRule* property, you can use the *ValidationText* property to specify the message to be displayed indicating the error.

> **TIP** ValidationRule and ValidationText are properties, so the names of each do not have spaces.

In this case, a message box will appear that displays the *validation text* specified by the ValidationText property. Validation rules are particularly important for number and currency data types that are used in calculations.

For example, in the Selections, Inc. e-commerce database, Price in the Products table and Quantity in the Order Detail table both must be positive values that are greater than zero. In the case of the quantity field, it will be an integer value. By changing the ValidationRule and ValidationText properties of these fields, you can ensure that the values entered are always positive, and greater than zero.

TASK 3: To Define Data Validation Criteria

1 Open the Products table in Design view.

2 Place the insertion point in any column of the Price field row and press F6 to move to the lower pane of the Table Design window.

3 Click the Validation Rule row and type **>0** as the validation expression.

4 Save these changes to the table. Since the table contains data, Access will inform you that the data integrity rules have been changed, and testing the existing data with the new rules may take a long time.

> **TIP** If you set a validation rule in a field that contains data, Microsoft Access will ask if you want to apply the new rule to existing data when you save the table.

5 Click Yes, as shown in Figure 3.8.

6 Close the table.

FIGURE 3.8

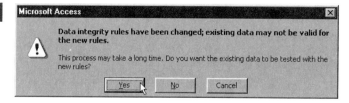

7 Open the Order Detail table in Design view.

8 Change the Data Validation property of the Quantity field to **>0**.

9 Save your changes to the table, and close it.

 Check Point

Why did you not receive a warning when you closed this table?

Setting Data Validation Text

Although you are not required to set the validation text property when you specify a validation rule, it is a good idea to do so. To specify the message that will appear when a user violates a validation rule, enter a text string in the Validation Text property of the field with the validation rule.

 TASK 4: To Set Validation Text

1 Open the Products table in Design view.

2 Click any column in the Price field in the upper pane of the Table Design grid.

3 Press F6 to move to the properties pane, and place the insertion point in the validation Text property row.

4 Type **The price for an item must be greater than zero.** The validation rule and associated validation text will appear as shown in Figure 3.9.

FIGURE 3.9

General | Lookup

Field Size	Double
Format	
Decimal Places	Auto
Input Mask	
Caption	
Default Value	
Validation Rule	>0
Validation Text	or an item must be greater than zero.
Required	No
Indexed	No

The error message that appears when you enter a value prohibited by the validation rule. Press F1 for help on validation text.

TROUBLESHOOTING Since the text string is too long to fit in the column, all of the text is not visible at this time.

5 Save this change to the table design and close the table.

6 Open the Order Detail table in Design view.

7 Place the insertion point in the Quantity field row in the upper pane, and press (F6).

8 Type **The quantity of any item on an order must be greater than zero.** as the validation text property for this field.

9 Save these changes and close the table.

Testing Validation Rules

Now that you have defined validation rules and set the associated validation text, you can check the rule in two ways. One method will check the existing data in a table to see if any fields violate the validation rule. This is useful if you change the validation rule that applies to a specific field. The second method is to change the data of a field to a value that violates the rule. You will then see the associated validation text as a message when the rule is violated.

TASK 5: To Test a Validation Rule

1 Open the Products table in Design view.

2 Right-click the Title bar for the table and choose Test Validation Rules, as shown in Figure 3.10.

FIGURE 3.10

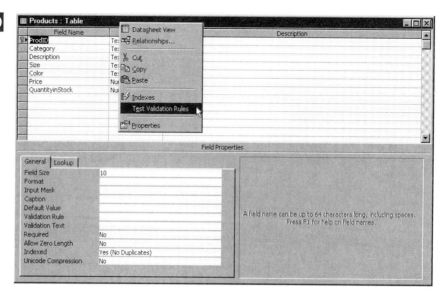

3 The message shown in Figure 3.11 will appear. Click Yes.

FIGURE 3.11

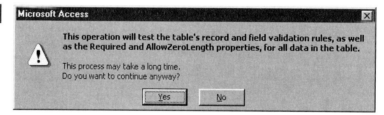

4 Access will apply the validation rule to all data in the table. In this case, no errors are found.

5 Click the Datasheet button ![button] to switch to Datasheet view.

6 Select the price in the first record.

7 Type **-1** as the new value, and press (ENTER). The validation text message shown in Figure 3.12 appears.

FIGURE 3.12

ProdID	Category	Description	Size	Color	Price	QuantityinStoc
RCX2001100	Clothing	Team Ritchey -	Child	White	-1	16
RCX2001110	Clothing	Team Ritchey -	Medium	White	16.95	18
RCX2001120	Clothing	Team Ritchey -	Large	White	16.95	25
RCX2001130	Clothing	Team Ritchey -	Extra Large	White	16.95	35
RCX3052110	Clothing	Team Ritchey C	Medium	Team Colors	49.95	6
RCX3052120	Clothing	Team Ritchey C	Large	Team Colors	49.95	8
RCX3052130	Clothing	Team Ritchey C	Extra Large	Team Colors	49.95	10
RCX3082110	Clothing	Team Ritchey C	Medium	Team Colors	69.95	4
RCX3082120	Clothing				69.95	6
RCX3082130	Clothing				69.95	8
RCX5007210	Clothing				29.95	10
RCX5007220	Clothing				29.95	12
RCX5007230	Clothing				29.95	16
RCX5007240	Clothing				29.95	10
RLA1001110	Accessories	Team Ritchey V	Small	White	4.95	125
RLA1001120	Accessories	Team Ritchey V	Large	White	4.95	100
RLA1001210	Accessories	Team Ritchey V	Small	Clear	4.95	125
RLA1001220	Accessories	Team Ritchey V	Large	White	4.95	100
RLA2007350	Accessories	CPR-4 Multi-Pu	Standard	Silver Anodized	2.95	25
RLA2007370	Accessories	CPR-4 Multi-Pu	Standard	Black Anodized	2.95	25
RLA6001120	Accessories	Team Ritchey V	Standard	Silver Anodized	9.95	30
RMD2001248	Mountain Bicyc	Ritchey P-20	48 cm	Standard	1799	1

Microsoft Access ⚠ The price for an item must be greater than zero. [OK] [Help]

Record: 1 of 48

8 Click OK to remove the message.

9 Press (ESC) to cancel the operation.

10 Close the Products table.

Break Point

If necessary, you can close your database, exit Access, and continue this project later.

Using Input Masks

An **input mask** ensures that the data will fit in the format you define, and you can specify the kind of values that can be entered in a field. You can use the **InputMask property** to display literal characters in the field with blanks to fill in. Access has a number of predefined input masks, and once you create one, you can easily modify it.

Web Tip

For more information on input masks, visit
http://msdn.microsoft.com/library/officedev/off2000/acproInputMaskX1.htm

TASK 6: To Create Input Masks

1 Launch Access if it is not currently running, and open the *Selections* database if necessary.

2 Open the Customers table in Design view.

3 Place the insertion point anywhere in the ZipCode field row in the upper pane of the Table Design grid.

4 Click the Input Mask row in the Properties pane, and click the Build Button ▦ ▾ that appears next to the Property row, as shown in Figure 3.13.

FIGURE 3.13

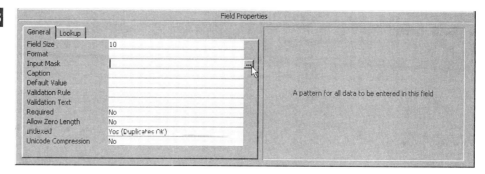

5 The Input Mask Wizard will appear, as shown in Figure 3.14.

TROUBLESHOOTING If the Input Mask Wizard does not appear, the wizards may not be installed on your computer. If this is the case, you will need to enter the input mask manually in the Input Mask property row. Type *00000-9999;0;_* as the property setting.

FIGURE 3.14

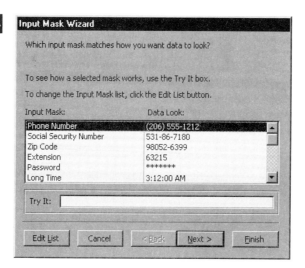

6 Click Zip Code in the list, and then click Next.

7 The Input Mask Wizard will now ask you to verify the settings for the input mask. Accept the default settings shown in Figure 3.15 and click Next.

FIGURE 3.15

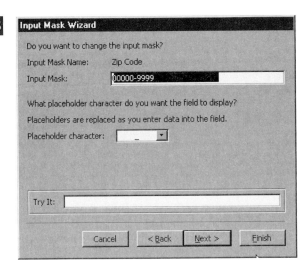

8 In the next step of the Input Mask Wizard, you will be asked to specify how data is stored in the field. The field size for the ZipCode field is 10, so check the option to store the literal character with the zip codes. Since you do not need to set any other properties, click Finish, as shown in Figure 3.16.

FIGURE 3.16

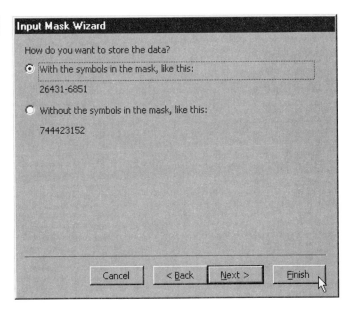

9 Press (F6) to return to the upper pane of the Table Design grid, and click the HomePhone field.

10 Use the Input Mask Wizard to specify an input mask for this field. Accept all the default values, except specify that the mask will contain literal characters. When you are finished, the input mask will appear as shown in Figure 3.17.

FIGURE 3.17

Field Properties

General	Lookup
Field Size	14
Format	
Input Mask	!(999) 000-0000;0;_ ...
Caption	
Default Value	
Validation Rule	
Validation Text	
Required	No
Allow Zero Length	No
Indexed	No
Unicode Compression	No

A pattern for all data to be entered in this field

TROUBLESHOOTING If you do not have the Access Wizards installed, enter the input mask as shown in Figure 3.17.

11 Press F6 to return to the upper pane of the Table Design grid, and click the State field.

12 Press F6 to return to the properties pane.

13 Type **>LL** as the input mask for this field.

Check Point

What does this input mask do? Search the Help System for examples of input masks to determine how the greater than symbol (>) and the capital letter L will display data for this field.

14 Save your changes to the table.

15 Close the table.

TIP Later in this module you will add records to the Customers table. At that time, you will see how the input masks you set will simplify data entry.

Using Lookup Fields

A database with data stored in multiple tables is efficient because you can table data when it is needed. For example, by adding a lookup field to the Orders table, you can look up a specific customer by Customer ID and associate this data with each time card record. From an end user perspective, this means that by simply selecting a customer number in a drop-down list, the name and address information will appear in a form, as you will see in Project 5. A *lookup field* displays values looked up from a related table and displays them in a list. The data can be looked up because the foreign key in the table displaying the looked up list corresponds to the primary key in the table that contains the values. A lookup list is based upon existing data in a table or query, or upon a value list that you create.

Web Tip

For more information on lookup fields, visit
http://msdn.microsoft.com/library/officedev/off2000/acdecWorkingWith
LookupFieldsS.htm

Why use lookup fields? In a database containing relationships, a related (child) table must have a value as the foreign key that matches a primary key value in the parent table. If you have enforced referential integrity, an error message will occur if an invalid value is entered into the foreign key field of the child table because there is no associated primary key. To prevent an error such as this from occurring, you can look up a corresponding value in the parent table. Because the user can select the values from a list instead of typing it into the field, you will always have a valid entry in the foreign key field.

> **TIP** A lookup field requires a relationship between tables. If one does not exist, Access will create it.

You will also add a lookup field to the Order Detail table. What data will you look up? As a customer places an order, each order detail record specifies a single item that will appear in the customer's invoice. Therefore, by looking up a product using its product number, a customer can specify each item appearing on the order. In the task that follows, you will create and modify a lookup field in the Orders table.

TASK 7: To Create and Modify a Lookup Field in the Orders Table

1. Open the Orders table in Design view.

2. Click the CustID field in the upper pane of the Table Design grid to select it.

3 Press (F6) to switch to the Properties pane.

4 Click the Lookup tab.

> **TIP** You can also create a lookup Field when designing or modifying a table by selecting Lookup Wizard as a field's data type.

5 Click the drop-down list button next to the Display Control property setting and choose Combo Box, as shown in Figure 3.18.

> **TIP** The ***Display Control*** is the specific database control that will appear in the table's field for selecting a lookup value.

FIGURE 3.18

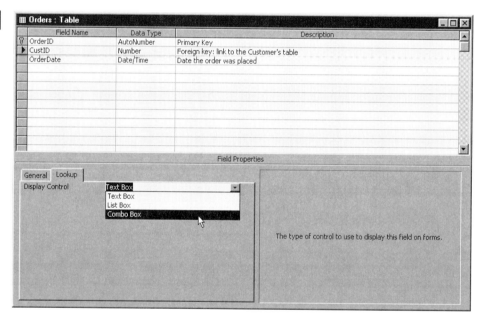

6 The properties pane will specify that the lookup field will use a table or a query as its row source type. The ***row source*** is the underlying database object that contains the data you want to look up. To specify which row of data is the source, click the drop-down list next to the row source.

7 Choose the Customers table from the list, as shown in Figure 3.19.

FIGURE 3.19

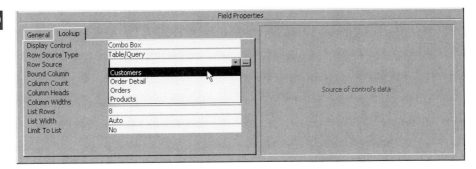

8 Save the table and switch to Datasheet view.

9 Click the CustID field to select it. A drop-down list for the lookup field will appear.

10 Click the drop-down arrow. The customer numbers appear as the looked up data, as shown in Figure 3.20.

FIGURE 3.20

11 Switch to Design view and select the CustID field.

12 Click the Column count row in the Properties pane. Select 1 and type **3** as the new value.

> **TIP** This property specifies the number of fields that will display when a value is looked up. In the design of the Customers table, the first column displays.

13 Save your changes to the table, and switch to Datasheet view.

14 Click and drag the border between the CustID and OrderDate fields, and increase the field width to approximately three times its current width.

15 Select the CustID field and click the drop-down list button. Access now looks up three fields of data from the Customers table, as shown in Figure 3.21.

FIGURE 3.21

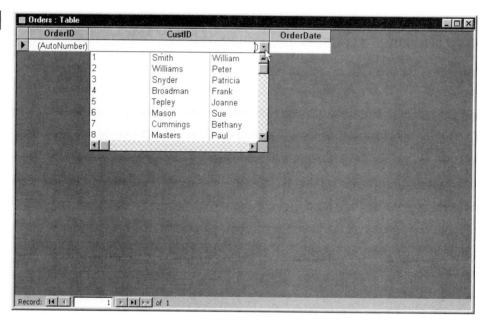

TROUBLESHOOTING Do not select a customer from the list, or you will create a record in the Orders table!

16 Close the table and save your changes to the table design.

Check Point

What changes to the table design did you save in step 16 above?

You are now ready to add a lookup field to the Order Detail table.

TASK 8: To Create and Modify a Lookup Field in the Order Detail Table

1 Open the Order Detail table in Design view.

2 Click the ProdID field in the upper pane of the Table Design grid.

3 Click the Lookup tab in the Properties pane.

4 Select Combo Box as the Display Control for this field.

5 Set the Row Source property to the Products table.

6 Set the Column Count property to 3. Setting this property to 3 will instruct Access to display the ProdID, Category, and Description fields in the lookup list.

7 Save your changes to the table design.

8 Close the table.

You have successfully implemented all the table design specifications that Mr. Traylor gave you. This concludes Part I of this module, in which you have focused upon designing and modifying the table structure of your database solution. In Part II you will learn how to build queries for combining data from the four tables in your database solution, how to create screen forms for order fulfillment, and how to create reports for printing information from the database.

Summary and Exercises

Summary

- Once you have created a table structure, you can modify the properties of specific fields in the table using the Table Design grid in Table Design view.
- To validate data as it is entered into fields, set the DataValidation property of one or more fields in a table.
- When you add data validation specifications to a field, it is a good idea to set the ValidationText property of the field as well, so that a descriptive message is displayed when the validation criterion is violated.
- An input mask provides a preset format for entering data into a field.
- You can use a lookup field to assist data entry by looking up corresponding records in a related table.

Key Terms and Operations

Key Terms

display control	validation rule
input mask	validation text
InputMask property	ValidationRule property
lookup field	ValidationText property
row source	

Operations

change the field size property of text fields	create an input mask
change the ValidationText property of fields	modify a lookup field
	rename a primary key field
create a lookup field	specify validation rules
	test a validation rule

Study Questions

Multiple Choice

1. You should always change the validation text property of a field when you enter a(n):
   a. input mask.
   b. lookup field.
   c. relationship.
   d. validation rule.
   e. row source.

2. Validation rules are especially important when defining fields using which data type?
   a. Memo
   b. Date/Time
   c. Text
   d. Currency
   e. Yes/No

3. A Lookup field list cannot contain:
   a. data from a table.
   b. data in a value list you create.
   c. data from a query.
   d. data from a form.
   e. All of the above.

4. You can change the ValidationText property of a field using:
   a. Datasheet view.
   b. the upper pane of the Table Design window.
   c. the lower pane of the Table Design window.
   d. the Relationships window.
   e. the Title bar of a table.

5. An input mask is appropriate for which of the following fields?
   a. Last Name
   b. Address
   c. Customer ID
   d. Telephone number
   e. Quantity in stock

6. Which field property specifies a message that will appear when invalid data is entered into a field?
   a. Row source
   b. ValidationRule
   c. Display Control
   d. Field Size
   e. ValidationText

7. When you add a lookup field to a table, which table contains the lookup list?
   a. The parent table
   b. The child table
   c. The table containing the foreign key
   d. The table containing the primary key
   e. Both a and d

8. Which property specifies the number of fields that will be displayed in a lookup list?
   a. Row source
   b. Column Count
   c. Field Size
   d. Display Control
   e. Row Source Type

9. Which property specifies the object from which a lookup list is generated?
   a. Row source
   b. Column Count
   c. Field Size
   d. Display Control
   e. Row Source Type

10. To look up data in field, what must exist in the database?
    a. A form bound to the field containing the values you want to look up.
    b. A relationship.
    c. A text field.
    d. A foreign key.
    e. Both b and d.

Short Answer

1. What are the three sources for a lookup list?
2. What does a lookup field require between tables?
3. What happens when you specify Lookup Wizard as a data type?
4. Where do you define validation criteria?
5. How do you change the field size property for a text field?
6. How do you modify the number of columns displayed in a lookup list?
7. How do you rename a primary key?
8. What happens if you violate a validation rule?
9. Which view do you use to change the ValidationText property of a field?
10. How can you test a validation rule?

Fill In the Blank

1. A _____ is a list of data that exists in a table, query, or field list you create.

2. The _____ property specifies how much space Access reserves to store data in a text field.

3. Before you create a lookup field, the _____ key in the child table must relate to the primary key in the parent table.

4. A validation text string will appear in the screen when a _____ is violated.

5. The _____ property specifies what kind of a control will display a lookup list.

6. To rename a field, use the _____ pane of the Table Design grid.

7. The _____ property specifies how many columns of data are displayed in a lookup list.

8. You can _____ a validation rule by right-clicking the Title bar of a table in Design view.

9. When you set the validation rule of a field, you should also consider changing the _____ property.

10. Data looked up by a lookup field in a child table looks up the data in the _____ table.

For Discussion

1. What kind of relationship is required for a lookup field and why?

2. How does the ValidationText property of a field differ from the ValidationRule property?

3. By default, a lookup field will display the leftmost field in a associated parent table. How can you display more information in the lookup list?

4. How do you rename a primary key? What are the implications of doing so?

5. How do you change the amount of space Access reserves for a text field? What may happen to record data when you reduce the field size?

Hands-On Exercises

1. Modifying an Input Mask

After creating an input mask, there may be times when you need to modify it. In this exercise you will open a database with Customer information, and modify the input mask specifying how data is entered into the State field.

To Modify an Input Mask

1. Open the *My Customer.mdb* database from your floppy diskette.

 Web Tip

If you do not have a copy of this file, you may download it from the Select Web site at http://www.prenhall.com/selectadvanced.

2. Open the CustomerList table in Design view.

3. Click the State field in the upper pane of the Table Design grid. The input mask property appears as shown in Figure 3.22.

FIGURE 3.22

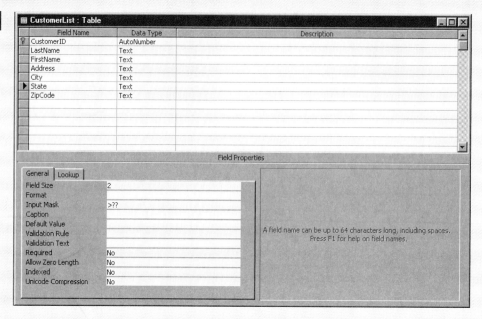

The greater than symbol (>) in this input mask forces all entries to appear in uppercase. Using this code, although a data entry person types the two-character State abbreviation in lowercase, it will always appear in uppercase, which is useful for printing address labels and reports. The two question mark (?) characters, however, specify that the field data is optional

4. Select the current input mask and type **>LL** as a replacement property setting. This will force any entries to uppercase.

5. Save your changes to the table.

6. Close the database.

2. Adding a Lookup Field to the Employees Database

As you learned in this project, lookup fields are very useful when you have related tables in a database and referential integrity is enforced in relationships. In this exercise you will modify the *Employees.mdb* database so that the TimeCards table contains a lookup field to look up employees by number.

To Add a Lookup Field to the TimeCards Table

1. Open the *Employees.mdb* database file you modified in Project 2.

2. Open the TimeCards table in Design view.

3. Click the first row in the table, and click Insert, Rows.

4. Create a field named **TimeCardID** using the AutoNumber data type. Set this field as the primary key.

TIP In Project 2 you created this table without a primary key. Access recommends that all tables have a primary key, so you are adding it here. Using the AutoNumber data type will optimize this field.

5. Select the EmpID field and click the Lookup tab in the Properties pane.

6. Enter the settings shown in Figure 3.23.

FIGURE 3.23

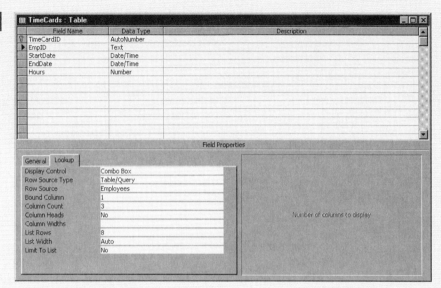

7. Save your changes to the table.

8. Close the *Employees* database.

On Your Own Exercises

1. Adding an Input Mask and Data Validation to the Employees Database

The Employees database does not contain any input masks or data validation specifications. Using the procedures you learned in Project 2, create a copy of this database named *My Employees.mdb*. Open this file and add an appropriate input mask to the EmpID field. Then, add a validation rule specifying that the pay rate must be at least $12 per hour. Add the appropriate validation text message to explain a violation of the rule. Update the table design and close the database when you are finished.

2. Learning More About Input Masks

As you learned in this project, the Input Mask Wizard makes it easy to add an input mask to fields holding data such as telephone numbers, zip codes, and Social Security Numbers. However, once you know the elements of input masks, you can easily create them. In this exercise you will see examples of input masks that are listed in the Help System. Launch Access if it is not running. Press (F1) to open the Help system. Type **Input mask examples** as a search topic and click Search. Select the Examples of input masks topic, which is shown in Figure 3.24. Read about input masks and review the examples. Close Access when you are finished.

FIGURE 3.24

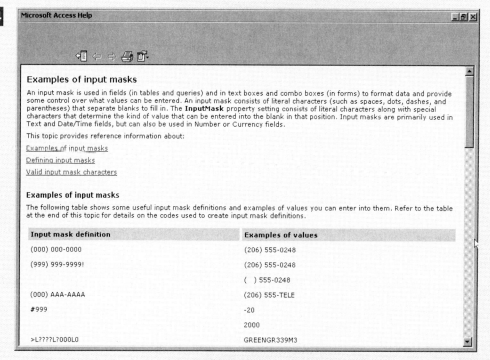

Microsoft Access Help

Examples of input masks

An input mask is used in fields (in tables and queries) and in text boxes and combo boxes (in forms) to format data and provide some control over what values can be entered. An input mask consists of literal characters (such as spaces, dots, dashes, and parentheses) that separate blanks to fill in. The **InputMask** property setting consists of literal characters along with special characters that determine the kind of value that can be entered into the blank in that position. Input masks are primarily used in Text and Date/Time fields, but can also be used in Number or Currency fields.

This topic provides reference information about:

Examples of input masks

Defining input masks

Valid input mask characters

Examples of input masks

The following table shows some useful input mask definitions and examples of values you can enter into them. Refer to the table at the end of this topic for details on the codes used to create input mask definitions.

Input mask definition	Examples of values
(000) 000-0000	(206) 555-0248
(999) 999-9999!	(206) 555-0248
	( ) 555-0248
(000) AAA-AAAA	(206) 555-TELE
#999	-20
	2000
>L????L?000L0	GREENGR339M3

Part II: Manipulating and Reporting Data Using Queries, Forms, and Reports

Microsoft Access 2000 is one of the most powerful microcomputer relational database management systems available today for building database solutions. In Part I of this module, you learned how to model database solutions, create tables, establish relationships, and modify table design to optimize database performance. In Projects 4 through 6, you will learn how to manipulate and report data using queries, forms, and reports.

Queries are an important object in Access. End users need some way of viewing information from the database that meet specific criteria, or combine records for multiple tables. By designing and running queries, you are able to see the data you need to consolidate data, create reports, and make business decisions. Access supports multiple query types. In this section you will design both simple and complex queries.

In a well-designed database, forms are the database objects created for end users who will use the database. Tables hold data, queries return data, and forms make it easy to work with records in a database. Most of the information in a form comes from an underlying record source—a table or query. Other elements on the form—the controls that display data and enable functionality—are stored in the form's design. You will learn how to create the forms a user needs to enter and edit records in a database.

Reports are an effective way to present your data in a printed format. Because you have control over the size and appearance of everything included in a report, you can display the information exactly how you want to see it printed. You will conclude this section by learning how to prepare records from an Access database for printing and distribution.

Creating Queries

Most databases contain large amounts of data, not all of which are needed for review at a specific time. Therefore, it is often necessary to work with a subset of the data that relates to a specific task. Stated another way, you need some way of viewing information from the database that meet specific criteria, or combining records for multiple tables. By designing and running queries, you are able to see the data you need to consolidate information, create reports, and make business decisions.

Objectives

After completing this project, you will be able to:

➤ Describe the types of queries you can create in Access

➤ Create a select query based on multiple tables

➤ Add fields to a select query using the Query Design Grid

➤ Create a parameter query

➤ Add a calculated field to a parameter query

➤ Specify AND and OR conditions in a query

➤ Create an update query

Running Case

In Access, queries are used for a variety of purposes. In the Selections, Inc. database, you want to build screen forms that will enable users to enter sales order data easily. By first designing a query that returns the specific fields in the order you want the form to display, you will have a much easier time creating the order form in Project 5.

The Challenge

Mr. Traylor is very pleased with the work you have done on the Selections, Inc. database. Now that you have designed the underlying table structure, he wants you to begin creating the database objects that will support customer transactions and product invoices. Before creating forms and reports, however, you will need to create a few queries. Here's what he wants you to do.

First, he wants you to design a query that will combine data from each of the four tables in the database. When you create screen forms for order processing, they will be based on this query.

Second, Mr. Traylor wants you to create a method for reviewing products easily in the database by product category. Currently there are not many products listed, but Mr. Traylor knows that very soon the product offering will be greatly expanded. He wants to be able to review the Product Number, Description, Price, and Quantity in Stock fields for specific groupings of products by simply specifying a product category. In addition, he wants this query to also display the retail value of the inventory in a category.

Finally, Mr. Traylor knows that each week Selections, Inc. receives additional customer names and addresses through the Selections, Inc. Web site. This data is stored in a separate Access table. He wants you to find some way of automating the process of adding these names and addresses to the Customers table.

The Solution

Fortunately, Access has powerful database query capabilities that will enable you to deliver the exact information that Mr. Traylor has requested. To meet his first request, you can create a multi-table select query. Although the users of the Selections, Inc. database will enter orders using screen forms, you will create this query as the database object on which two of the forms will be based. You will create these forms in Project 5. Figure 4.1 displays the Design view for the select query you will create.

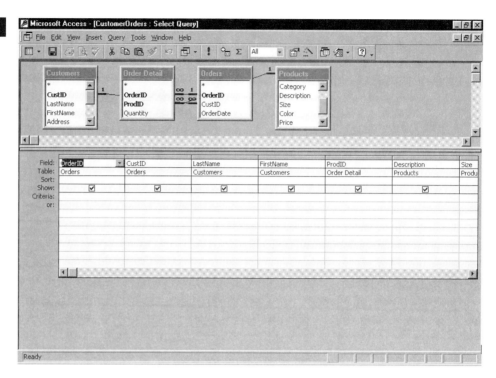

FIGURE 4.1

So that Mr. Traylor can review products easily by category, you can create a parameter query. This query will be based on a single table in the database, but will ask the user to input a category name each time the query is run. Figure 4.2 displays seven records from the Accessories category that are returned when the ProductByCategory query is run.

FIGURE 4.2

ProductByCategory : Select Query

ProdID	Description	Price	QuantityinStock	Inventory Value
RLA1001110	Team Ritchey Water Bottle	4.95	125	$618.75
RLA1001120	Team Ritchey Water Bottle	4.95	100	$495.00
RLA1001210	Team Ritchey Water Bottle	4.95	125	$618.75
RLA1001220	Team Ritchey Water Bottle	4.95	100	$495.00
RLA2007350	CPR-4 Multi-Purpose Tool	2.95	25	$73.75
RLA2007370	CPR-4 Multi-Purpose Tool	2.95	25	$73.75
RLA6001120	Team Ritchey Water Bottle Cage	9.95	30	$298.50

Record: 1 of 7

To enable Mr. Traylor to add customer information easily from the Web site data into the Selections, Inc. database, you can create an append query. This query will automatically append records from one database table to another. Figure 4.3 shows the Customers table with ten additional records that were appended to the table using the Append Customer Records *update query*.

FIGURE 4.3

		CustID	LastName	FirstName	Address	City	State	ZipCode
	+	15	Jackson	Lawrence	925 S. Bull Run	Amazon	MI	65122-7888
	+	16	Petersen	Ivan	1211 Moscow	Duane	CA	98812-6700
	+	17	Lilley	Warren	P.O. Box 121	Jackson	NY	21198-2111
	+	18	Allison	Fraiser	9001 Tucson Ct	Arizona City	CA	98766-9090
	+	19	Peterson	Janet	12122 S. Marion	Georgian	MI	47812-6755
	+	20	Ward	Sylvia	307 N. Hines	Bridge	MA	10123-0000
	+	21	Rogers	Tasha	4 Courtside #31	Albans	NY	20233-9090
	+	22	Collins	Toby	301 E. Cross	Holy Cross	NY	31129-1200
	+	23	Burns	James	98077 SE 44th	Madison City	CA	90655-9077
	+	24	Williams	Beth	101 E. Remingt	Ft. Washington	WA	89211-0000
	+	25	Banes	Donald	455 S. Clover	Sunnyside	CA	78344-1000
	+	26	Nelson	Rebecca	201 S. Tulip	Grand Rapids	MI	67712-1212
	+	27	Smith	Robert L.	677 E. Madison	Downsville	NY	21190-2333
	+	28	Carter	Jason	55 Gun Club	Red River	CA	98766-9000
	+	29	Dover	Annie	130 Bowling Gre	Boston	MA	02312-9000
	+	30	Tarkenton	Rebecca	7612 South Rive	Carson	CA	90866-0000
	+	31	Jackson	Melissa	30123 E. Cente	San Francisco	CA	91234-0000
	+	32	Mendoza	Eduardo	377 SE Ridgevie	Littleton	CO	81244-0000
	+	33	Anderson	Richard	401 Humboldt	Mission	KS	79214-9212
	+	34	Stevens	Amanda	3072 S. Temple	Salt Lake City	UT	97823-0000
▶	+	35	Stipanov	Darcy	21135 Vincenne	Englewood	NJ	07459-1233
*	+	(AutoNumber)						

Record: ◄◄ ◄ 35 ► ►► ►* of 35

The Setup

To design the queries specified above, launch Microsoft Access, open the *Selections.mdb* database you modified in Project 3, and make sure that you select the settings listed in Table 4.1. If you need additional assistance setting these options, refer to Figure 1.1 through 1.3 of Project 1. This will ensure that your screen matches the illustrations and the tasks in this project function as described.

Table 4.1   Access Settings

Location	Make these settings:
Office Shortcut Bar	If the Office Shortcut bar is visible, close it by right-clicking the Office icon on the shortcut bar and choosing Exit.
Office Assistant	Hide the Office Assistant.
Tools, Customize	Click the Toolbars tab and display the Database toolbar and the Menu Bar, as shown in Figure 1.1 of Project 1, if they are not currently visible.
Tools, Customize	Click the Options tab, and make sure the check box to display recently used menu commands first is deselected, as shown in Figure 1.2 of Project 1.
Tools, Options	Click the View tab and display Status bar, Startup dialog box, New object shortcuts, and Windows in Taskbar, as shown in Figure 1.3 of Project 1.

Creating Queries in Microsoft Access

What is a query? As you learned in Project 1, designing a database includes deciding how to display data from one or more tables that meet specific conditions. An Access *query* is a database object that you create to view, change, and analyze data in different ways. You can also use queries as the source of records for forms and reports. Sometimes you will want to see information from the database that requires a *calculated field*—a field that displays data resulting from an expression rather than stored data.

Think of a query as a subset of data from one or more tables. Data returned by a query isn't stored in the query, but in the tables underlying the query. Therefore, the query will always display the most recent data in the database. Queries are similar to tables in that they display records in a datasheet. If you have followed sound principles in designing your database, users will never interact directly with tables. As you know from Part I of this module, the purpose behind creating multiple tables in a relational database is to arrive at a data structure that avoids unnecessary repetition of data, thereby improving the overall integrity of the database. Queries are an extension of tables—they display records in a record set. Sometimes queries are used to *filter* records, or to return only those records from one or more tables that meet specific criteria. At other times you might use a query to return information from all the records in one or more tables, but displaying only certain fields. For example, you might need to review employee salary information, so you create a query that displays only the Social Security Number, Last Name, and annual salary for each employee in the database. Queries are also useful for performing calculations and updating information in tables. Table 4.2 summarizes the kinds of queries you can create in Microsoft Access.

Table 4.2

Query Type	Purpose
Select Query	This is the most common type of query and retrieves data from one or more tables and displays the results in a datasheet where you can update the records. You can also use a select query to group records and calculate sums, counts, averages, and other types of totals.
Parameter Query	Displays its own dialog box prompting you for information, such as criteria for retrieving records or a value you want to insert in a field. You can design the query to prompt you for more than one piece of information; for example, you can design it to prompt you for two dates. Microsoft Access can then retrieve all records that fall between those two dates.
Crosstab Query	Displays summarized values (sums, counts, and averages) from one field in a table and groups them by one set of facts listed down the left side of the datasheet and another set of facts listed across the top of the datasheet.
Action Query	Makes changes to many records in just one operation. There are four types of action queries:
	Delete Deletes a group of records from one or more tables. You could use a delete query to remove products that are discontinued or for which there are no orders. With delete queries, you always delete entire records, not just selected fields within records.
	Update Makes global changes to a group of records in one or more tables. For example, you can raise prices by 10 percent for all bicycle accessories, or you can raise salaries by 5 percent for employees within a certain department. With an update query, you can change data in existing tables.
	Append Adds a group of records from one or more tables to the end of one or more tables. For example, suppose your business acquires new customers, and you need to add multiple customer records to the database in one operation.
	Make-table Creates a new table from all or part of the data in one or more tables. Make-table queries are helpful for creating a table to export to other Microsoft Access databases, creating data access pages that display data from a specified point in time, or making a backup copy of a table. They are also helpful in creating a history table that contains old records, or improving performance of forms, reports, and data access pages based on multiple-table queries or SQL statements.
SQL Query	A query you create using an SQL statement. Examples of SQL-specific queries are the union query, pass-through query, data-definition query, and subquery. For information on each of these SQL query types, consult the Office Assistant.

Creating Select Queries

The most common kind of query is a **select query** that retrieves data from one or more tables and displays the results in a datasheet where you can update the records. Select queries often include calculated fields. In the tasks that follow, you will create a select query in Query Design view, add fields to the query, and then view the results.

TASK 1: To Use Query Design View to Create a Select Query Based on Multiple Tables

1 Click the Queries button on the Database Objects toolbar.

2 Click the New button ⊞New.

3 Select Design View in the New Query dialog box and click OK, as shown in Figure 4.4.

FIGURE 4.4

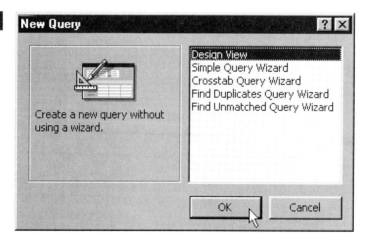

4 The Show Table dialog box will appear. Click the first table in the list, then drag a selection to include all tables in the Show Table dialog box, as shown in Figure 4.5. Click Add.

FIGURE 4.5

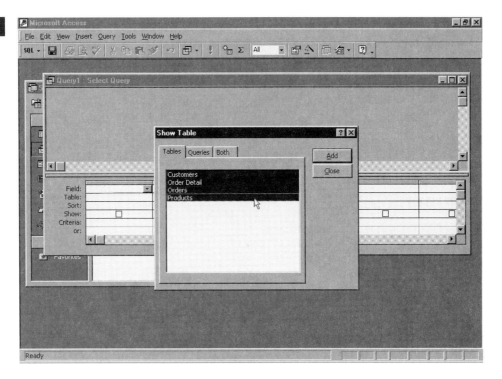

5 Click the Close button in the Show Table dialog box to remove it from the screen. The Query Design window now displays the tables in the Selections, Inc. database. Figure 4.6 identifies important screen elements you will use.

TROUBLESHOOTING If your Query Design window appears differently that the one shown here, you can resize it as you would any window in the Windows environment.

6 The Query Design window consists of two panes. The upper pane includes the tables containing the fields that you will use in the query. The lower pane consists of columns where you will define the fields of data the query will display. This is the *query design grid*. Notice that the default name of the query is displayed in the query's title bar.

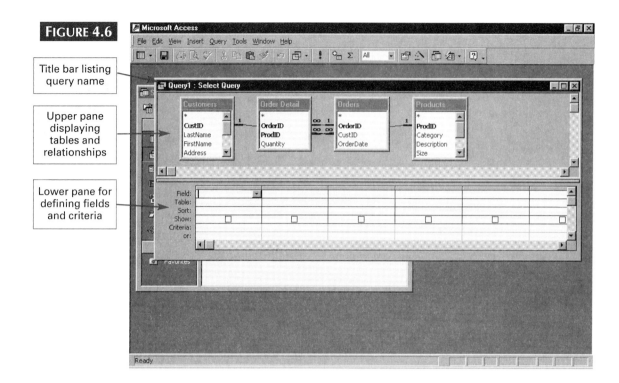

FIGURE 4.6

Title bar listing query name

Upper pane displaying tables and relationships

Lower pane for defining fields and criteria

TIP The query design grid was formally called the QBE (Query By Example) grid. In some Access documentation, you will still see references to the QBE grid.

7 Click the Save button 🖫 on the Query Design toolbar.

8 Type **CustomerOrders** in the Save As dialog box, as shown in Figure 4.7.

FIGURE 4.7

TIP When you name a query, you cannot give it the same name as an existing table in the database. As with tables, consider a descriptive name for your query. If you anticipate creating SQL statements in the database, consider omitting spaces from the names you give to your database objects.

9 Click OK.

Adding Fields to a Select Query

Similar to a table, an Access query has multiple views. You use **query design view** to create the query specifications. You can then run a query. When you **run** a query, Access will load your specifications and display the results in a query datasheet. A **query datasheet** is almost identical to a table datasheet—you can use it to modify field data and add records to the underlying table or tables.

> **TIP** Although a query datasheet will display the results of calculated fields, you cannot modify the contents of a calculated field via a query datasheet.

Before a query datasheet can display any records, you need to specify which fields the query will return. These are added to the query design grid. You can add fields in a variety of ways.

> **TIP** When you are designing a select query using fields from multiple tables, you need to carefully choose the fields you include in the query. In Project 3 you added a lookup field to the Customers table, and also to the Products table. These will be available in the CustomerOrders query, but only if you add the fields from a table on the many side of the relationship.

As you add fields to the query, keep in mind that the primary way to reference order information is by the order number. Thus, you will design the query using this table first.

TASK 2: To Add Fields to the Query Design Grid

1 Click the OrderID field in the field list of the Orders table in the upper pane of the Query Design window, as shown in Figure 4.8.

2 While holding down the left mouse button, drag the field name from the upper pane to the first available row and column in the lower pane. Access will display the icon shown in Figure 4.9, representing the field you are currently adding to the lower pane of the design grid.

FIGURE 4.8

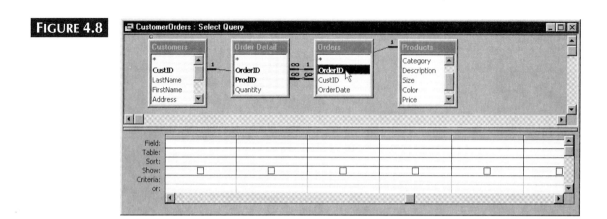

FIGURE 4.9

Icon representing the selected field

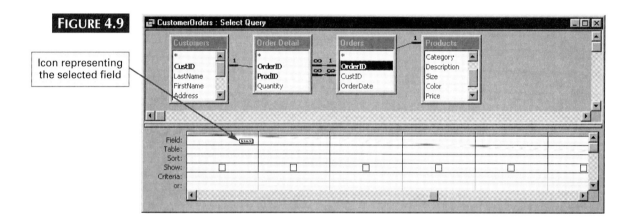

3 Release the left mouse button. The OrderID field from the Orders table is now displayed in the leftmost column of the query design grid, as shown in Figure 4.10.

FIGURE 4.10

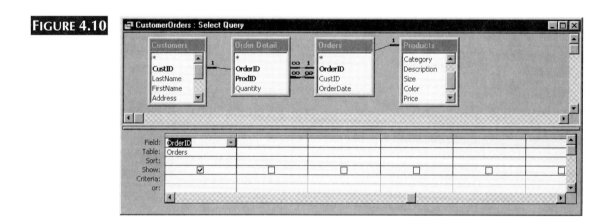

4 Move the mouse pointer inside the first row of the next available column in the lower pane and click the left mouse button. A drop-down list button will appear.

5 Click the drop-down list button. Scroll through the list and select the CustID field from the Orders table, as shown in Figure 4.11. The CustID field is now added to the first column of the query design grid.

FIGURE 4.11

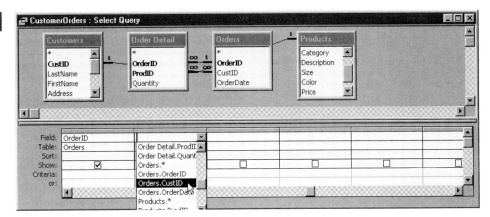

 Check Point

The Orders table contains a lookup field. Why are you adding the CustID field from the Orders table, and not the Customers table?

6 Using either method, add the fields shown in Table 4.3 to the query design grid.

Table 4.3

Table	Field
Customers	LastName
Customers	FirstName
Order Detail	ProdID
Products	Description
Products	Size
Products	Color
Products	Price
Order Detail	Quantity

TIP As you add these fields to the query design grid, you will need to use the scrollbar to display more available columns. Also, notice that the Show: button for each field is checked. If you need to use a field for the query but do not want it to show in the query datasheet, deselect the field's Show: button.

7 Click the Save button 🖫 on the Query Design toolbar to update the changes to your query.

Viewing the Results of a Query

So far you have not seen how the query datasheet will look when you run the query. One of the advantages of using a graphical query design tool such as the Query Design window is that you can run your query at any time while you are designing it to see what data it will display.

TASK 3: To View the Results of a Select Query

1 Click the Run button ⏸ on the Query Design toolbar.
The query will return records in a datasheet displaying the fields you selected, as shown in Figure 4.12.

FIGURE 4.12

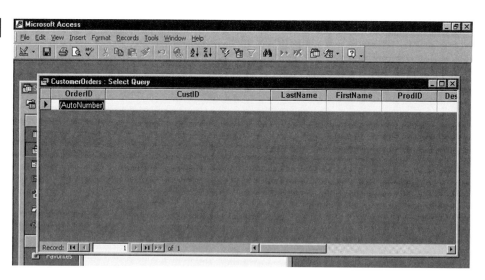

TIP You can also use the View menu to switch between Query Design and Query Datasheet view.

2 Notice that the title bar identifies the datasheet as belonging to a select query. You will also notice that the query datasheet contains many of the same elements that a table datasheet does, but no records are returned. Access will display records in a query that are based on the underlying table data. Because there are currently no records in either the Orders or the Order Detail tables, the query datasheet is empty.

3 Close the query.

You are finished with this query. In Project 5, you will see that Access often creates select queries as the basis for other database objects. When you create two forms based on this query, Access will create an SQL query on which two forms are based. You will modify that query so it includes a calculated field to display the extended price for each item on any given order.

Creating a Parameter Query

You are now ready to create the query that will enable Mr. Traylor to view products by category. A *parameter query* is a select query that will display its own dialog box prompting you for information every time you run the query. By entering the information, Access will return only records meeting the specified criteria every time you run the query. To create a parameter query, you create a select query and add a criteria expression in the criteria row of the field with the parameter data. A *criteria expression* is the text string that will appear in the parameter test box. The criteria expression is enclosed in square brackets. In the next task you will create a parameter query and then run it.

TASK 4: To Create and Run a Parameter Query

1 Click the Queries button in the Database window, if the Query pane is not currently active.

2 Click New ⒶNew.

3 Select Design view in the New Query dialog box.

4 Select the Products table in the Show Table dialog box and click Add, as shown in Figure 4.13.

FIGURE 4.13

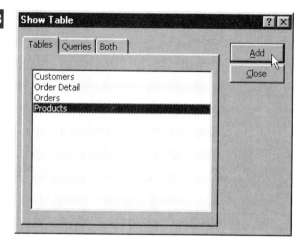

5 Click Close.

6 Add the following fields to the lower pane of the query design grid: **ProdID**, **Category**, **Description**, **Price**, and **QuantityInStock**. Your query will now appear as shown in Figure 4.14.

FIGURE 4.14

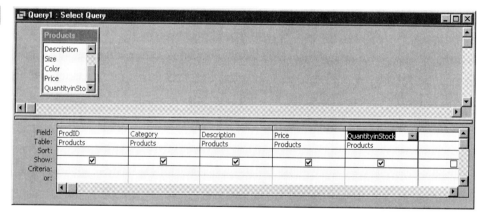

 Check Point

The Category field must appear in the query design because it contains the parameter data, but it should not appear as a column in the query datasheet. How can you prevent this field from being displayed when the query is run?

7 Deselect the Show: check box for the Category field.

8 Place the insertion point in the criteria row for the Category field. Type **Please enter a category** as the criteria expression.

9 Save the query as **ProductByCategory**.

10 Click the Run button ![run] to run the query.

11 The Enter Parameter Value text box shown in Figure 4.15 will appear.

FIGURE 4.15

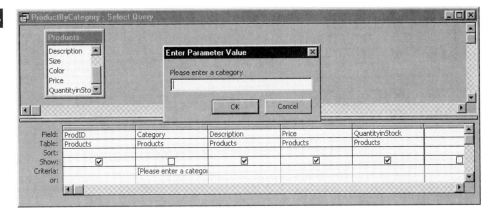

12 Type **Accessories** as the parameter value and click OK, as shown in Figure 4.16.

FIGURE 4.16

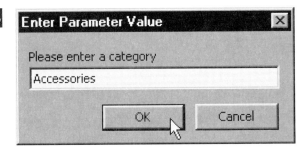

13 The query returns the fields and records shown in Figure 4.17.

FIGURE 4.17

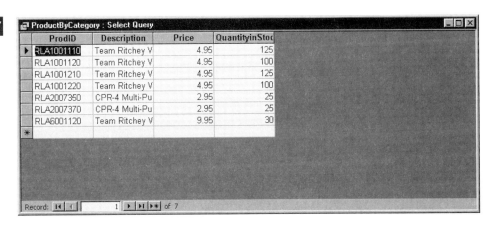

14 Click the View button to return to Design view.

Web Tip

Did you know that you could create a parameter query that gets information from a custom dialog box? Visit http://msdn.microsoft.com/library/ officedev/ off2000/achowCreateAQuerytGetsCriteriaFromAFormS.htm for more information.

Adding a Calculated Field to a Parameter Query

To determine the value of each inventory item displayed in the ProductBy-Category query, you must create a calculated field to calculate this value for each record. A **calculated field** is a field you create in the query design grid. You will recall that a calculated field is a field that returns data according to some expression. An **expression** is a combination of object identifiers, arithmetic or logical operators, and values that produce a result. Access includes an **Expression Builder** - a graphical workspace - that you can use to create an expression.

TASK 5: To Add an Expression to Calculate Inventory Value

1 Use the scrollbar in the query design grid to display additional columns in the lower pane.

2 Place the insertion point over the next available column, right click, and select Build from the shortcut menu, as shown in Figure 4.18.

FIGURE 4.18

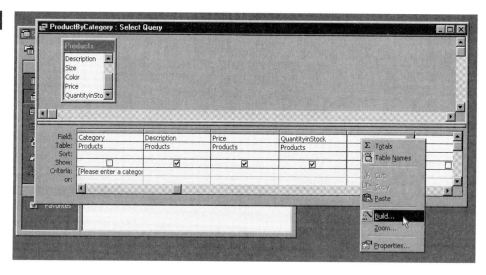

The Expression Builder will appear. Notice that the leftmost pane displays the available database objects, and the center pane displays the fields in the active object, the ProductByCategory query.

3 Select Price in the center pane and click the Paste button, as shown in Figure 4.19.

FIGURE 4.19

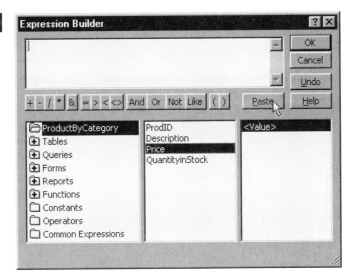

4 Click the Multiplication button ⊞ or press ⊛ (the asterisk) on the keyboard. The expression shown in Figure 4.20 specifies that the Price field will be multiplied by an additional value you will specify.

FIGURE 4.20

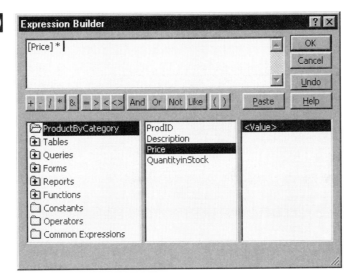

5 Select the QuantityinStock field and click Paste.

6 Click the OK button to close the Expression Builder.

7 Save your changes to the query.

Now that you have added an expression defining a calculated field, you can run the query to see the results. After viewing the results, you will format the calculated field.

TASK 6: To View the Results of the Expression and Modify its Format

1 Click the Run button [!] on the Query Design toolbar, and type **Accessories** as the parameter value. The calculated field data will appear as shown in Figure 4.21.

FIGURE 4.21

ProductByCategory : Select Query				
ProdID	Description	Price	QuantityinStock	Expr1
▶ RLA1001110	Team Ritchey V	4.95	125	618.75
RLA1001120	Team Ritchey V	4.95	100	495
RLA1001210	Team Ritchey V	4.95	125	618.75
RLA1001220	Team Ritchey V	4.95	100	495
RLA2007350	CPR-4 Multi-Pu	2.95	25	73.75
RLA2007370	CPR-4 Multi-Pu	2.95	25	73.75
RLA6001120	Team Ritchey V	9.95	30	298.5
*				

Record: |◄ ◄| 1 |► ►I ►*| of 7

You will notice that the calculated field has the default name of Expr1, and that the data does not appear in currency format.

2 Click the View button to return to Design view.

3 Highlight the text *Expr1* in the first row of the column containing the calculated field expression and type **Inventory Value** as the new field label, as shown in Figure 4.22.

FIGURE 4.22

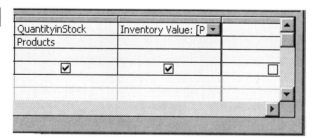

TROUBLESHOOTING Make sure you do not highlight the colon character!

4 Click the Properties button on the Query Datasheet toolbar.

5 Click the Format row in the Field Properties dialog box.

6 Click the drop-down list button. Select Currency from the list, as shown in Figure 4.23.

FIGURE 4.23

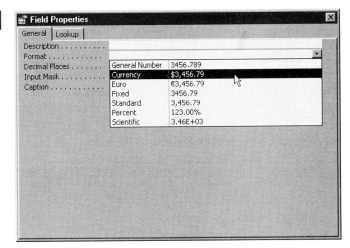

7 Close the Field Properties dialog box and run the query to view your changes. Remember to type **Accessories** as the parameter value.

8 In the query datasheet, double-click or click and drag the border between each field heading to resize the entire column. The field will now be formatted as shown in Figure 4.24.

FIGURE 4.24

ProdID	Description	Price	QuantityinStock	Inventory Value
RLA1001110	Team Ritchey Water Bottle	4.95	125	$618.75
RLA1001120	Team Ritchey Water Bottle	4.95	100	$495.00
RLA1001210	Team Ritchey Water Bottle	4.95	125	$618.75
RLA1001220	Team Ritchey Water Bottle	4.95	100	$495.00
RLA2007350	CPR-4 Multi-Purpose Tool	2.95	25	$73.75
RLA2007370	CPR-4 Multi-Purpose Tool	2.95	25	$73.75
RLA6001120	Team Ritchey Water Bottle Cage	9.95	30	$298.50

Record: 1 of 7

9 Save your changes.

Break Point

If necessary, you can close Access and continue this project later.

Specifying Query Conditions

Queries are powerful not only because they return records with data from fields in multiple tables, but also because you can specify criteria further defining which records will be returned. Remember that Mr. Traylor wants to see a listing of products by category. Suppose he also wanted to see only those records where the quantity in stock was over 100 items, and the total value of the inventory exceeded $400 for each item. You can accomplish this in two ways: by adding additional criteria expressions that request parameter values when the query is run, or by entering a literal expression specifying a condition in one or more criteria rows. A *condition* is a specification that must be met for data to be returned, such as the inventory value or the quantity in stock. A *literal expression* is a literal value and expression, such as >400. In the tasks that follow you will specify literal conditions for the parameter query.

There are two kinds of conditions you can add to a query. An *AND condition* returns records that meet every multiple condition specified. An *OR condition* returns records that meet any of the multiple criteria specified.

TASK 7: <u>To Specify an AND Condition</u>

1 Launch Access if it is not currently running, open the *Selections.mdb* database file, and open the ProductByCategory query in Design view.

2 Type **>100** in the Criteria: row for the QuantityinStock field in the lower pane of the Query Design Window.

3 Type **>400** in the Criteria: row of the Inventory Value calculated field. The conditions should appear as shown in Figure 4.25.

FIGURE 4.25

Price	QuantityinStock	Inventory Value: [P	
Products	Products		
☑	☑	☑	☐
	>100	>400	

Query with an AND condition specified

TIP This is an AND condition because the only records that will be returned when the query is run are those where the QuantityinStock is greater than 100 AND the Inventory Value is greater than $400 per hour.

4 Run the query, typing **Accessories** as the parameter value. The two records displayed in Figure 4.26 are returned in the datasheet.

FIGURE 4.26

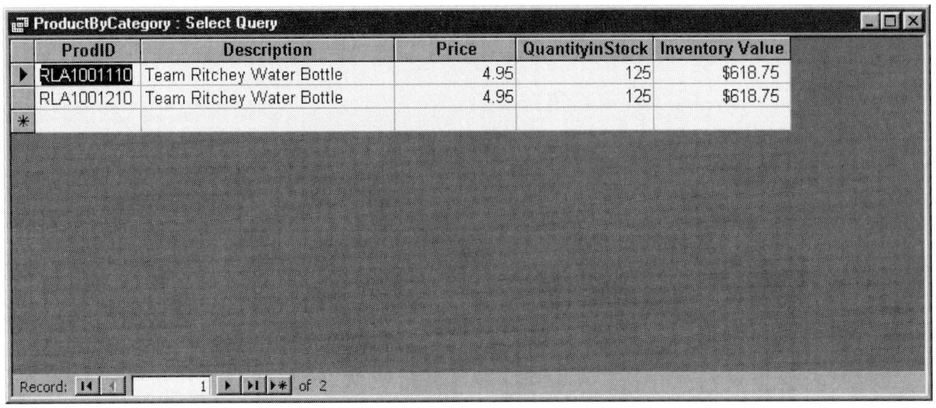

ProductByCategory : Select Query

ProdID	Description	Price	QuantityinStock	Inventory Value
RLA1001110	Team Ritchey Water Bottle	4.95	125	$618.75
RLA1001210	Team Ritchey Water Bottle	4.95	125	$618.75
*				

Record: |◄| ◄| 1 |►| |►►| |►*| of 2

5 Switch to Design view.

You will now enter the specifications for an OR condition in the query design grid.

TASK 8: To Specify an OR Condition

1 Delete the entry in the Criteria: row of the Inventory Value calculated field.

2 In the Inventory Value field, Type **>1000** in the row immediately below the current entry in the Or: row, as shown in Figure 4.27.

FIGURE 4.27

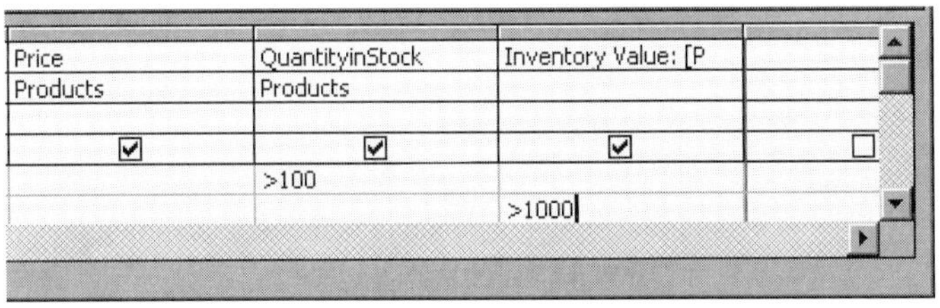

Price	QuantityinStock	Inventory Value: [P	
Products	Products		
☑	☑	☑	☐
	>100		
		>1000	

TIP This is an OR condition, because only records will be returned when the query is run that have a Quantity in Stock value greater than 100, or a Total Inventory Value greater than $1000.

3 Run the query. This time, do not enter any expression as a parameter value. This will cause Access to return all records meeting the specified criteria. The records shown in Figure 4.28 are returned.

FIGURE 4.28

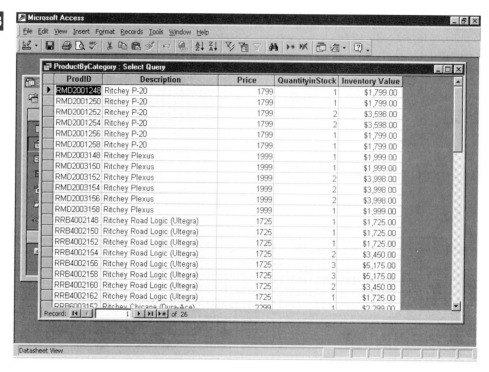

④ Switch to Design view.

⑤ Remove all conditions from the query.

Modifying Query Properties

When you run the parameter query, you might have noticed that the price of each inventory item does not appear in Currency format. In this next task you will change the query properties so that this field displays all values as currency.

Check Point

What property would you change to make sure all database objects using this data would be formatted as currency?

TASK 9: <u>To Change Additional Query Properties</u>

① Right-click the Price field and select Properties from the shortcut menu.

② Click the Format row to select it.

③ Click the drop-down arrow and choose Currency as the format.

4. Close the Field Properties dialog box.
5. Save these changes to the query.
6. Run the query. When prompted, type **clothing** as the parameter value. Access will display the records shown in Figure 4.29. Notice that the Price field now displays in currency format.

FIGURE 4.29

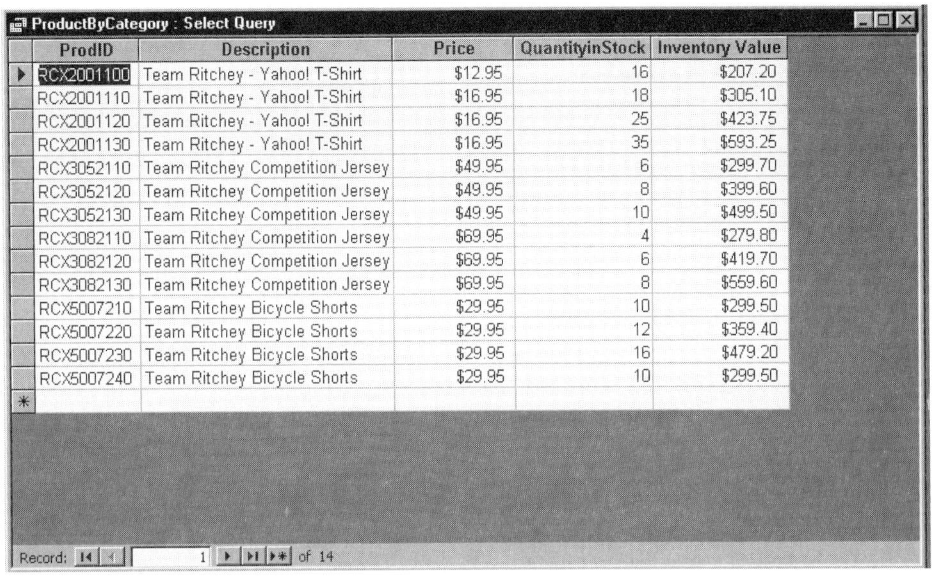

ProdID	Description	Price	QuantityinStock	Inventory Value
RCX2001100	Team Ritchey - Yahoo! T-Shirt	$12.95	16	$207.20
RCX2001110	Team Ritchey - Yahoo! T-Shirt	$16.95	18	$305.10
RCX2001120	Team Ritchey - Yahoo! T-Shirt	$16.95	25	$423.75
RCX2001130	Team Ritchey - Yahoo! T-Shirt	$16.95	35	$593.25
RCX3052110	Team Ritchey Competition Jersey	$49.95	6	$299.70
RCX3052120	Team Ritchey Competition Jersey	$49.95	8	$399.60
RCX3052130	Team Ritchey Competition Jersey	$49.95	10	$499.50
RCX3082110	Team Ritchey Competition Jersey	$69.95	4	$279.80
RCX3082120	Team Ritchey Competition Jersey	$69.95	6	$419.70
RCX3082130	Team Ritchey Competition Jersey	$69.95	8	$559.60
RCX5007210	Team Ritchey Bicycle Shorts	$29.95	10	$299.50
RCX5007220	Team Ritchey Bicycle Shorts	$29.95	12	$359.40
RCX5007230	Team Ritchey Bicycle Shorts	$29.95	16	$479.20
RCX5007240	Team Ritchey Bicycle Shorts	$29.95	10	$299.50

7. Close the query.

Creating an Append Query

You are ready to complete the last task Mr. Traylor has assigned to you. To automate the task of adding new customer records to the Selections.mdb database, you can create an Action query. Remember that an ***action query*** is a query that makes changes to many records in just one operation. In this case you create an Append action query.

The Selections, Inc. IT (Information Technology) department has created a sample Access database file named *Additions.mdb* containing one table, New Customers. This table contains name and address information submitted to the Selections, Inc. Web site. In this next task you will create an action query to append this data to the Customers table in the *Selections.mdb* database file.

To complete the next two tasks, you need a copy of your *Selections.mdb* database file, along with the Additions.mdb database file. The following task assumes that both of these files are in the root directory of your floppy disk.

Web Tip

To complete this task, you need a copy of the Additions.mdb Access database file. If you do not have a copy of this file, you can download it from the Select Web site at http://www.prenhall.com/selectadvanced.

TASK 10: To Create an Append Query

1 Open the *Additions.mdb* database from your floppy diskette.

2 Click the Queries button in the Database window.

3 Create a new query in Design view.

4 Select the New Customers table in the Show Table dialog box and add it to the query design grid.

5 Maximize the Query Design window, and add the following fields to the query: LastName, FirstName, Address, City, State, ZipCode, and HomePhone. Your query will appear as shown in Figure 4.30.

FIGURE 4.30

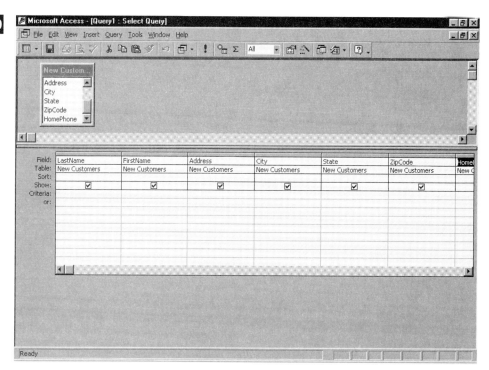

TROUBLESHOOTING Since the Customers table in the *Selection.mdb* database contains an AutoNumber field as the primary key, you do not need to add the ID field to the query design grid.

6 Click Query, Append Query, as shown in Figure 4.31.

FIGURE 4.31

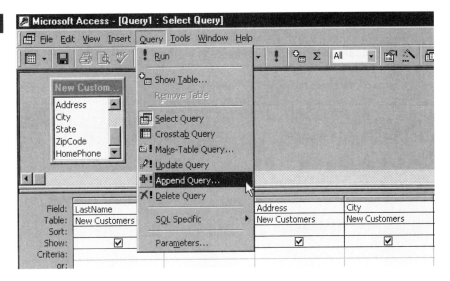

7 The Append dialog box will appear. Type **Customers** as the table name, click the option button to append the records to another database, and type **a:\selections.mdb** as the path and database name. When your settings match those shown in Figure 4.32, click OK.

FIGURE 4.32

TROUBLESHOOTING If your floppy disk does not use A as the drive letter, enter the appropriate drive letter in the path.

8 Save the query as **Append Customer Records**. The query design will now appear as shown in Figure 4.33. Notice that the Title bar indicates that this is an append query.

FIGURE 4.33

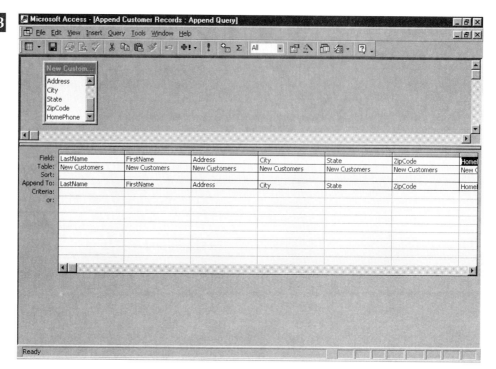

⑨ Click the View button  on the Query Design toolbar. The query will append the records shown in Figure 4.34 when you actually run the query in the next step.

FIGURE 4.34

	LastName	FirstName	Address	City	State	ZipCode	HomePhone
▶	Jackson	Melissa	30123 E. Center	San Francisco	CA	91234-0000	(719) 821-2011
	Mendoza	Eduardo	377 SE Ridgeview	Littleton	CO	81244-0000	(720) 971-2131
	Anderson	Richard	401 Humboldt	Mission	KS	79214-9212	(401) 766-8933
	Stevens	Amanda	3072 S. Temple	Salt Lake City	UT	97823-0000	(801) 399-1723
	Stipanov	Darcy	21135 Vincennes	Englewood	NJ	07459-1233	(201) 377-2884
*							

⑩ Switch to Design view and click the Run button on the Query Design toolbar. Access displays a warning, indicating that five rows will be appended to the Customers table. Click Yes, as shown in Figure 4.35.

FIGURE 4.35

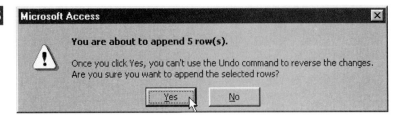

> **Microsoft Access**
>
> ⚠ You are about to append 5 row(s).
>
> Once you click Yes, you can't use the Undo command to reverse the changes. Are you sure you want to append the selected rows?
>
> [Yes]   [No]

11 Close the *Additions.mdb* database.

12 Open the *Selections.mdb* database.

13 Open the Customers table in Datasheet view and navigate to the last record in the table. The table now contains 35 records, as shown in Figure 4.36.

FIGURE 4.36

Customers : Table

	CustID	LastName	FirstName	Address	City	State	ZipCode
	16	Petersen	Ivan	1211 Moscow	Duane	CA	98812-6700
	17	Lilley	Warren	P.O. Box 121	Jackson	NY	21198-2111
	18	Allison	Fraiser	9001 Tucson Ct	Arizona City	CA	98766-9090
	19	Peterson	Janet	12122 S. Marior	Georgian	MI	47812-6755
	20	Ward	Sylvia	307 N. Hines	Bridge	MA	10123-0000
	21	Rogers	Tasha	4 Courtside #31	Albans	NY	20233-9090
	22	Collins	Toby	301 E. Cross	Holy Cross	NY	31129-1200
	23	Burns	James	98077 SE 44th	Madison City	CA	90655-9077
	24	Williams	Beth	101 E. Remingt	Ft. Washington	WA	89211-0000
	25	Banes	Donald	455 S. Clover	Sunnyside	CA	78344-1000
	26	Nelson	Rebecca	201 S. Tulip	Grand Rapids	MI	67712-1212
	27	Smith	Robert L.	677 E. Madison	Downsville	NY	21190-2333
	28	Carter	Jason	55 Gun Club	Red River	CA	98766-9000
	29	Dover	Annie	130 Bowling Gre	Boston	MA	02312-9000
	30	Tarkenton	Rebecca	7612 South Rive	Carson	CA	90866-0000
	31	Jackson	Melissa	30123 E. Cente	San Francisco	CA	91234-0000
	32	Mendoza	Eduardo	377 SE Ridgevie	Littleton	CO	81244-0000
	33	Anderson	Richard	401 Humboldt	Mission	KS	79214-9212
	34	Stevens	Amanda	3072 S. Temple	Salt Lake City	UT	97823-0000
▶	35	Stipanov	Darcy	21135 Vincenne	Englewood	NJ	07459-1233
*	(AutoNumber)						

Record: ◄◄ ◄ 35 ► ►► ►* of 35

14 Close the *Selections.mdb* database.

You have now completed each task Mr. Traylor asked you to do. In Project 5 you will learn more about working with select queries in conjunction with forms.

Summary and Exercises

Summary

- Queries are database objects that you use to view, change, and analyze data in different ways.
- Queries are often used as the source of records for forms and reports.
- A select query retrieves data from one or more tables and displays the results in a datasheet.
- You use the Query Design window to create queries in Access.
- The Query Design window consists of two panes — the upper pane contains a list of tables and fields; the lower pane contains the query design grid.
- Fields appearing in the query design grid return information in a query datasheet when the query is run.
- Queries can be based on one or more tables.
- A parameter query is a special kind of select query that prompts the user for a parameter value that limits the records that are returned by the query.
- Queries can contain calculated fields that return data according to an expression.
- You can easily create expressions using the Expression Builder.
- You can add AND and OR criteria specifications to return specific records in a query.
- An append query is a kind of action query that will append records to a specified table.

Key Terms and Operations

Key Terms

action query	OR condition
AND condition	parameter query
calculated field	query
condition	query datasheet
criteria expression	query design grid
expression	query design view
Expression Builder	run
filter	select query
literal expression	update query

Operations

add a calculated field to a query using the Expression Builder
add fields to a query using the query design grid
add tables to a query
create a new query

create a parameter query
create an append query
define AND and OR criteria for a query
run a query

Study Questions

Multiple Choice

1. The query design grid appears in the:
   a. Database window.
   b. query datasheet.
   c. upper pane of the Query Design window.
   d. lower pane of the Query Design window.
   e. Relationships window.

2. Which type of query will prompt the user for a value before returning a datasheet?
   a. Select
   b. Append
   c. Update
   d. Parameter
   e. Create Table

3. When you run a query based on one table, the results are displayed in:
   a. the Database Window.
   b. a query datasheet.
   c. a table datasheet.
   d. the query design grid.
   e. the lower pane of the query design grid.

4. Which kind of query often includes a calculated field?
   a. Select
   b. Parameter
   c. Append
   d. Both a and b
   e. Both a and c

5. Where do you add fields when designing a query?
   a. The Database window
   b. The upper pane of the Query Design window
   c. The query design grid
   d. The query datasheet
   e. The Relationships window

6. What do you use to create a calculated field in a query?
   a. A formula
   b. An expression
   c. A filter
   d. A condition
   e. A data source

7. Which of the following statements is true?
   a. Select queries cannot be used to change field data in tables.
   b. Queries return records in a datasheet.
   c. Select queries do not reflect the most recent changes to an underlying table.
   d. Queries can be used as the source object for an Access form.
   e. A parameter query will not prompt the user to enter a value.

8. The expression =[Quantity]*[Price] will most likely return the:
   a. purchases made by an employee.
   b. total membership fee charged to a club member.
   c. total number of members belonging to a club.
   d. value of an inventory item.
   e. total customers in one city.

9. Where is the data in a calculated field stored?
   a. In the Database window
   b. In a query datasheet
   c. In a table
   d. Calculated fields are not stored anywhere in a database
   e. In the Query Design grid

10. Which of the following statements is false?
    a. Query results are returned in a datasheet.
    b. A query must be based on one or more tables or another query.
    c. A query is similar to a table but often includes calculated fields.
    d. A query cannot be saved.
    e. A query can prompt the user for a parameter value.

Short Answer

1. What is the query design grid?

2. What does the upper pane of the Query Design window display?

3. What do the columns in the query design grid represent?

4. How do you run a query?

5. What options are available for sorting records returned by a query?

6. When you run a query, where is the data displayed?

7. How many criteria rows are required in the query design grid for an AND condition?

8. How do you specify conditions in a query?

9. What database objects can be used to create an AutoForm?

10. What kind of query returns data meeting a parameter value?

Fill in the Blank

1. The table or tables used in a query are added to the Query Design window using the _____ _____ dialog box.

2. A query returning records that meet one condition or another is called a(n) _____ query.

3. Queries are modified in _____ view.

4. A _____ _____ uses an expression to return data in a query.

5. Fields appearing in a query are displayed in the _____ pane of the Query Design window.

6. You can prompt the user for a specific value for returning records by creating a _____ query.

7. When you run a query, the results are displayed in a _____.

8. The _____ property of a field determines whether currency data is displayed as such.

9. Queries can be based on one or more _____ or _____.

10. A query returning records meeting two conditions simultaneously is called a(n) _____ query.

For Discussion

1. How does a query datasheet differ from a table datasheet?

2. What is a calculated field and where does it store data?

3. How do you create a parameter query?

4. How does an AND condition differ from an OR condition?

5. How do you create a query based on more than one table?

Hands-On Exercises

1. Filtering Records in a Query

There might be times when you need to quickly filter records returned by an Access query. When you filter a query datasheet, the procedure is identical to filtering a table's datasheet. You have two options: filter by form, and filter by selection. In this exercise you will filter a query's datasheet using these two methods.

To Filter a Query Using Filter By Selection and Filter By Form.

1. Open the *Products.mdb* database.

 **Web Tip**

If you do not have a copy of this file, you can download it from the Select Web site at http://www.prenhall.com/selectadvanced.

2. Open the Inventory query in Datasheet view.

3. Highlight Clothing in the Category field of the first record, as shown in Figure 4.37.

FIGURE 4.37

ProdID	Category	Description	Price	QuantityinStock	Inve
RCX2001100	Clothing	Team Ritchey - Yahoo! T-Shirt	$12.95	16	
RCX2001110	Clothing	Team Ritchey - Yahoo! T-Shirt	$16.95	18	
RCX2001120	Clothing	Team Ritchey - Yahoo! T-Shirt	$16.95	25	
RCX2001130	Clothing	Team Ritchey - Yahoo! T-Shirt	$16.95	35	
RCX3052110	Clothing	Team Ritchey Competition Jersey, Short Sleeve	$49.95	6	
RCX3052120	Clothing	Team Ritchey Competition Jersey, Short Sleeve	$49.95	8	
RCX3052130	Clothing	Team Ritchey Competition Jersey, Short Sleeve	$49.95	10	
RCX3082110	Clothing	Team Ritchey Competition Jersey, Long Sleeve	$69.95	4	
RCX3082120	Clothing	Team Ritchey Competition Jersey, Long Sleeve	$69.95	6	
RCX3082130	Clothing	Team Ritchey Competition Jersey, Long Sleeve	$69.95	8	
RCX5007210	Clothing	Team Ritchey Bicycle Shorts	$29.95	10	
RCX5007220	Clothing	Team Ritchey Bicycle Shorts	$29.95	12	
RCX5007230	Clothing	Team Ritchey Bicycle Shorts	$29.95	16	
RCX5007240	Clothing	Team Ritchey Bicycle Shorts	$29.95	10	
RLA1001110	Accessories	Team Ritchey Water Bottle	$4.95	125	
RLA1001120	Accessories	Team Ritchey Water Bottle	$4.95	100	
RLA1001210	Accessories	Team Ritchey Water Bottle	$4.95	125	
RLA1001220	Accessories	Team Ritchey Water Bottle	$4.95	100	
RLA2007350	Accessories	CPR-4 Multi-Purpose Tool	$2.95	25	
RLA2007370	Accessories	CPR-4 Multi-Purpose Tool	$2.95	25	
RLA6001120	Accessories	Team Ritchey Water Bottle Cage	$9.95	30	

Record: 1 of 48

4. Click the Filter By Selection button on the Query Datasheet toolbar. Access filters the record set, as shown in Figure 4.38.

FIGURE 4.38

ProdID	Category	Description	Price	QuantityinStock	Invent
RCX2001100	Clothing	Team Ritchey - Yahoo! T-Shirt	$12.95	16	
RCX2001110	Clothing	Team Ritchey - Yahoo! T-Shirt	$16.95	18	
RCX2001120	Clothing	Team Ritchey - Yahoo! T-Shirt	$16.95	25	
RCX2001130	Clothing	Team Ritchey - Yahoo! T-Shirt	$16.95	35	
RCX3052110	Clothing	Team Ritchey Competition Jersey, Short Sleeve	$49.95	6	
RCX3052120	Clothing	Team Ritchey Competition Jersey, Short Sleeve	$49.95	8	
RCX3052130	Clothing	Team Ritchey Competition Jersey, Short Sleeve	$49.95	10	
RCX3082110	Clothing	Team Ritchey Competition Jersey, Long Sleeve	$69.95	4	
RCX3082120	Clothing	Team Ritchey Competition Jersey, Long Sleeve	$69.95	6	
RCX3082130	Clothing	Team Ritchey Competition Jersey, Long Sleeve	$69.95	8	
RCX5007210	Clothing	Team Ritchey Bicycle Shorts	$29.95	10	
RCX5007220	Clothing	Team Ritchey Bicycle Shorts	$29.95	12	
RCX5007230	Clothing	Team Ritchey Bicycle Shorts	$29.95	16	
RCX5007240	Clothing	Team Ritchey Bicycle Shorts	$29.95	10	

Record: 1 of 14 (Filtered)

5. Click the Remove Filter button to remove the filter specifications.
6. Click the Filter By Form button .
7. Click the Price field to select it, click the drop-down list arrow, and choose $29.95, as shown in Figure 4.39.

FIGURE 4.39

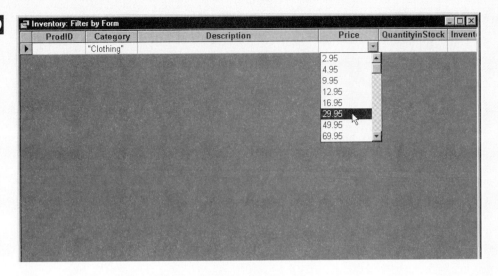

8. Click the Apply Filter button ![filter]. Access filters the recordset, as shown in Figure 4.40.

FIGURE 4.40

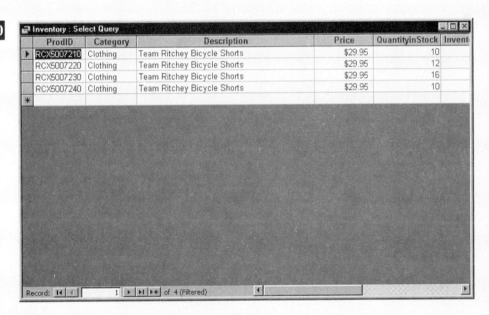

9. Remove the filter, and close the database.

2. Creating a Totals (Crosstab) Query

There are times when you need to aggregate data and display totals in unique ways. In this exercise you will aggregate totals in a crosstab query to display the total value of inventory by item category, tabulated according to price.

To Create a Crosstab Query

1. Open the *Products.mdb* database file from your floppy disk.

2. Create a new query using the Crosstab Query Wizard by clicking on the New button and then choosing Crosstab Query Wizard.

3. Click the queries option button to view queries, highlight the Inventory query, and click Next, as shown in Figure 4.41.

FIGURE 4.41

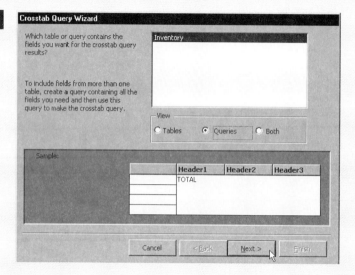

4. Add the Price field as the Row Heading field and click Next, as shown in Figure 4.42.

FIGURE 4.42

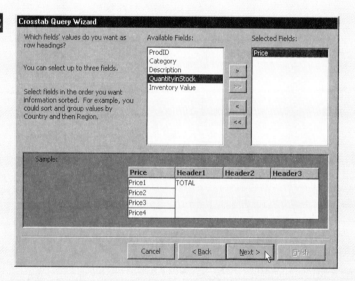

5. Add Category as the column heading and click Next, as shown in Figure 4.43.

6. Choose Inventory Value as the calculated field, and click Sum as the aggregate function. Click Next, as shown in Figure 4.44.

7. Accept the default filename for the Crosstab query and click Finish. Access cross tabulates the data as shown in Figure 4.45.

8. Close the database.

FIGURE 4.43

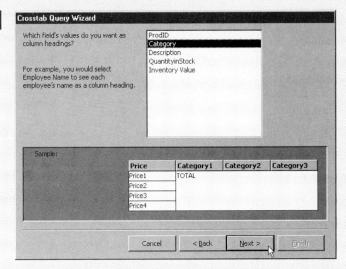

FIGURE 4.44

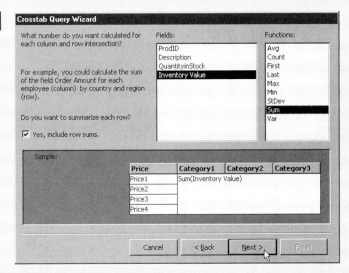

FIGURE 4.45

Price	Total Of Invent	Accessories	Clothing	Mountain Bicy	Road Bicycles
$2.95	147.5	147.5			
$4.95	2227.5	2227.5			
$9.95	298.5	298.5			
$12.95	207.2		207.2		
$16.95	1322.1		1322.1		
$29.95	1437.6		1437.6		
$49.95	1198.8		1198.8		
$69.95	1259.1		1259.1		
$1,725.00	24150				24150
$1,799.00	14392			14392	
$1,999.00	17991			17991	
$2,299.00	16093				16093

Record: 14 ◄ | 1 ► ►I ►* of 12

Web Tip

For a brief explanation of Crosstab queries, visit http://msdn.microsoft.com/library/officedev/off2000/acconUnderstandingCrosstabQueries AndWhenUseThemS.htm.

On Your Own Exercises

1. Optimizing Queries Using Indexes

When you repeatedly query data from an underlying table, there are times when performance might deteriorate. To speed up accessing data in tables and queries, consider adding an index to the fields on which a query filters or otherwise organizes data. Open the *Selections.mdb* database file. Open the Products table in Design view. Select the Category field, and then click the Index row in the lower pane. Click the drop-down arrow, and then choose Yes (Duplicates OK), as shown in Figure 4.46.

FIGURE 4.46

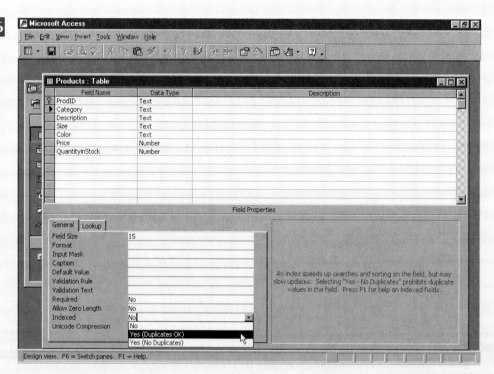

Save your changes to the table and close the database. Now, when you run a parameter query using the Category field, performance will improve.

2. Querying the Web Sites Database

Create a query in the *Web Sites.mdb* database that returns records meeting an AND condition of your choosing. Save the query with an appropriate name. Save your changes when you are finished.

3. Creating a Parameter Query of Web Site Ratings

Open the *Web Sites.mdb* database you modified in the previous exercise. Create a parameter query that prompts the user for the type of site. Save and close the database when you are finished.

4. Using the Office Assistant

Open the *Inventory* database. Choose 'Show The Office Assistant' from the Help menu. Search the help system for information about AND versus OR queries. Build an OR query, and save it with a unique name. Save the changes you make to the database.

5. Adding a Query to the Employees Database

Open the *Employees.mdb* database you modified in Project 3. Add two time card records for two of the employees in the database. Then, create a select query that lists the time card data for each employee. Save the query as **GrossPay**. Add a calculated field to the query that calculates the employee's total pay for the period. Save your changes to the query and close the database when you are finished.

Creating and Modifying Forms

In Access, forms are the primary way in which users enter, edit, and delete records. Tables hold data, queries return data, and forms make it easy to work with records in a database. Most of the information in a form comes from an underlying record source, such as a table or query. Other elements of the form—the controls that display data and enable functionality—are stored in the form's design. You can design forms after you have designed tables and queries in a database.

Objectives

After completing this project, you will be able to:

➤ Create an AutoForm

➤ Modify controls on a form

➤ Create a form in Design view

➤ Add controls to a form in Design view

➤ Create a main form with a synchronized subform

➤ Add fields to the main form

➤ Add a calculated field to the Footer section of the subform

➤ Add an order with two items to the database using the Orders form

Running Case

Mr. Traylor has reviewed the work you've done on the Selections, Inc. database. He knows that you have taken great care in defining the tables, establishing relationships, and building queries—all of which are building blocks for an effective user interface. He now wants you to design forms so a user can work with data in the database.

The Challenge

Mr. Traylor wants you to design an attractive and functional user interface for the Selections, Inc. database. He has asked you to create the following screen forms.

First, he wants you to design a form for entering and editing customer records. As with any e-commerce database, there will most likely be thousands of customer transactions each week, so you need to design a customer form that allows data entry personnel to add new customers to the database as well as search for existing customer records.

Mr. Traylor anticipates that the online product offering will expand greatly, thus he wants you to design a form displaying the products in the database. This form should allow users to locate current products as well as add new product records to the database.

Finally, Mr. Traylor needs you to create a form for entering customer orders. This form should display customer, product, order, and order detail information. In addition, it should also list the extended price for each item on a customer's order, and display the order total.

The Solution

Access has the tools and capabilities that will enable you to meet each of Mr. Traylor's interface design objectives. The easiest way to create a form displaying customer information is to create an AutoForm based upon the Customers table. Once you have created the AutoForm, you can use Form Design view to make any necessary modifications. Figure 5.1 displays the Customers form you will create.

FIGURE 5.1

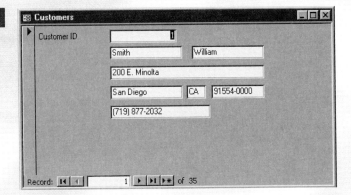

You can create a form displaying product information the same way you created the Customers form, although when you create a form using Form Design view, you have more control over how the form will appear. Once you have created a Products form, you can make additional modifications, if necessary. Figure 5.2 shows how the Products form will appear when it is completed.

FIGURE 5.2

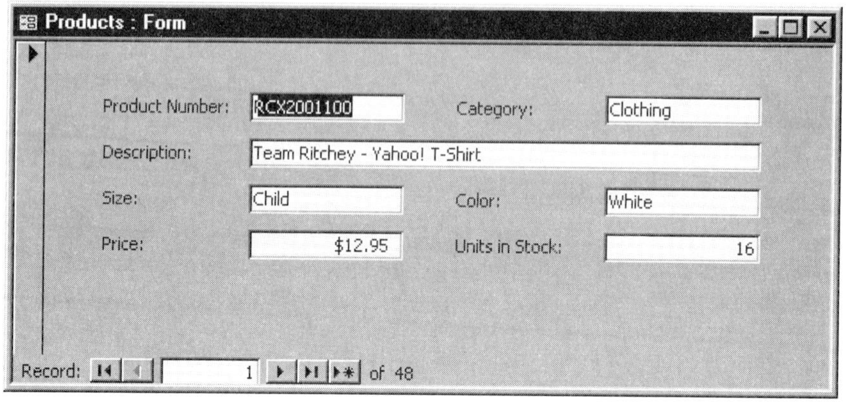

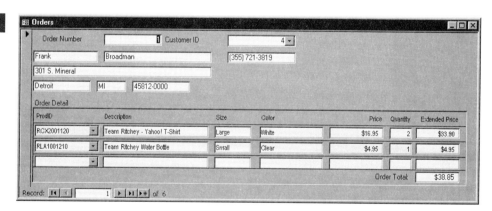

You will find it challenging to create the customer order form since it will combine data from all four tables in your database. You will recall that in Project 4 you created a query based on all four tables: the CustomerOrders query. You can use a Form Wizard in Access 2000 to create a form based upon this query. The form you create will list customer and order information on a main form, and will list the order detail information on a synchronized subform. In addition, this form will contain calculated controls and fields to display order subtotals and totals. Figure 5.3 displays the main form and the associated subform you will create in this project.

FIGURE 5.3

The Setup

To create the forms described above, launch Microsoft Access, open the *Selections.mdb* database file you modified in Project 4, and make sure that you select the settings listed in Table 5.1. If you need additional assistance setting these options, refer to Figure 1.1 through 1.3 of Project 1. This will ensure that your screen matches the illustrations and the tasks in this project function as described.

Table 5.1   Access Settings

Location	Make these settings:
Office Shortcut Bar	If the Office Shortcut bar is visible, close it by right-clicking the Office icon on the shortcut bar and choosing Exit.
Office Assistant	Hide the Office Assistant.
Tools, Customize	Click the Toolbars tab and display the Database toolbar and the Menu Bar, as shown in Figure 1.1 of Project 1, if they are not currently visible.
Tools, Customize	Click the Options tab, and make sure the check box to display recently used menu commands first is deselected, as shown in Figure 1.2 of Project 1.
Tools, Options	Click the View tab and display Status bar, Startup dialog box, New object shortcuts, and Windows in Taskbar, as shown in Figure 1.3 of Project 1.

Creating Forms

In Project 1 you used the AutoForm Wizard to create the Employees form currently in the database. Remember that a form is always based upon a *record source*—a table or query that contains the records the form displays. You bind the table or query field data displayed on a form using graphical objects called *controls*. A control is an object such as a textbox that displays information in a form.

Access offers many options for creating forms. In the tasks that follow you will create an AutoForm based upon the Customers table, and then modify the form using Form Design view.

TASK 1: <u>To Create the Customers AutoForm</u>

1 Open the *Selections.mdb* database from your floppy disk.

2 Click the Forms button in the Database window.

3 Click the New button 🔲 New on the Database toolbar.

4 The New Form dialog box will appear. Select AutoForm: Columnar as the form type, and choose the Customers table as the object underlying the form, as shown in Figure 5.4.

FIGURE 5.4

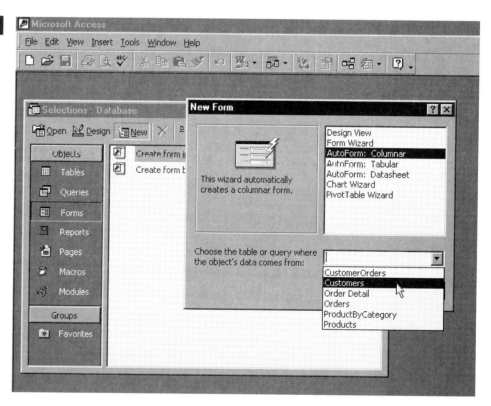

5 Click OK. Access will create the form shown in Figure 5.5.

FIGURE 5.5

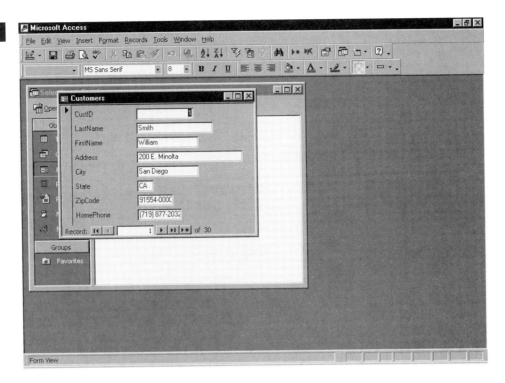

The form displays the first record of a total of 35 records. You will also notice that the form contains navigation controls. Figure 5.6 shows the purpose of each control appearing at the bottom of the form.

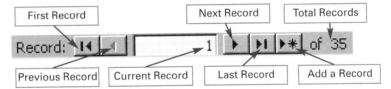

FIGURE 5.6

Modifying a Form Using Form Design View

You will notice that when Access created the Customers AutoForm, it placed objects on the form that display descriptive titles as well as the data from the first record in the table. These objects are called controls. A **control** is an object such as a textbox, label, command button, line, option button, check box, or a variety of other objects that give a form its functionality. Controls have **properties**, which are settings that govern how a control appears and how it behaves. For example, a textbox control has numerous font properties that specify the appearance of text in the control. When you modify controls on a form, you often change one or more of the control's properties. In this next task you will modify the form by resizing the textboxes it contains, and changing the appearance of the labels appearing next to certain textboxes.

TASK 2: <u>To Modify the Controls on a Form</u>

1 Click the View button to switch to Form Design view.

2 Maximize the form using the Maximize button on the form. Close the Toolbox, if it is visible.

3 Select the text within the CustID label, as shown in Figure 5.7.

FIGURE 5.7

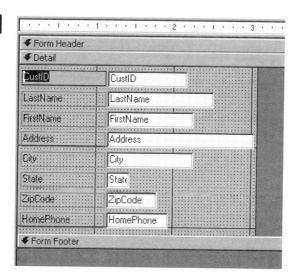

4 Type **Customer ID** and press (ENTER).

5 Click the label appearing next to the LastName textbox to select it. While holding down (SHIFT), select each additional label, except for the Customer ID label. When you have selected all the remaining labels, the selection will appear as shown in Figure 5.8.

FIGURE 5.8

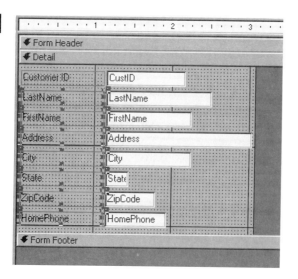

6 Press (DEL). The selected labels are deleted from the form.

7 Click the right edge of the form in the Detail section. The mouse pointer will change, as shown in Figure 5.9.

FIGURE 5.9

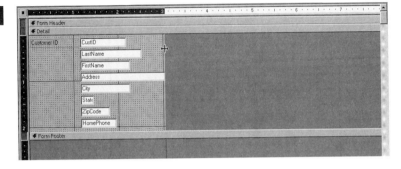

8 Drag the mouse to the 4.25 inch position on the ruler to resize the form (see Figure 5.10).

FIGURE 5.10

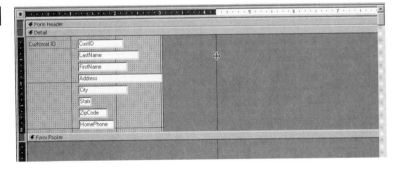

9 Release the left mouse button. The form is resized, as shown in Figure 5.11.

FIGURE 5.11

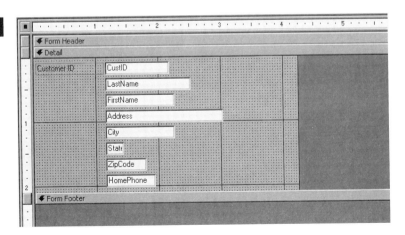

10 Click the FirstName textbox and drag it to the position displayed in Figure 5.12. As you drag the textbox, notice that the hand pointer indicates that you are repositioning the control, and that a faint gray border marks the new location of the control.

FIGURE 5.12

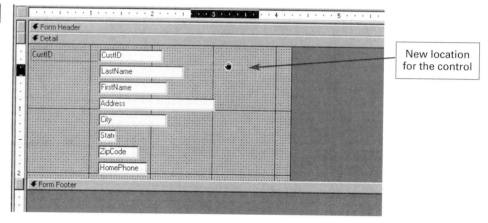

New location for the control

11 Release the left mouse button. The control is repositioned on the form, as shown in Figure 5.13.

FIGURE 5.13

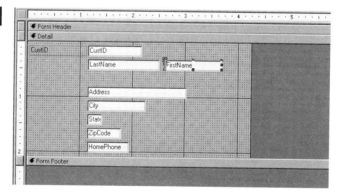

12 Reposition and resize the remaining controls on the form to the locations shown in Figure 5.14.

TIP To resize the controls, click and drag a sizing handle.

FIGURE 5.14

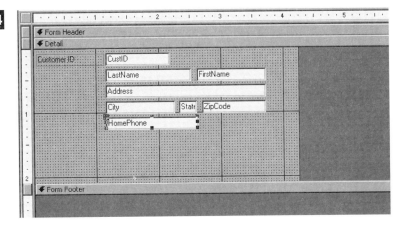

13 Click the Restore button on the Form's title bar. Resize the form as shown in Figure 5.15.

FIGURE 5.15

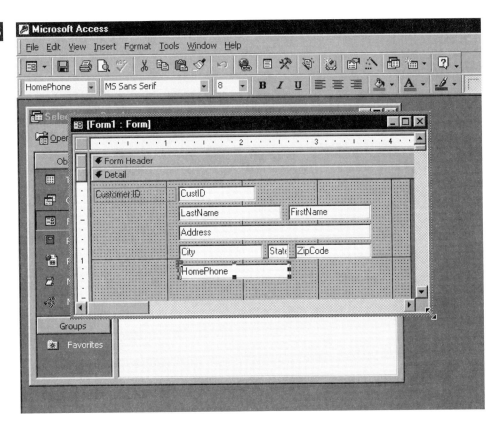

14 Your form will now appear similar to Figure 5.16.

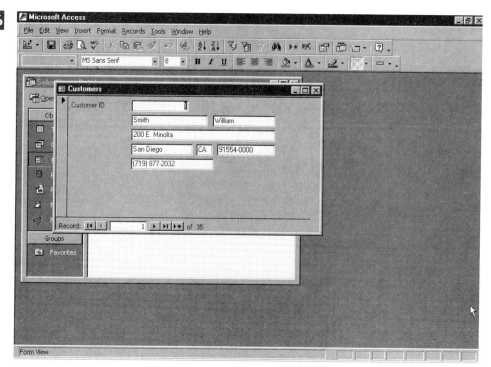

FIGURE 5.16

15 Close the form. When prompted to save changes, click Yes. Accept the default name and click OK, as shown in Figure 5.17.

FIGURE 5.17

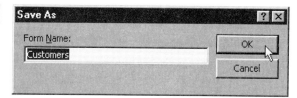

Creating a Form Using Form Design View

You are now ready to create the Products form, which will be based on the Products table. As you will see, Access provides numerous tools for creating forms using design view. You create a form by adding controls to the form's **Detail section**, which is the area of the Form Design window that displays when you create a new form in Design view.

TASK 3: To Create a New Form Using Design View

1 Click the New button ![New] in the Database window.

2 Select Design View to create a form without using a wizard, and base the form on the Products table, as shown in Figure 5.18.

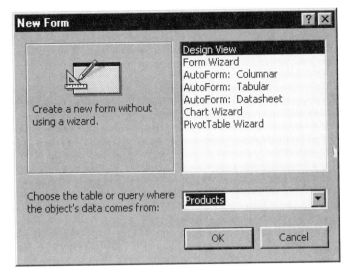

FIGURE 5.18

New Form

Create a new form without using a wizard.

Design View
Form Wizard
AutoForm: Columnar
AutoForm: Tabular
AutoForm: Datasheet
Chart Wizard
PivotTable Wizard

Choose the table or query where the object's data comes from:

Products

OK   Cancel

3 Click OK. A blank form will appear in Form Design view (see Figure 5.19).

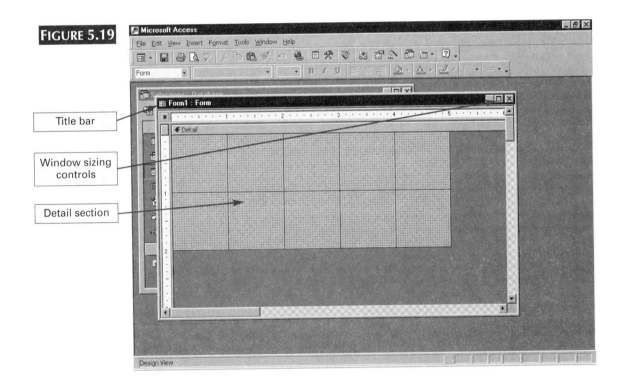

FIGURE 5.19

Title bar

Window sizing controls

Detail section

TROUBLESHOOTING If any tool palettes are displayed in the window, close them.

Note that a default name for the form appears in the form's Title bar. The Form Design window contains controls for minimizing, maximizing, and closing the form. You will add controls for the form's Detail section.

4 Click the Maximize control in the form's Title bar.

5 Save the form. Type **Products** as the form name.

Adding Controls to the Form

Now that you have created the form, you are ready to add controls that give the form functionality.

TASK 4: **To Add Controls to the Form**

1 Click the Field List button 🗉 on the Form Design toolbar.

2 Reposition the Field List box near the top of the screen.

3 Click the ProdID field name to select it. While holding down the left mouse button, drag the field to the position shown in Figure 5.20. Notice that as you drag, the mouse pointer changes to a graphic representation of the field.

FIGURE 5.20

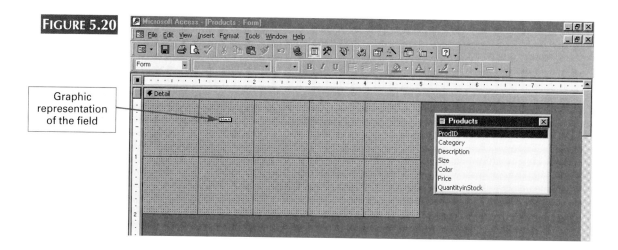

4 Release the mouse button. Figure 5.21 displays the two controls that appear on the form.

FIGURE 5.21

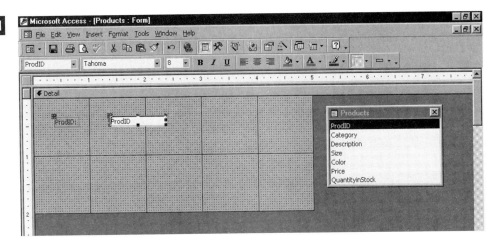

Notice in Figure 5.21 that both controls have ProdID inside them. As was the case with the AutoForm you modified earlier, the control on the right is a **bound control**, meaning that it is bound (or linked) to a specific database object (a field, in this case). The leftmost control is a **label control**, which will display descriptive text. The bound control is a **textbox control**, which is used to display field data that can be edited in the form.

TIP As you add controls to the form, the order in which you add them is important! Access assigns a tab index property to each control. When you view the form in **Form view**, you can move from control to control in index order by pressing (TAB). Therefore, add controls to the form in the order in which you want users to be able to tab through them.

5 Using the same procedure, drag the remaining controls shown in Figure 5.22 to the detail section of the form, approximately in the position shown. Resize the Description textbox as shown.

FIGURE 5.22

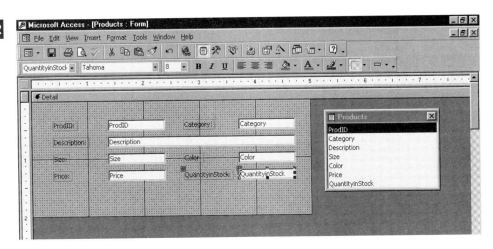

TROUBLESHOOTING As you move the controls on the form you will notice that the label and the textbox for each field move as a unit. If you inadvertently click the square selection handle in the upper-left portion of each control, it will move independent of the associated control.

6 Restore the form to its previous size by using the Restore button on the Title bar. Save these changes to the form.

7 Click the View button 📧 ▾ on the Form Design toolbar. The form will display the first record in the Members table in Form view (see Figure 5.23).

FIGURE 5.23

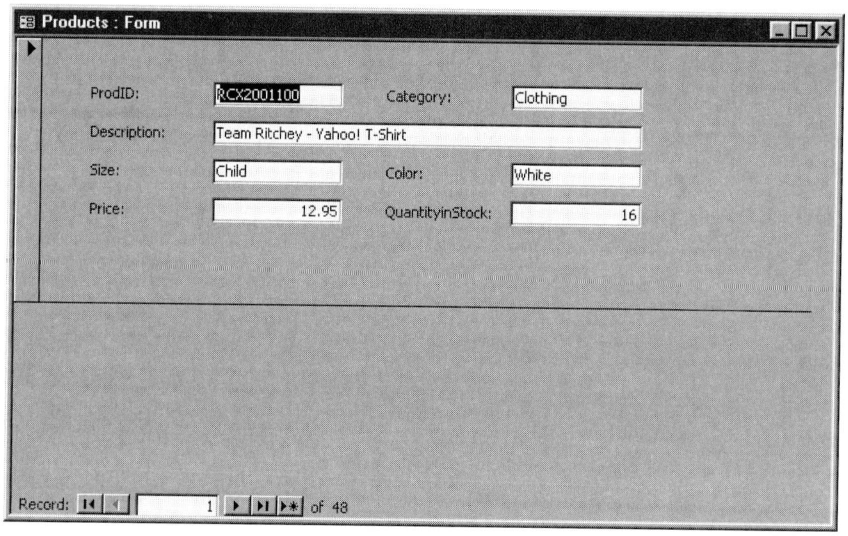

8 Switch to Design view.

Modifying Controls on the Products Form

As you know from modifying the Customers form, Design view has the advantage of giving you complete control over the location and format of each control on a form. Once you add controls to a form in Design view, the next step in designing a form is modifying the controls.

Some of the Products form labels need modifications. Also, the Price field does not appear in Currency format. In this next task you will modify controls on the Products form.

TASK 5: <u>To Modify Controls on the Products Form</u>

1 Close the Field list, if it is still visible.

2 Select the caption in the ProdID label, type **Product Number**, and press (ENTER).

3 Select the QuantityinStock caption, type **Units in Stock**, and press (ENTER).

4 Right-click the Price textbox and choose Properties, as shown in Figure 5.24.

FIGURE 5.24

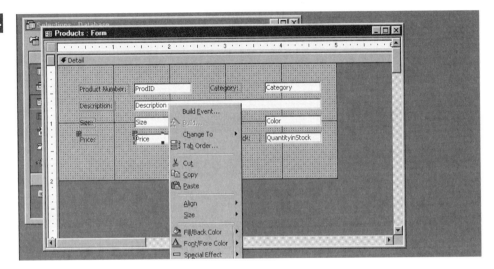

5 The Properties dialog box for the Price textbox will appear. Click the format row to select it, and then click the drop-down arrow and choose Currency (see Figure 5.25).

FIGURE 5.25

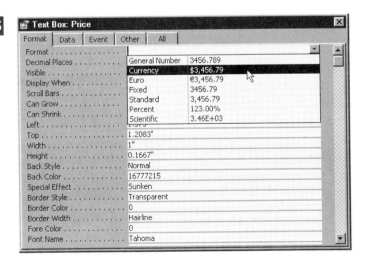

Check Point

Will the fields in the Products table now appear in currency format?

6 Close the Properties dialog box and then save these changes.

7 Switch to Form view. The form will now appear as shown in Figure 5.26.

FIGURE 5.26

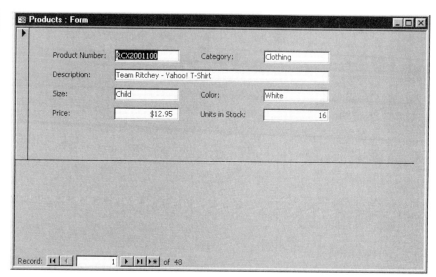

8 Close the form.

 Break Point

If necessary, you can close Access and continue this project later.

Creating a Main Form with a Synchronized Subform

When you have data in Access tables where there is a one-to-many relationship, you will often need to create a ***main form*** with a synchronized (linked) ***subform***. A subform is essentially a form within a form. The primary form is called the main form, and the form within the form is called the subform. A main form/subform combination is often referred to as a hierarchical form, a master/detail form, or a parent/child form.

TIP You can create a main form with a synchronized subform by adding a Subform/Subreport control to a form.

Subforms are especially effective when you want to show data from tables or queries with a one-to-many relationship. In this case, you will create a main form based upon the Orders and Customers table, and the subform will display information from the Products and Order Detail tables. The main form and subform are linked so that the subform displays only product and detail records that are related to the current order and record in the main form.

When you create a form and subform based on tables that have a one-to-many relationship, the main form shows the *one* side of the relationship and the subform shows the *many* side of the relationship. The main form is synchronized with the subform so that the subform shows only records related to the record in the main form. This example is complicated by the fact that your database contains a many-to-many relationship, which consists of multiple one-to-many relationships with a junction table. Designing a complex main form/subform such as this is challenging. In this project, you will create the forms using the Form Wizard, and then you will modify the forms.

TASK 6:   To Create a Main Form with a Synchronized Subform

1   Launch Access if it is not currently running, open the *Selections.mdb* database file and click the Forms button in the Database window.

2   Click the New button ⌐ᵍ New in the Forms pane.

3   In the New Form dialog box, select Form Wizard, and choose the *CustomerOrders* query as the object upon which the form will be based. Click OK, as shown in Figure 5.27.

FIGURE 5.27

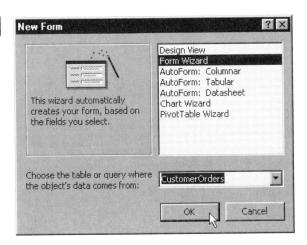

4   The Form Wizard will now appear. Click the double arrow button to add all fields to the form (see 5.28).

FIGURE 5.28

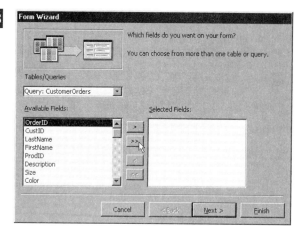

5 Access will move all the fields in the query from the Available Fields list to the Selected Fields list. Click Next.

6 By default, Access will suggest viewing the data by orders, since there is a one-to-many relationship between Orders and Customers. By default, Access will create a main form with a subform. When your settings match those shown in Figure 5.29, click Next.

FIGURE 5.29

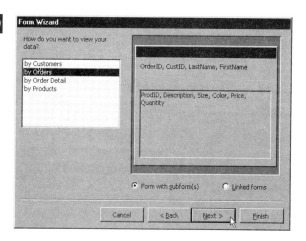

TROUBLESHOOTING It is essential that your settings match Figure 5.28 exactly. If they do not, the wizard will not create a main form/subform solution.

7 Choose the layout for the subform in the next step of the Form Wizard. Accept the Datasheet default and click Next.

8 Choose Standard as the layout in the next step of the Form Wizard, and click Next.

9 In the last step of the Form Wizard, Access will recommend names for the main form and subform. Accept the defaults and click Finish, as shown in Figure 5.30.

FIGURE 5.30

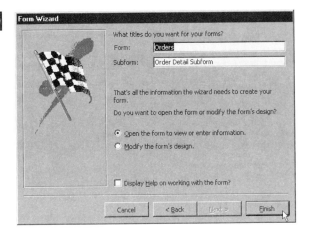

10 Access creates the main form/subform shown in Figure 5.31.

FIGURE 5.31

Main form displaying order and customer information

Subform displaying product and order detail information

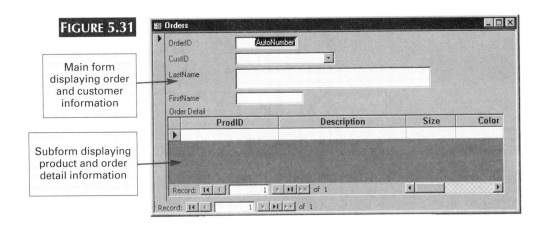

TIP In Project 4 you created the CustomerOrders query for the sole purpose of being able to create this main form/subform solution. The hard work is over—you can now modify the main form and the subform to produce the exact results you want.

11 Save the form.

Adding Fields to the Main Form

When you open the Orders form in Form view, it displays only the Customer ID, Last Name, and First Name of each customer. Because you will want to print mailing labels for each customer who places an order, you will need to add additional fields to the Orders main form.

When you created the main form using the Form Wizard, Access created a query that underlies the form. To add additional fields to the main form, you will first need to add them to the query underlying the form.

> **TIP** The query underlying the form is not stored in the Queries pane of the Database window. It is generated via a Structured Query Language (SQL) statement each time the form is opened.

TASK 7: To Add Fields to the Main Form

1 Change the view to Form Design view.

2 Click the Properties button 📇 on the Form Design toolbar.

3 The Properties dialog box for the form will appear. Click the Data tab.

4 Click the Build button next to the Recordsource row, as shown in Figure 5.32.

FIGURE 5.32

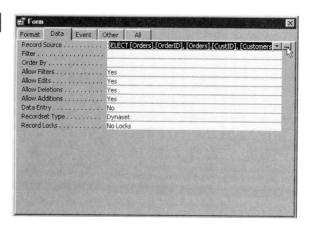

5 An SQL Statement query will appear in Design view. Add the following fields from the Customers table to the Query Design Grid: Address, City, State, ZipCode, and HomePhone. The query will now contain the fields shown in Figure 5.33.

FIGURE 5.33

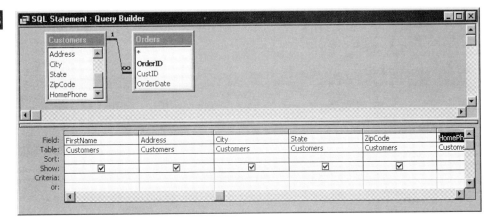

6️⃣ Close the query. The message shown in Figure 5.34 will appear. Click Yes to save changes to the query.

FIGURE 5.34

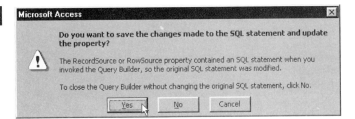

7️⃣ Close the Properties dialog box, and click the Field List button 📄 to display the Field List.

8️⃣ Resize the list as necessary. Add the following fields to the main form: Address, City, State, ZipCode, and HomePhone. Close the Field List when you are finished.

9️⃣ Change the captions for the OrderID and CustID labels to **Order Number** and **Customer ID**, respectively.

🔟 Delete all other labels from the form.

1️⃣1️⃣ Position the textbox controls as shown in Figure 5.35.

FIGURE 5.35

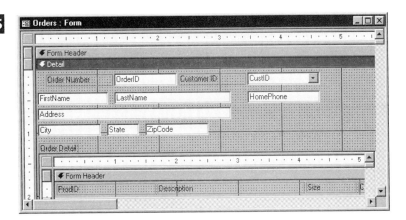

12 Save the form, and switch to Form view. It will now appear as is shown in Figure 5.36.

FIGURE 5.36

FIGURE 5.36

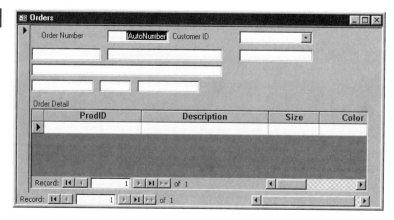

13 Close the form.

Check Point

Why does the form not display any customer data?

Break Point

If necessary, you can close Access and continue this project later.

Adding a Calculated Field to a Subform

You are now ready to modify the subform by adding a calculated field. As customers place orders where they order multiple quantities of a given item, you will want to display an extended total for the items on the order.

In Project 4 you added a calculated field to a parameter query. In this next task the process will be similar, except that you will add the calculated field to the SQL statement underlying the subform.

TASK 8: To Add a Calculated Field to the Subform

1 Launch Access if it is not running, and open the *Selection.mdb* database if it is not open. Open the Order Detail Subform in Design view.

2 Click View, Properties.

3 Click the Data tab. Open the Recordsource query in Design view.

4 Use the scrollbar to display the next available column in the lower pane of the Query Design window.

5 Right-click over the first row of the next available column and choose Build, as shown in Figure 5.37.

FIGURE 5.37

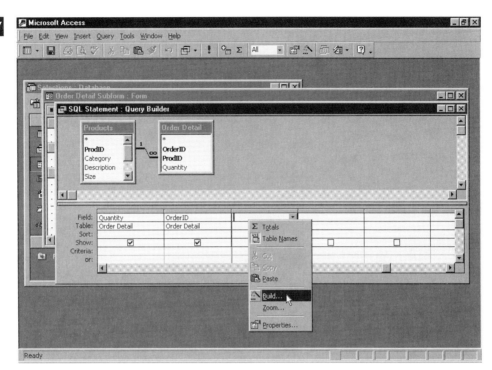

6 Type the following expression in the work area of the Expression Builder:
Extended Price: [Order Detail]![Quantity]*[Products]![Price]
When your expression matches the one shown in Figure 5.38, click OK.

FIGURE 5.38

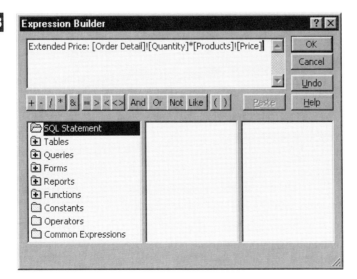

7 Close the query. Make sure you save your changes. Close the Properties dialog box.

8 In the Form Design window, scroll the form so that the Price and Quantity fields are visible.

9 Click the Toolbox button 🛠 on the form Design toolbar. Reposition the Toolbox if necessary.

10 Click the Textbox tool **ab|** and drag a textbox in the Detail section of the form, as shown in Figure 5.39.

FIGURE 5.39

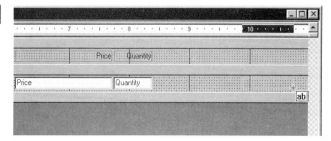

11 Access adds an unbound control to the form. Click the Properties button 📰 on the Form Design toolbar. An **_unbound control_** is a control on a form or report that is not bound to a specific field.

12 Click the Data tab, and choose Extended Price as the control source for this control, as shown in Figure 5.40.

FIGURE 5.40

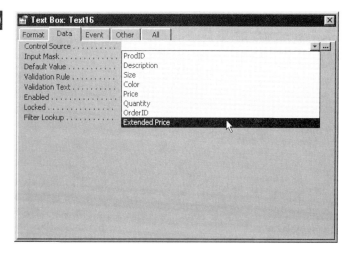

13 Close the Properties dialog box. Click the label that accompanies this textbox to select it and press the [Delete] key to remove it from the form.

14 Reposition the Extended Price textbox so that it appears next to the Quantity textbox. Click the Data tab and set the Name property for the control to **Extended Price**. The control will appear as shown in Figure 5.41.

FIGURE 5.41

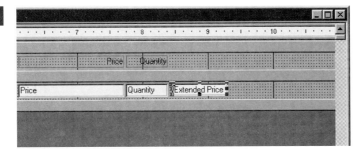

15 Save these changes to the form.

Check Point

Is this a bound or an unbound control?

Modifying the Subform

The subform needs further modification. There is no label above the Extended Price field, and the subform is wider than the main form, because of the number of fields it contains. In this next task you will add a label above the Extended Price field, change the font property of the textbox, label controls on the subform, and change the width of each control.

TASK 9: To Change the Properties of Other Controls on the Subform

1 Click the Label button **Aa** in the Control Toolbox.

2 Add a label to the Form Header section of the subform, as shown in Figure 5.42.

FIGURE 5.42

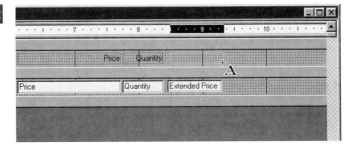

3 Type **Extended Price** as the caption for the label and press (ENTER). Set the alignment of the control to right aligned.

4 Close the Control Toolbox.

5 Click the Extended Price label. While holding down (SHIFT), click each additional control in the Form Header and Detail sections of the form. The selected controls will appear as shown in Figure 5.43.

FIGURE 5.43

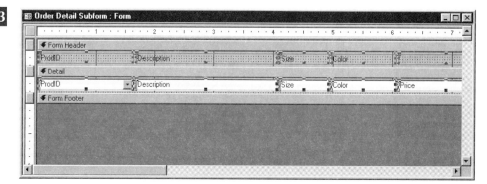

6 Click the Properties button [icon], and then click the Format tab.

7 Set the Font Name property to Arial Narrow, as shown in Figure 5.44.

FIGURE 5.44

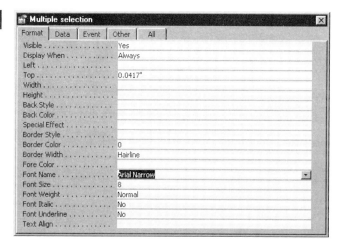

8 Maximize the subform and resize the controls (see Figure 5.45).

FIGURE 5.45

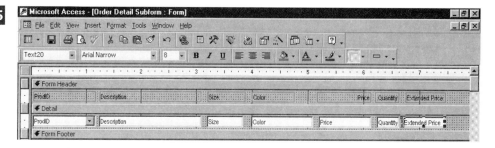

9 Click the Price textbox, hold down (SHIFT), and click the Extended Price textbox. Using the Properties dialog box, change the format of the selected controls to Currency.

Check Point

How do you change the format property of the selection?

10 Click below the form footer to deactivate the current selection. This will also select the entire form.

> **TROUBLESHOOTING** Make sure you click the area below the Form Footer bar to select the form.

11 Open the Properties dialog box for the form. Set the Default View property to Continuous forms, the Scroll Bars property to Vertical Only, the Record Selectors property to No, and the Navigation Buttons property to No. The properties for the form will appear as shown in Figure 5.46.

FIGURE 5.46

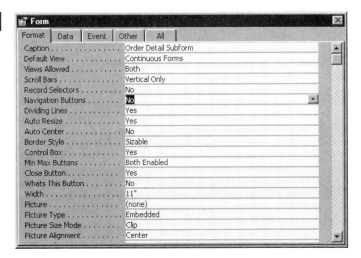

12 Close the Properties dialog box.

13 Save these changes and close the form.

14 Open the Orders form in Form view. The form and the subform will now appear as shown in Figure 5.47.

FIGURE 5.47

Orders

Order Number [AutoNumber] Customer ID

Order Detail

ProdID	Description	Size	Color

Record: 1 of 1

Modifying the Main Form

You still need to make a few modifications to the main form. Notice that all of the order detail information is not displayed. You can resize the form and the subform/subreport control so that all information is displayed.

TASK 10: To Modify the Main Form

1 Switch to Design view.

2 Maximize the form in the Database window.

3 Click the Subform/Subreport control, and resize it to 7 5/8 inches, as shown in Figure 5.48.

TROUBLESHOOTING Depending upon the order in which you open the forms (Form view or Design view), the appearance of the subform may differ slightly.

FIGURE 5.48

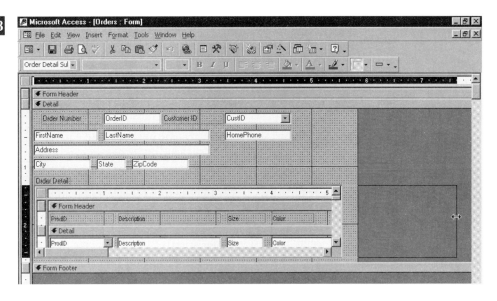

4 Restore the form, and resize it as shown in Figure 5.49.

FIGURE 5.49

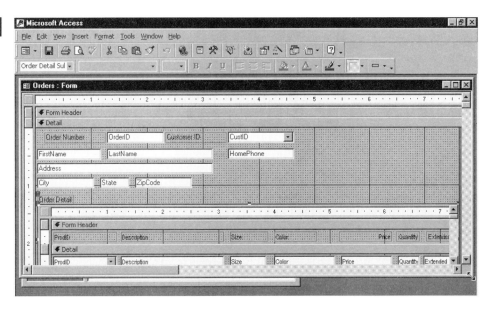

5 Switch to Form view. The form now appears as shown in Figure 5.50.

FIGURE 5.50

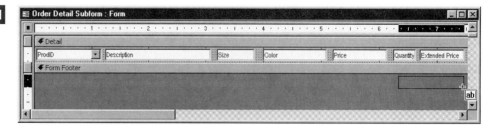

6 Save your changes and close the form.

Adding a Calculated Control to the Subform

You are almost finished designing the Orders form. Your last task is to modify the subform so that it will display the total for each order. You can accomplish this by adding a calculated control to the Footer section of the subform. A **calculated control** is a control that contains an expression. After you design this control, you will add one Orders record, with two Order Detail records.

TASK 11: To Add a Calculated Control to the Subform

1 Open the Order Detail Subform in Design view.

2 Display the Toolbox.

3 Add a textbox control to the Form Footer section, as shown in Figure 5.51.

FIGURE 5.51

4 Display the Properties dialog box and click the Data tab.

5 Type **=sum([Extended Price])** as control source for the textbox.

6 Set the Enabled property to No, and the Locked property to Yes. When your settings match Figure 5.52.

FIGURE 5.52

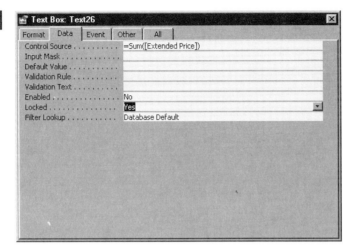

7 Click the Format tab and change the format to Currency.

8 Change the label caption to **Order Total:** and right-align the caption.

9 Resize the textbox and the caption as shown in Figure 5.53.

FIGURE 5.53

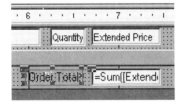

10 Save these changes and close the form.

Adding an Order with Two Items to the Database Using the Orders Form

You are now ready to add an order to the database using the Orders form. So far, the database only contains Customer and Product records. In the final task of this project you will add an order to the database. To add the order, you will first select the customer using the lookup field. Then, you will specify two items for the order. To complete the order, you will specify the quantities of each item appearing on the order. The form will calculate the extended price, and display the order total.

TASK 12: To Add an Order with Two Items
to the Database Using the Orders Form

1 Open the Orders form in Form view.

2 Click the drop-down list for a customer, scroll the combo box to display last names, and select Broadman, as shown in Figure 5.54.

FIGURE 5.54

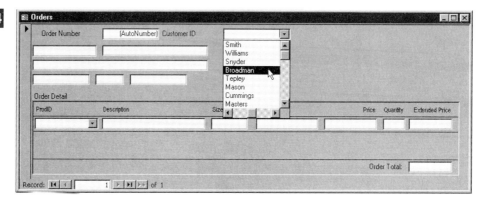

Access returns the customer information shown in Figure 5.55.

FIGURE 5.55

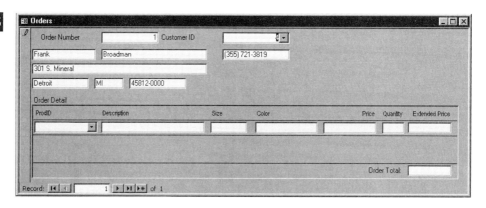

3 Click the ProdID drop-down list in the Detail section of the form. Choose product number RCX2001120 (see Figure 5.56).

FIGURE 5.56

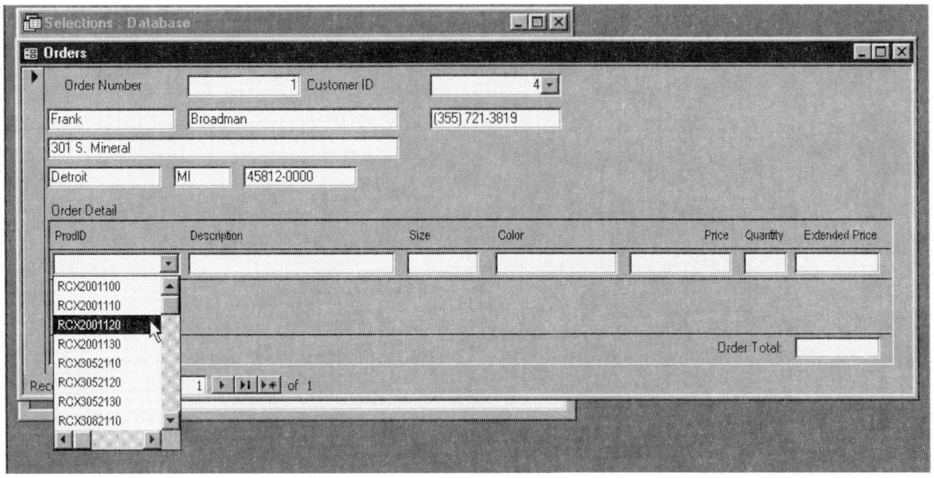

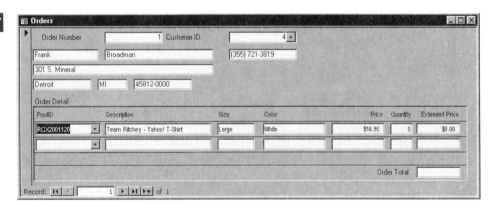

Access returns the product information shown in Figure 5.57.

FIGURE 5.57

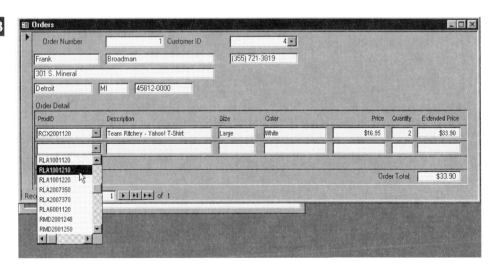

4 Change the quantity for the item to 2 by typing **2** in the Quantity textbox.

5 Click the drop-down list button for the second product. Scroll the list and choose Product RLA1001210, as shown in Figure 5.58.

FIGURE 5.58

6 Type **1** as the quantity for this item.

7 Click the Quantity textbox for the next item. This will cause Access to recalculate the order total. The order will now appear (see Figure 5.59).

FIGURE 5.59

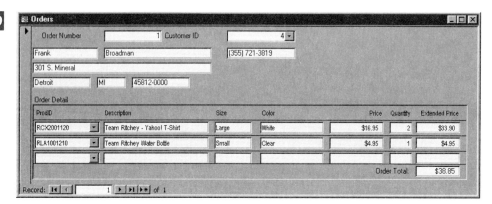

8 Close the Order form.

 **Web Tip**

In this project you learned how to create a main form with a synchronized subform. At times, you may want to create a single form that displays records from more than one table. Visit http://www.microsoft.com/TechNet/Access/Tips/mo99766.asp for more information.

You have completed the forms Mr. Traylor asked you to create. In addition, you now are able to see how forms in an Access database are used to enter data into the underlying tables.

Summary and Exercises

Summary

- The easiest way to create a form is to use the AutoForm option.
- You have a great deal of flexibility in how you create a form using Design view.
- Forms often contain both bound and unbound controls.
- Bound controls are linked to an underlying record source such as a table or a query.
- Unbound controls are normally used to add descriptive information to a form.
- A main form with a synchronized subform is very useful for displaying information from related tables.
- To add a calculated field to a main form/subform solution, modify the SQL query underlying the form.
- To add a calculated control to a subform, add a textbox to the form footer section and create a valid expression as the control source.
- A main form with a synchronized subform can be used to enter records into a database with a many-to-many relationship.

Key Terms and Operations

Key Terms

> bound control
> calculated control
> control
> Detail section
> Form view
> label control
> main form
> properties
> record source
> subform
> textbox control
> unbound control

Operations

> add a calculated control to the Footer Section of a subform
> add a calculated field to an SQL query underlying a subform
> add fields to a form
> add fields to the SQL query underlying a main form
> add records to tables in a database using a main form and its synchronized subform

add unbound controls to a form's header and footer
create a main form with a synchronized subform
create a new form using Design view
modify bound controls

Study Questions

Multiple Choice

1. When you create a main form with a synchronized subform, which element contains the subform?
   a. Textbox
   b. Form Detail Section
   c. Label
   d. Subform/Subreport control
   e. B and D

2. To add controls to a form, you use:
   a. form view.
   b. the Toolbox.
   c. design view.
   d. Both b and c.
   e. Both a and c.

3. In Access, a form normally:
   a. is bound to a field.
   b. is based upon a record source.
   c. uses another form as its record source.
   d. contains only unbound controls.
   e. is bound to a report.

4. You can easily add fields to a form using:
   a. the Toolbox.
   b. Form view.
   c. the Field List.
   d. the View button.
   e. the Properties dialog box for a form.

5. Label controls are used to display:
   a. descriptive text.
   b. data that is bound.
   c. field data.
   d. images or graphics.
   e. calculated expressions.

6. A form displays records in:
   a. Form Design view.
   b. Form Datasheet view.
   c. the Database window.
   d. a bound control.
   e. a calculated control.

7. To add fields to a main form that are not in the record source, you must first modify the:
   a. Footer section.
   b. name of the form.
   c. Header section.
   d. SQL query underlying the form.
   e. Detail section.

8. Which of the following statements is false?
   a. Label controls can be deleted from a form.
   b. A label can be resized on a form.
   c. A label can be moved on a form using the mouse.
   d. A label is a bound control.
   e. You can easily change the caption property of a label.

9. You created a form using Form Design View, and specified a query as the form's data source. How many record sources does the form have?
   a. One
   b. Two
   c. Three
   d. Four
   e. Eight

10. A form can be based upon all except which of the following?
    a. A table
    b. A query
    c. Either a table or a query
    d. A form
    e. A report

Short Answer

1. What do you use to add fields to a form in Design view?

2. What kind of control do you use to add descriptive text to a form?

3. What database objects can be used to create a form?

4. A textbox is which kind of control?

5. What screen element assists in adding fields to a form?

6. Where do you find the tools you need to add controls to a form?

7. Do you use a bound or an unbound control to display field data?

8. A label is which kind of control?

9. A subform is usually synchronized with what?

10. Which category of controls in a main form is used to display a subform on a main form?

Fill in the Blank

1. Bound controls get their data from a(n) _____.

2. A main form displays a subform using a _____ control.

3. To display a form's SQL query, open the _____ for the form.

4. The _____ contains buttons for selecting the kinds of controls you will add to a form.

5. To create a form without using a wizard, select _____ view.

6. A subform is _____ with its associated main form.

7. A _____ _____ is a control containing an expression.

8. You can display the _____ _____ to quickly and easily add fields to a form in Design view.

9. All controls on a form have _____ that you can set.

10. A _____ control accompanies a textbox when you add fields from the field list to a form in Design view.

For Discussion

1. How does Form Design view differ from Query Design view and Table Design view?

2. How do you remove controls from a form?

3. How do bound controls differ from unbound controls?

4. What is a calculated control? How does it differ from a calculated field?

5. What is an SQL query? Why might you want to modify an SQL query?

Hands-On Exercises

1. Adding Additional Records to the Selections Database Using the Orders Form

In Project 6 you will learn how to create reports, such as an invoice specifying the items on a customer's order. In this exercise you will add five additional order records to the Selections Database. Complete the following steps:

1. Launch Access and open the *Selections.mdb* database from your floppy disk.

2. Open the Orders form in Form view.

3. Click the New Record button at the bottom of the form.

4. Enter the orders specified in Table 5.2. Each row in Table 5.2 represents a unique order.

Table 5.2

Customer Last Name	Product ID	Quantity
Tepley	RMD2001248	1
	RCX5007210	1
	RCX3052110	1
Ward	RCX2001120	2
	RLA2007350	1
Banes	RCX5007220	2
Nelson	RLA6001120	4
	RLA1001120	2
Stipanov	RCX3052120	2
	RCX5007230	1

5. Navigate through the Orders form and verify the items on each order.

6. Close the Orders form when you are finished.

2. Adding ControlTips to a Form

In this project you modified the Customer's form by removing the labels associated with many of the bound controls. It is easy to see which controls are bound to specific fields when a record is displayed in the form, but when entering new records, users will need to know which data goes in each field. ControlTips are descriptive labels accompanying the bound controls on a form. In this exercise you will add ControlTips to the Customers form.

To Add ControlTips to the Customers Form

1. Open the *Selections.mdb* database.

2. Open the Customers form in Design view.

3. Select the LastName textbox.

4. Display the Properties dialog box.

5. Click the Other tab.

6. Type **Enter the Customer's Last Name here** as the ControlTip text, as shown in Figure 5.60.

FIGURE 5.60

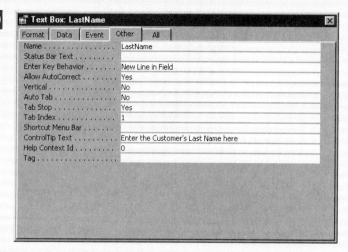

7. Save the form, close the Properties dialog box, and switch to Form view.

8. Click the New Record button on the Navigation bar.

9. Move the insertion point over the Last Name field. The ControlTip will appear as shown in figure 5.61.

FIGURE 5.61

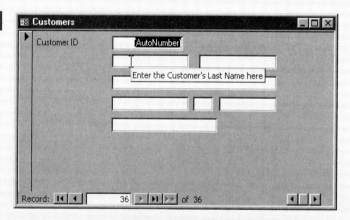

10. Switch to Design view. Add ControlTips for the remaining fields.

11. Save these changes.

12. Close the database.

 Web Tip

Did you know you can display context-sensitive help in Access forms using Visual Basic? Visit http://msdn.microsoft.com/library/officedev/odeopg/ decondisplayingcontextsensitivehelpaccessforms.htm for more information.

3. Adding an Image to a Form

There are times when you will want to enhance the appearance of a form by adding one or more images to it. In this exercise, you will add the Selections, Inc. company logo to the Customers form. To add an image to the form complete the following:

1. Open the *Selections.mdb* database.

2. Open the Customers form in Design view, and maximize the form.

3. Click View, Toolbox.

4. Click the Image tool, as shown in Figure 5.61.

5. Draw an image control in the lower portion of the form, as shown in Figure 5.62.

 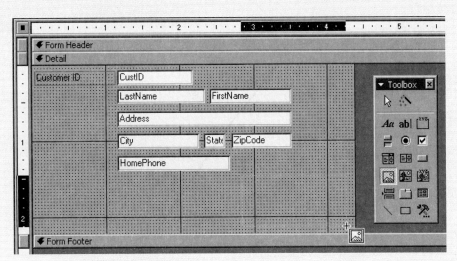

FIGURE 5.62

7. Release the mouse button. The Insert Picture dialog box will appear. Navigate to your floppy disk, select the *Selections Logo.bmp* file, and click OK, as shown in Figure 5.63.

 Web Tip

If you do not have a copy of this file, you may download it from the Select Web site at http://www.prenhall.com/selectadvanced.

FIGURE 5.63

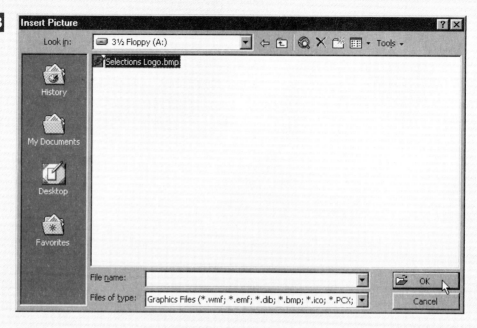

8. Save the form, and restore it.

9. Click the View button to switch to Form view. The form will now appear as shown in Figure 5.64.

FIGURE 5.64

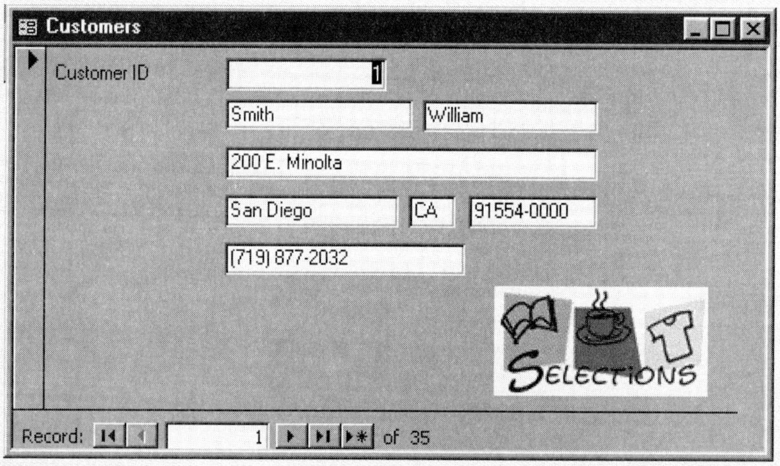

10. Close the form.

On Your Own Exercises

1. Building a Form Based on a Query with an AND Condition

Open the *Web Sites* database file. Using Form Design view, create a form based upon the query displaying records meeting the AND condition you specified in Project 4. Update the database when you are finished.

2. Compacting the Selections Database

Because you made significant changes to the *Selections.mdb* database in this Project, you should compact it. Open the *Selections.mdb* database from your floppy disk. Click Tools, Database Utilities, and Compact and Repair Database. Close the database when you are finished.

3. Creating a Main Form Subform Solution in the Employees Database

Now that you have learned how to create a main form with a synchronized subform, you will know how to modify the *Employees.mdb* database to display the time card data associated with each employee. Open the database and create a main form/subform solution. The main form will display employee information, and the subform will display the associated time cards for each employee. Compact the database when you are finished.

Creating and Modifying Reports

A report is an effective way to present your data in a printed format. Because you have control over the size and appearance of everything included in a report, you can display the information exactly how you want to see it printed.

Objectives

After completing this project, you will be able to:

➤ Create a report using the Report Wizard

➤ View a report in the Print Preview window

➤ Modify report properties

➤ Create a report using Report Design view

➤ Import database objects into an Access database

➤ Create a report using the Subform/Subreport control

➤ Modify a report's underlying query to include parameter information

Running Case

Mr. Traylor has reviewed the work you have completed on the Selections, Inc. database. He knows that you have taken great care in defining the tables, establishing relationships, building queries, and designing forms for data entry. He now wants you to create three reports for printing information from the database.

The Challenge

Now that you have designed the interface for the Selections, Inc. database, Mr. Traylor has asked you to create the following reports.

First, he wants you to design a report for printing customer records. As with any e-commerce database, the Marketing Department will conduct an ongoing analysis of customer data. Therefore, it is important that they be able to see a listing of all customers, sorted by last name. Next, Mr. Traylor wants to be able to print a list of all products in the database. The Product report should first show products by category, and then by product number.

Finally, Mr. Traylor needs you to create a report for printing each customer's invoice. This report must list customer, product, order, and order detail information, and it should be flexible enough to enable database users to specify which customer invoice to print.

The Solution

As you might anticipate, Access offers the tools that will enable you to meet each of Mr. Traylor's interface design objectives. The easiest way to create a Customer report is to create an AutoReport based upon the Customers table. Once you have created the report, you can use Report Design view to specify the order for the records in the report. Figure 6.1 displays the customer report you will create.

FIGURE 6.1

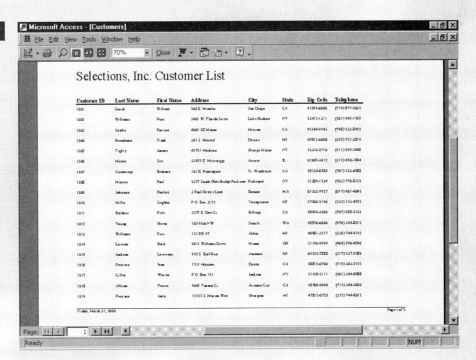

You can create the product list report in a manner similar to how you created the Customer report. When you create a report using Report Design view, though, you have more control over how the report will appear. Once you have created a product report, you can make additional modifications, if necessary. Figure 6.2 shows how the completed product report will appear.

FIGURE 6.2

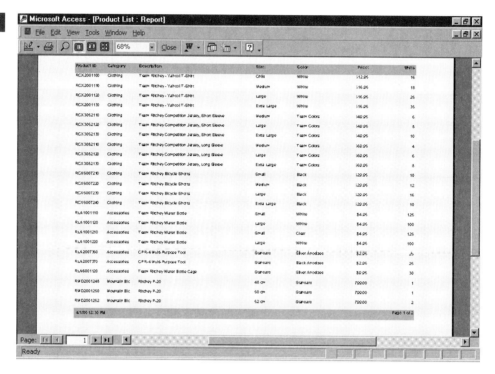

The Invoice report will be the most challenging to create, because it will combine data from all four tables in your database. You will recall from Project 5 that you created a form based upon all four tables: the Orders form. You can use a similar process to create the Invoice report, and like the Orders form, the Invoice report will contain a subform/subreport control. The report will list customer and order information on the main report, as well as the specific order detail information on the synchronized subreport. In addition, this report will contain calculated controls and fields to display order subtotals and totals. To specify a specific customer invoice to print, you can modify the report properties and add parameter specifications to the underlying query. Figure 6.3 displays the Invoice report you will create in this project.

FIGURE 6.3

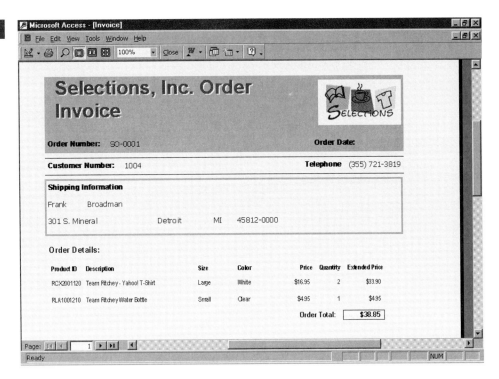

The Setup

To create the reports specified above, launch Microsoft Access, open the *Selections, Inc.* database you modified in Project 5, and make sure that you select the settings listed in Table 6.1. If you need additional assistance setting these options, refer to Figure 1.1 through 1.3 of Project 1. This will ensure that your screen matches the illustrations and the tasks in this project function as described.

Table 6.1   Access Settings

Location	Make these settings:
Office Shortcut Bar	If the Office Shortcut bar is visible, close it by right-clicking the Office icon on the shortcut bar and choosing Exit.
Office Assistant	Hide the Office Assistant.
Tools, Customize	Click the Toolbars tab and display the Database toolbar and the Menu Bar, as shown in Figure 1.1 of Project 1, if they are not currently visible.
Tools, Customize	Click the Options tab, and make sure the check box to display recently used menu commands first is deselected, as shown in Figure 1.2 of Project 1.
Tools, Options	Click the View tab and display Status bar, Startup dialog box, New object shortcuts, and Windows in Taskbar, as shown in Figure 1.3 of Project 1.

Creating Reports

Creating reports is similar to creating forms. The **Report Design window** contains a graphical workspace displaying the report's bound and unbound controls. The Report Design window contains five sections where you can add controls. You add various controls to a specific section of the report, depending upon where you want the information to appear. For example, information appearing at the beginning or end of the report requires a control in either the **Report Header** or **Report Footer** section. If your information needs to appear on every page of the report add a control to the **Page Header** or **Page Footer** section. For information that is bound to a specific field in the record source, use a bound control such as a text box and add it to the **Report Detail** section in the Report Design window. These sections are identified in Figure 6.4.

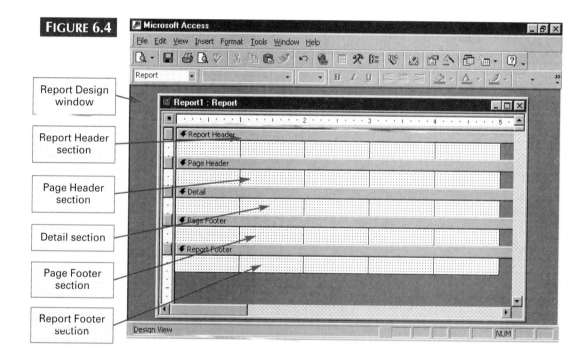

FIGURE 6.4

- Report Design window
- Report Header section
- Page Header section
- Detail section
- Page Footer section
- Report Footer section

Creating a Report Using the Report Wizard

The easiest way to create a report is to use the Report Wizard, view the report, and then switch to the Report Design window to make any necessary modifications.

TASK 1: To Create a Report Using the Report Wizard

1 Click the Reports button on the Database Objects toolbar.

2 Click the New button ![New].

3 Select AutoReport: Tabular as the report type and base the report on the Customers Table, as shown in Figure 6.5.

FIGURE 6.5

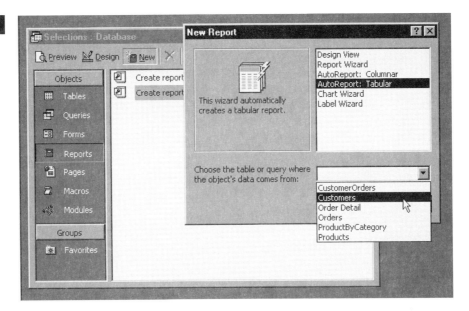

4 Click OK. Access creates the report shown in Figure 6.6. The report appears in the Print Preview window. Figure 6.6 selects important elements of Print Preview.

FIGURE 6.6

Print Preview toolbar

Print Preview window

Scroll bars

Last Page

Next Page

Previous Page

First Page

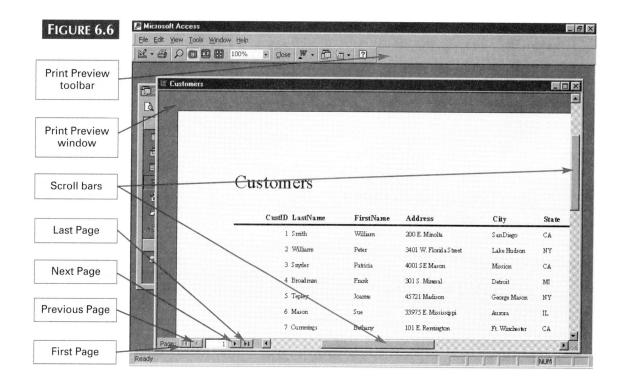

5 Click File, Save. Accept the default name Customers and Click OK, as shown in Figure 6.7.

FIGURE 6.7

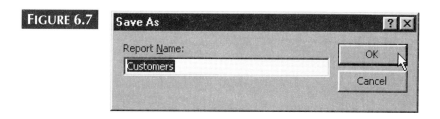

Access saves the report.

Viewing a Report in the Print Preview Window

When you create a new report using the Report Wizard, or preview an existing report, Access displays the report information in the Print Preview/Layout window. The information is displayed here exactly as it will appear when printed.

The preview normally displays at 100% of its size. You can use the scrollbars in the Print Preview window or the Zoom box on the Print Preview toolbar to change how the preview displays.

TASK 2:   To Change the Preview Display

1 Drag the horizontal scrollbar to reposition the preview. At 100%, it is difficult to see the entire layout of the report.

2 Select the Zoom box 100% ▼ on the Print Preview toolbar, type **80**, and press (ENTER).

3 Maximize the Preview window.

4 Reposition the preview using the scrollbars. The entire report layout is now visible, as shown in Figure 6.8.

FIGURE 6.8

TIP Reports have three views: Design, Print Preview, and Layout. You use Design view to create or change a report. Print Preview displays the report's data as it will appear on every page. Layout displays the position of the report's controls, and includes a sample of the data in the report.

5 Close the Print Preview window.

6 Close the Report in Report Design view.

7 Restore the Database window. The Customers report is listed on the Reports page.

Modifying the Design of the Customers Report for Printing

Rarely does a wizard create a report that does not need to be modified. You can modify a report's layout easily by adjusting the size and position of the report's bound and unbound controls in the Report Design window. Once you have modified the Customers report, it will be ready for printing.

TASK 3: <u>To Modify the Design of the Customers Report for Printing</u>

 Click the Reports button on the Database Objects toolbar if it is not currently active, select the Customers report, and click the Design button. Maximize the Report Design window so it appears as shown in Figure 6.9.

FIGURE 6.9

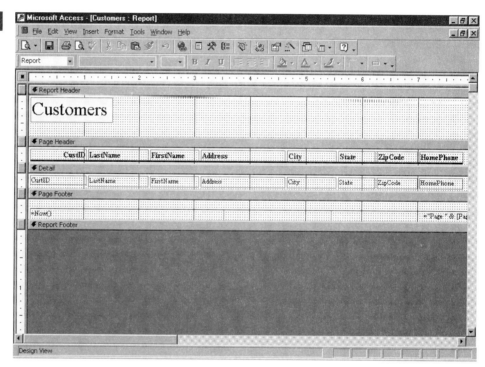

Notice that the current report has four sections.

 Check Point

Is the label control in the Report Header section bound or unbound? Since the label control displays descriptive text that does not originate from a record source, it is an unbound control.

2 Click the caption of the label in the Report Header section to select the caption. Type **Selections, Inc. Customer List** as the new caption for the control, as shown in Figure 6.10.

FIGURE 6.10

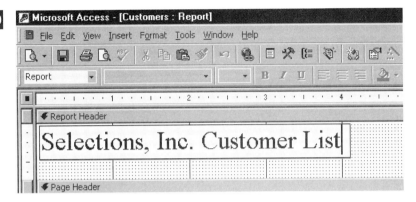

3 Press (ENTER).

4 Select the text in the CustID label in the Page Header section. Type **Customer ID** and press (ENTER).

5 Click the Left-Align button on the Formatting Toolbar to change the alignment for the heading.

6 Change the caption for the LastName label from LastName to **Last Name** (add a space) and press (ENTER).

7 Change the caption for the FirstName label from FirstName to **First Name** (add a space) and press (ENTER).

8 Select the text in the HomePhone label in the Page Header section. Type **Telephone** and press (ENTER). The labels will now appear as shown in Figure 6.11.

FIGURE 6.11

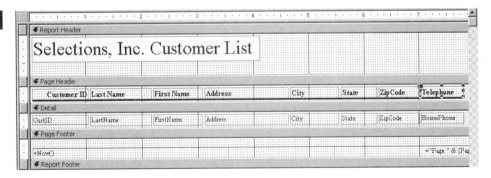

9 Select the CustID text box in the Detail section, right-click, and choose Properties. Select the Format tab if it is not active, and type **\1000** as the format property, as shown in Figure 6.12. This will format all customer numbers so they appear in a four-digit format.

FIGURE 6.12

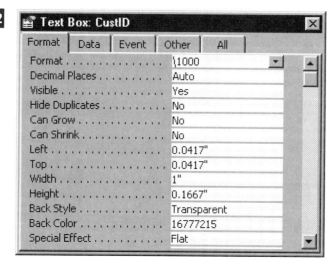

10 With the CustID field still selected, click the Left-align button to change the Text Align property to left aligned.

11 Close the Properties dialog box and save your changes.

12 Select the View button [icon] on the Report Design toolbar. Change the zoom to 80% and press (ENTER). The report now appears as shown in Figure 6.13.

FIGURE 6.13

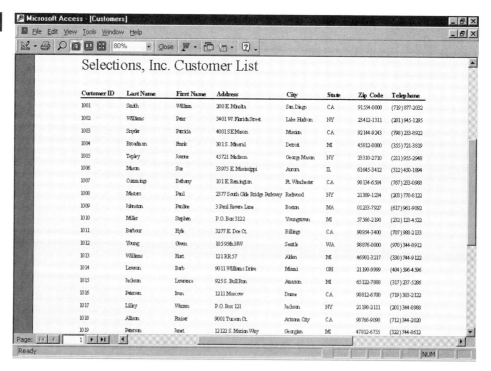

13 Close the report and restore the Database window.

Break Point

If necessary, you can close Access and continue this project later.

Creating a Report Using Report Design View

Although the Report Wizard generates reports quickly, you have the most control over what a report contains when you create a new report using Design view. By placing bound and unbound controls in the various sections of the report, you specify exactly how you want the report to look. In the next task you will use Report Design view to create the Product List report.

TASK 4: To Create a New Report Using Design View

1 Launch Access if it is not currently running, and open the *Selections.mdb* database if it is not open.

2 Click the New button 🔲 New in the Report Page of the Database window.

3 Click Design View and base the report on the Products table, as shown in Figure 6.14.

FIGURE 6.14

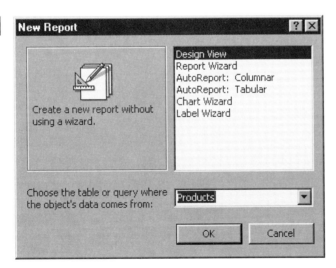

4 Click OK. Select the Field List button 🔲 on the Report Design toolbar to display the field list, if it is not currently visible.

5 Drag the ProdID, Category, Description, Size, Color, Price, and QuantityInStock fields to the Detail section of the report. Close the Field List when you are finished.

TIP Don't be concerned with where these fields are currently placed. You will modify the report design later.

6 Click the ProdID label and select Edit, Cut.

7 Click inside the Page Header section to select it and select Edit, Paste. The label is pasted into the Page Header section, as shown in Figure 6.15.

FIGURE 6.15

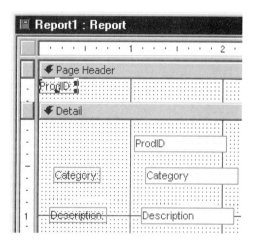

8 Maximize the Report window. Cut the remaining labels from the Detail section, paste them into the Page Header section, and reposition each one. Resize the report as necessary.

TIP To resize the report and make it wider, select and drag the right border of the detail section.

When you are finished, your report design should resemble Figure 6.16.

FIGURE 6.16

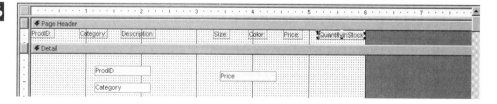

TROUBLESHOOTING You will have to reposition each control when you paste it into the Page Header section. By default, Access pastes the control in the upper left corner of the section.

9 Position and resize the text box and label controls as shown in Figure 6.17.

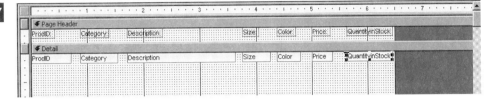

10 Select the text in the ProdID label caption and type **Product ID** as the new caption.

11 Select the text in the QuantityInStock label caption and type **Units** as the new caption. Change the alignment of the label to right aligned.

12 Place the insertion point near the lower edge of the Detail section. Click and drag the lower border of the Detail section, as shown in Figure 6.18.

Lower border of the Page Header section

Insertion point indicating new size of Detail section

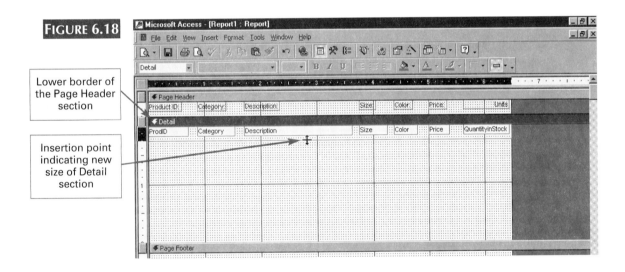

13 Save the report. Type **Product List** as the name of the report, as shown in Figure 6.19.

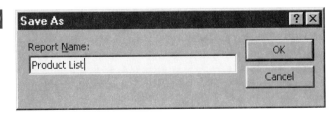

14 Click OK.

15 Click the View button to preview the report, and change the zoom to 75%. It will appear as shown in Figure 6.20.

FIGURE 6.20

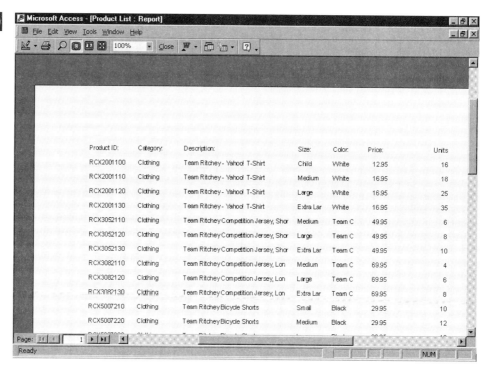

As you review the product information listed in the report, you will notice that the Description, Size, and Color fields are still truncated. In addition, the field headings do not stand out from the field data, the price for each item does not appear in currency format, and a footer might enhance the appearance of the report. In this next task you will make final modifications to the Product List report.

TASK 5: To Make Additional Modifications to the Report

1 Click the View Button to return to Report Design view.

2 Click File, Page Setup, and select the Page tab.

3 Set the orientation to Landscape and click OK, as shown in Figure 6.21.

FIGURE 6.21

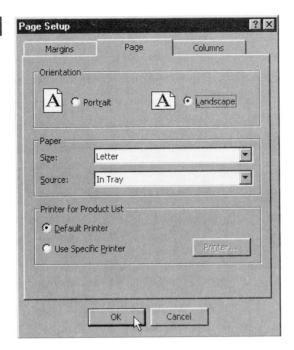

4 Drag the right border of the report to 9 inches.

5 Reposition and resize the Description, Size, Color, Price, and Quantity in Stock label and text box controls so they appear as shown in Figure 6.22. Right-click the Price field, choose Properties from the shortcut menu, and change the format to currency.

FIGURE 6.22

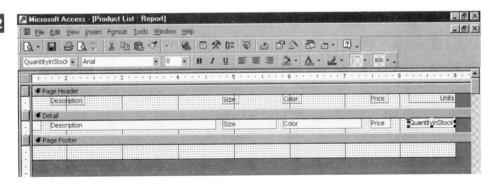

6 Select the Product ID label in the Page Header section, press (SHIFT), and select each additional label.

7 Click the Bold button on the Formatting (Form/Report) toolbar.

8 Select anywhere inside the Page Header section to deselect the current selection. Select View, Properties.

9 With the Format tab active, click the Back Color row and then click the Ellipsis button to choose a color. Set the back color as shown in Figure 6.23 and click OK. Close the Properties dialog box.

FIGURE 6.23

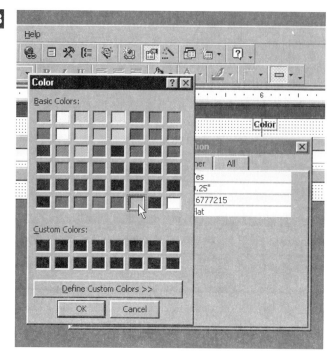

TIP You can also change the background color of a report section by right-clicking the section and choosing Fill/Back Color from the menu.

10 Select the Page Footer section.

11 Choose Insert, Page Numbers, as shown in Figure 6.24.

FIGURE 6.24

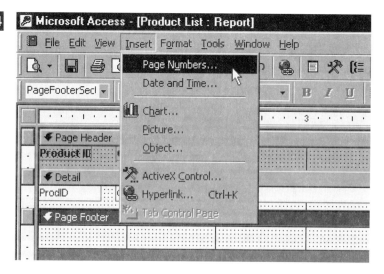

12 Set the page number options shown in Figure 6.25 and click OK. After Access adds the control to the Page Footer, select it and change the alignment to right aligned and the font style to Bold.

Check Point

What is the easiest method for changing the text alignment and font weight for this control?

FIGURE 6.25

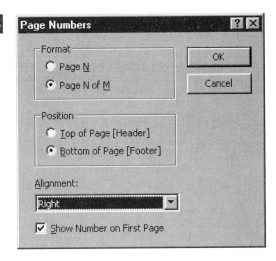

13 Click Insert, Date and Time. Set the date and time options shown in Figure 6.26 and click OK.

FIGURE 6.26

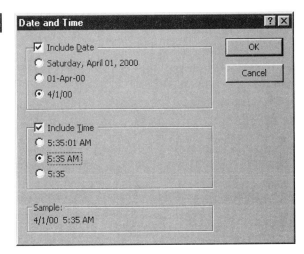

14 By default, Access adds the date and time control to the Detail section. Select the control and drag it to the Page Footer section, as shown in Figure 6.27. Change the control to bold.

FIGURE 6.27

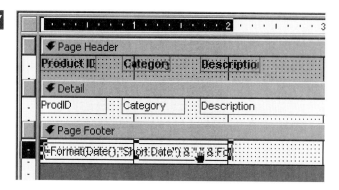

15 Using the same procedure as for the Page Header section, change the back color property of the Page Footer section for the report.

16 Save your changes and preview the report at 68% zoom. It will appear as shown in Figure 6.28. Close the report when you are finished previewing it and restore the Database window.

FIGURE 6.28

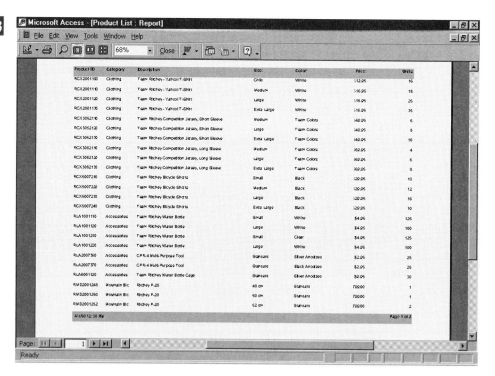

 Check Point

This report does not contain a title. How would you add a title to the report?

Creating the Invoice Report

Remember that Mr. Traylor wants you to create the Invoice report that displays information from four tables in the database. This report will be similar to the main form/subform solution you created in Project 5. The purpose of the Invoice report is to print an invoice that accompanies each order. Therefore, you will also need a method for locating a specific invoice for printing.

This report is potentially the most challenging to create, so some of the work has been completed for you. There are two ways you can create a report that links associated records in Access. The first method is similar to how you created the main form/subform solution in Project 5. You will recall that you created the main form by using the Form Wizard, and combining fields into the report from the CustomerOrders query, which returns fields from all four tables in the database. Using this method, the Form Wizard asked you how you wanted to view the data. When you chose to order the report by the Orders field, Access created a linked subform in the main form. When you create reports using the Report Wizard, you can easily create a report based upon multiple tables, or upon a multiple table query. However, using this method, Access will create a synchronized report, but will not automatically add a synchronized subreport using the subform/subreport control. If you use this method to create the report, you will also need to add calculated controls to display the extended price and order total information.

There is another method you can use to create attractive customer invoices that utilize the database objects you have already created. You will recall that in Project 5 you created the Order Detail subform, which displays order detail information for each associated order. This form contains all the logic necessary to calculate the extended price for each item on the order, as well as the order total. To create a customer invoice report you can create a main report that lists the order and customer information in the Page Header section of the report. You can then add a subform/subreport control in the Report Detail section, and bind this control to the Order Detail form.

In this example, you will use the second method to create the invoices. Two objects have been created for you: the InvoiceDetail form, and the Customer Invoice report. The InvoiceDetail form is a modified copy of the Order Detail subform you created in Project 5. The Customer Invoice report is a report with order and customer information appearing in the Page Header section of the report. Both of these objects are contained in the *Report Objects.mdb* database. In the tasks that follow, you will import these database objects into the *Selections.mdb* database, and then modify the Customer Invoice report so it displays the InvoiceDetail information using a subform/subreport control. You will then modify the SQL query underlying the Customer Invoice report so it requests an order number before displaying an invoice. To complete the next task, you need a copy of the *Report Objects.mdb* database.

Web Tip

If you do not have a copy of this database, you can download it from the Select Web site at http://www.prenhall.com/selectadvanced.

TASK 6: To Import the InvoiceDetail Form and the Customer Invoice Report Objects into the Selections.mdb Database

1 Click File, Get External Data, and choose Import.

2 Navigate to your floppy disk, select the *Report Objects.mdb* database, and select Import, as shown in Figure 6.29.

FIGURE 6.29

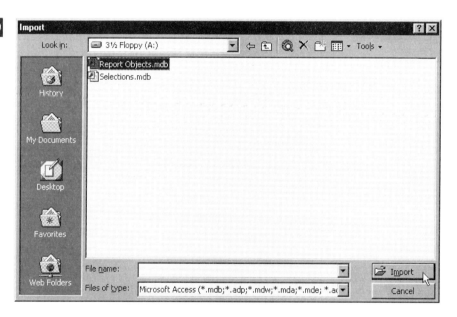

3 Click the Forms tab, select the InvoiceDetail form, and click OK, as shown in Figure 6.30.

FIGURE 6.30

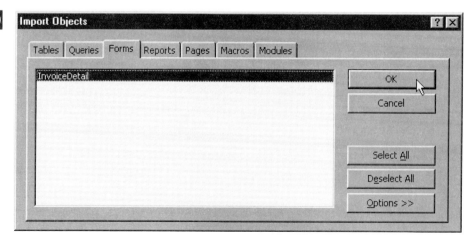

Access imports the object into the *Selections.mdb* database.

4 Click File, Get External Data, and choose Import.

5 Navigate to your floppy disk, select the *Report Objects.mdb* database, and select Import.

6 Click the Reports tab, select the Customer Invoice Report, and click OK, as shown in Figure 6.31. Access imports the Customer Invoice report into the *Selections.mdb* database.

FIGURE 6.31

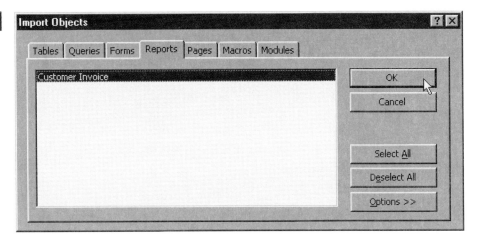

 Check Point

After importing objects into a database, it is a good idea to compact the database. How do you do this?

Adding a Subform/Subreport Control to the Detail Section of a Report

Now that you have imported these two objects into the *Selections.mdb* database, you are ready to modify the Detail section of the Customer Invoice report. In this next task you will add the control to the report in Report Design view, and then bind the control to the InvoiceDetail form. You will then synchronize the report and its associated subform object. The report will contain a ***subform/subreport control***, which is a control you use to display an associated form or report in the main form or report.

TASK 7: To Add a Subform/Subreport
Control to the Customer Invoice Report

1 Click the Report button in the Database window to display the Reports Page, if it is not currently active.

2 Open the Customer Invoice report in Design view, and maximize the Report Design window.

3 Click and drag the Detail section to 1 1/2 inches, as shown in Figure 6.32.

FIGURE 6.32

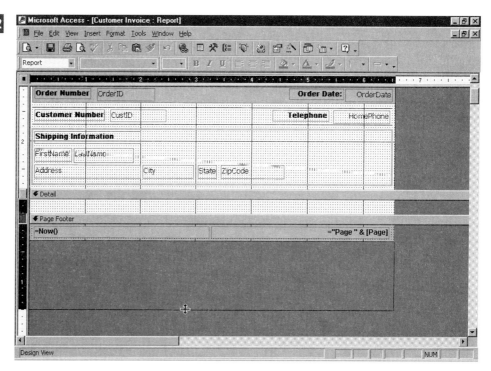

4 Click the Toolbox button 🛠 on the Report Design toolbar to display the Toolbox. Reposition the Toolbox so it appears at the right of the Report Design window.

5 Click the Subform/Subreport tool, as shown in Figure 6.33.

FIGURE 6.33

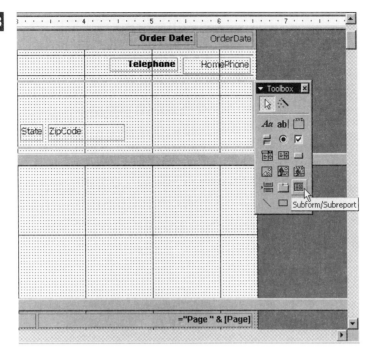

6 Add a subform/subreport control to the Detail section of the Customer Invoice report, as shown in Figure 6.34.

FIGURE 6.34

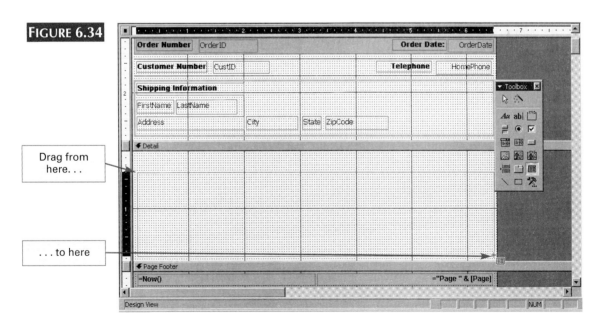

Drag from here. . .

. . . to here

7 Click the caption of the label associated with the control and type **Order Details** as the new caption, as shown in Figure 6.35. Press (ENTER), and then reposition the label so it appears slightly above the subform/subreport control.

TIP Use the larger sizing handle on either the label or the text box to move one independently from the other.

FIGURE 6.35

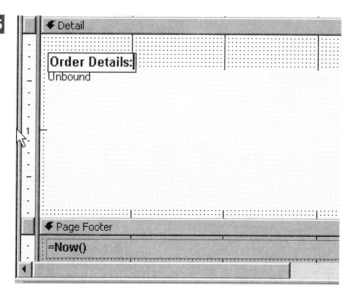

8 Right-click the unbound subform/subreport control and choose Properties from the menu.

9 Click the Data tab in the Subform/Subreport properties dialog box, if it is not active. Click the Source Object row to activate it, and then select the drop-down list arrow. Select Form, InvoiceDetail as the source object, as shown in Figure 6.36.

FIGURE 6.36

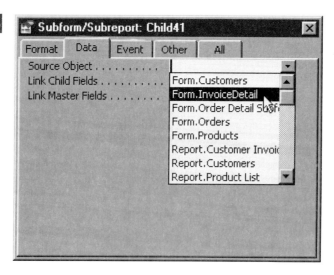

10 Click the Link Child Field row to activate it, and then click the Ellipsis button. The Subreport Field Linker dialog box will appear.

11 Click the drop-down arrow below the Master fields: list and select OrderID. Access will add this specification to the Child field list as well. When your settings match those shown in Figure 6.37, click OK. Close the Properties dialog box.

FIGURE 6.37

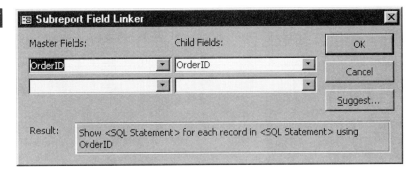

12 You need to add a page break below the subform/subreport control so that each invoice displays only the associated product and order detail information. Click the Page Break tool in the Toolbox, as shown in Figure 6.38.

FIGURE 6.38

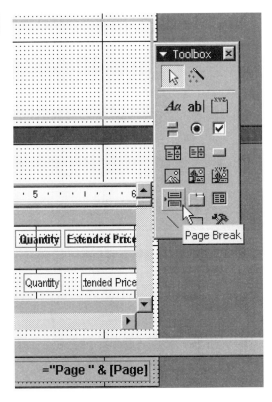

13 Add a Page Break control in the position shown in Figure 6.39.

FIGURE 6.39

Add the control here

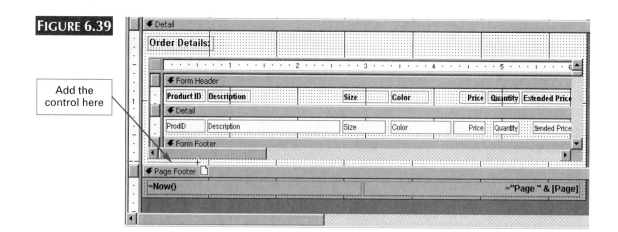

TROUBLESHOOTING Make sure you add the Page Break control below the Subform/Subreport control.

14 Close the Toolbox, and then save your changes to the Report.

15 Switch to Print Preview, and scroll through the Preview window to display the order details. The first invoice will appear as shown in Figure 6.40. Close the report when you are finished viewing it.

FIGURE 6.40

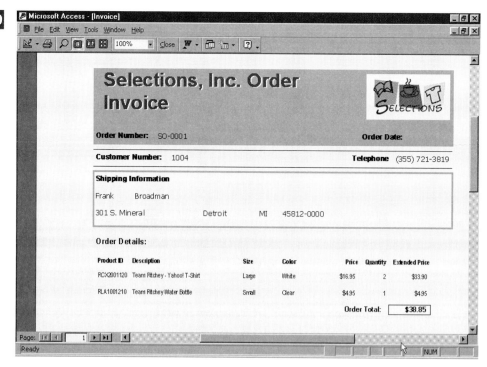

Check Point

Why does the order date not appear in this report?

Adding Parameter Specifications to the Customer Invoice Report

You are almost finished creating the Invoice report Mr. Traylor requested. You will recall that he wants database users to be able to quickly locate a specific invoice for printing. You can accomplish this by adding parameter information to the SQL query that underlies the Customer Invoice report. You will add the parameter specifications to the OrderID field in the query's design. The parameter criteria will specify an order number. Then, every time a user runs the report, Access will request an order number, and then display the appropriate customer invoice.

Check Point

Using the parameter specified above, how many records will the record set underlying the report return each time a valid parameter is entered?

TASK 8: To Add Parameter Specifications to the SQL Query Underlying the Customer Invoice Report

1. Open the Customer Invoice report in Design view.

2. Click View, Properties.

3. The Properties dialog box for the report will appear. Click the Ellipsis button next to the Record Source row, as shown in Figure 6.41.

FIGURE 6.41

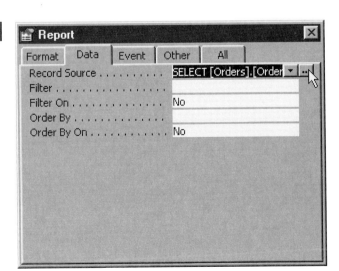

4 The SQL query for the report will appear. Select the Criteria Row for the OrderID field and type **[Please enter an Order number]** to specify the query parameters.

5 Close the query by clicking the Close button in the query's title bar. Access will verify that you want to update the query. Click Yes, as shown in Figure 6.42.

FIGURE 6.42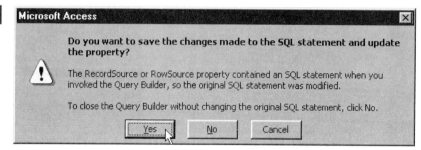

6 Close the Properties dialog box and save your changes to the report.

7 Switch to Print Preview. Access will request an Order Number, as shown in Figure 6.43.

FIGURE 6.43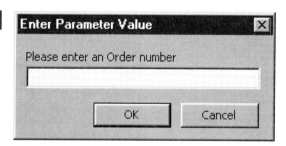

8 Type any number between 1 and 6. Access will display the appropriate invoice.

TROUBLESHOOTING If the report displays additional pages, you have one or more controls that extend beyond the printable area. If you resize the report and make it narrower, you will also need to resize any controls, such as lines or text boxes, that still extend into the area previously occupied by a report section.

9 Close the report.

10 Close the database.

You are now ready to meet with Mr. Traylor and show him the enhancements you have made to the Selections, Inc. database.

Summary and Exercises

Summary

- Database reports are used to print information from a database.
- You can create a report by using one of the Report Wizards or by using Report Design view.
- A report contains bound and unbound controls that specify where information will appear on the report.
- Once you create a report you can view it in the Print Preview window.
- You can modify a report by changing the properties of each control in the report.
- When you create a report in Design view, you must add controls to the report and then modify the control properties.
- You can import existing Access database objects from a separate database file into the current Access database.
- You can use the Subform/Subreport control to bind a report to an associated sub-report or subform.
- To display a specific record in an Access report, modify the SQL query underlying the report so it includes parameter specifications.

Key Terms and Operations

Key Terms

Page Footer
Page Header
Report Design window
Report Detail section
Report Footer
Report Header
subform/subreport control

Operations

add a subform/subreport control to the Detail section of a report
bind a database object to a subform/subreport control
change the Preview display
create a new report using Report Design view
create a report using the Report Wizard
import database objects from an Access database into the current database
modify a report in Design view
specify parameter information in a SQL query underlying a report

Study Questions

Multiple Choice

1. Which view displays all the data in a report exactly as it will be printed?
   a. Design
   b. Preview
   c. Layout
   d. Form
   e. Datasheet

2. To which section of a report will you normally add a subform/subreport control?
   a. Report Header
   b. Page Header
   c. Detail
   d. Page Footer
   e. Report Footer

3. To arrange controls on a report you must use:
   a. Design view.
   b. Layout view.
   c. Form view.
   d. Preview view.
   e. Datasheet view.

4. In which section of a report do bound controls normally appear?
   a. Page Header
   b. Detail
   c. Page Footer
   d. Report Header
   e. Report Footer

5. You can add fields to a report easily using the:
   a. toolbox.
   b. properties dialog box.
   c. database window.
   d. field list.
   e. report formatting toolbar.

6. Unbound controls usually appear in all sections of a report, except which section?
   a. Page Header
   b. Report Header
   c. Page Footer
   d. Detail
   e. Report Footer

7. Data entered in the Page Header section of a report appears:
   a. at the beginning of the report only.
   b. at the end of the report.
   c. at the top of every page
   d. at the bottom of every page.
   e. on every page of the report.

8. Field data from a query appears in which section of a report?
   a. Page Header
   b. Detail
   c. Page Footer
   d. Report Header
   e. Report Footer

9. A query displays an employee's Last Name, First Name, Address, Social Security Number, and time cards in an associated subreport. Each page of the report lists information for one employee only. To easily locate a given employee in a report based upon the query, you should:
   a. add parameter information to the query.
   b. sort the report by Social Security Number.
   c. use the Find feature.
   d. use the navigation controls to locate the record you want to print.
   e. None of the above.

10. You want to add a descriptive title to a report that appears only on the first page of the report. Which section should you add the control to?
    a. Page Header
    b. Detail
    c. Page Footer
    d. Report Header
    e. Report Footer

Short Answer

1. What is the main purpose of a report?

2. What is a subform/subreport control?

3. Where do bound controls normally appear in a report?

4. When should you use a query as the basis for a report?

5. How do you bind a subform or subreport to other data on a report?

6. What is the fastest method for creating a report?

7. How do you import objects from an external database into the active database?

8. How do you move labels from the Detail section of a report to the Page Header section?

9. How do you save a report?

10. What kind of unbound controls does a report usually contain?

Fill in the Blank

1. You can add _____ specifications to the SQL query underlying a report to limit the records displayed in the report.

2. The _____ _____ section displays information that appears only at the beginning of the report.

3. Data displayed in a subform/subreport control is _____ to data appearing elsewhere on a report.

4. A label appearing in the Page Header section of a report is a(n) _____ control.

5. Information displayed in the Report Detail section requires a(n) _____.

6. A report is normally based upon either a(n) _____ or a(n) _____.

7. To create a report using Design view, you add _____ to the various sections of a report.

8. A text box control appearing in the Report Detail section is a(n) _____ control.

9. The _____ view displays all the records in a report exactly as they will be printed.

10. The _____ _____ contains summary information for each page of a report.

For Discussion

1. What database objects can you use to create a report? When might you use one rather than the other?

2. When might you want to add a subform or subreport in a report?

3. When do you use bound versus unbound controls on a report?

4. Describe the three views associated with reports.

5. When should you consider parameter specifications to the SQL query underlying a report?

Hands-On Exercises

1. Adding an Image to a Report

In Project 5 you learned how to add an image to a form using an unbound image control. You can also add images to any section of a report. In this exercise you will add the Selections logo to the Customers report. Complete the following steps:

1. Open the *Selections.mdb* database from your floppy disk.

2. Click the Reports button on the Database Objects toolbar.

3. Open the Customers report in Design view.

4. Add an image control to the right side of the Report Header section.

5. Locate the *Selections Logo.bmp* file on your floppy disk.

 Web Tip

If you do not have a copy of this file, you can download it from the Select Web site at http://www.prenhall.com/selectadvanced.

6. Click OK, as shown in Figure 6.44.

FIGURE 6.44

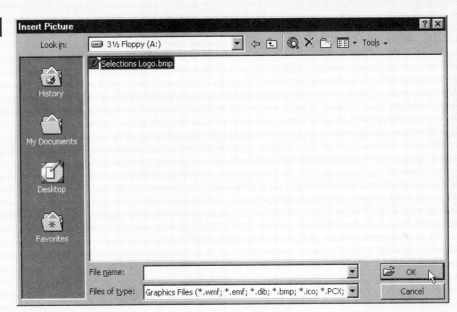

7. Change the Size Mode property of the image control to Stretch.

8. Reposition and resize the image control as necessary.

9. Save your changes.

10. Preview the report at 75% zoom. It will appear as shown in Figure 6.45.

FIGURE 6.45

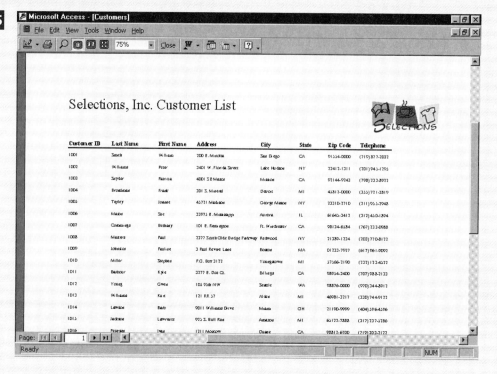

11. Close the report.

2. Modifying a Report's Design

The report you created in the previous exercise can still use modification. In this exercise you will add additional unbound controls to the report, modify text box properties, and change the location of some of the report's controls. Complete the following steps:

1. Open the *Selections.mdb* database file.

2. Open the Customers report in Design view.

3. Adjust the size of the Report Header section, if necessary.

4. Select the label control displaying the report caption. Change the back color property to gray, the font color property to blue, the italics property to true, the weight property to bold, the border style property to solid, and the font size property to 26.

5. Select all labels appearing in the Page Header section.

6. Change the Font Color property of the selection to Blue and the Italics property to Yes.

7. Modify the line at the bottom of the Page Header section so that it appears as blue. Add a line to the top of the Report Footer section. Change the color to blue.

8. Change the fill color of both the Report Header and Page Footer sections to gray.

9. Save your changes.

10. Preview the report, and change the zoom to 60%. Your preview should resemble the report shown in Figure 6.46.

FIGURE 6.46

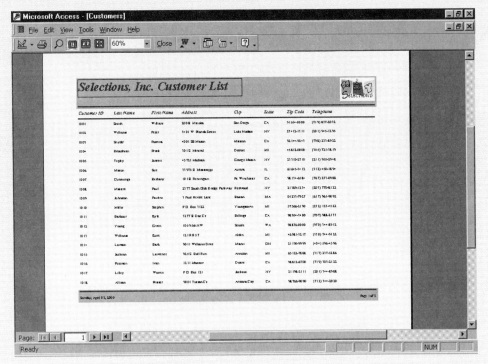

11. Close the preview and the report.

12. Close the database.

3. Creating a Time Cards Report

Open the *Employees.mdb* database and create a report listing the time card data associated with each employee. Modify the report header so it contains the company name, Selections, Inc. somewhere in the header. Save the report as *Time Cards*. Compact the database when you are finished.

On Your Own Exercises

1. Building a Report Based on a Query with an AND Condition

Open the *Web Sites* database file. Using Report Design view, create a report based upon the query displaying records meeting the AND condition you specified in Project 4. Update the database when you are finished.

2. Creating a Report Based on a Multi-table Query

Open the *Products.mdb* database from your floppy disk. Create a report using the Report Wizard based upon the Inventory query you created in Project 4. Include all of the query's fields in the report, and group the report by category. Modify the report as appropriate. Save your changes.

3. Using the Office Assistant

Open the *Products* database. Click Show The Office Assistant in the Help menu. Search the help system for information about creating calculated controls on reports. Create a control in the Report Footer section that lists the total value of the inventory, and format the field as currency. Save the changes you make to the database.

 **Web Tip**

Do you want to learn more about creating Acces reports? Visit http://www.microsoft.com/TechNet/Access/technote/ac210.asp for powerful tips and tricks to create sophisticated reports.

Part III: Maintaining and Customizing a Database

You are well on your way to being an expert Access user! You know the importance of designing efficient database solutions that minimize redundant data, and produce timely, accurate results. You also know how to use many features in Access to create and optimize the primary database objects. You are now ready to learn how you can customize your database solutions and share Access data with other Office and Windows applications. In this section you will explore features in Access for maintaining databases and sharing Access data with other applications.

In Access 2000 there are a number of features available for refining a database. In addition to creating a switchboard menu system, you can use additional Access 2000 features and tools to fine-tune database performance.

Visual Basic for applications (VBA) is the development environment all Office applications share for customization. In this section you will learn how to create Access macros, and you will also explore how to customize your database using VBA procedures. Access and Excel are common applications for storing and analyzing structured data. It should come as no surprise, therefore, that you can easily integrate data in Excel and Access. If you need to distribute components of your database to users who do not have Microsoft Access installed on their computers, you can create a database front end using Visual Basic. After packaging your Visual Basic solution, you can deploy it on individual computers or distribute it from a network.

Maintaining Databases Using Access Database Tools

Now that you have created each of the fundamental database objects for the Selections, Inc. database, you can focus on maintaining the database, and using additional Access tools and features to further refine its performance. In this project you will begin to explore methods for improving database performance.

Objectives

After completing this project, you will be able to:

➤ Specify join properties in relationships

➤ Set Cascade Update and Cascade Delete options

➤ Use the Database Performance Analyzer

➤ Set and modify a database password

➤ Create a database switchboard using Form Design view

➤ Add command button controls to a switchboard

➤ Set startup options

Running Case

Mr. Traylor is very pleased with the progress you have made in the Selections, Inc. e-commerce prototype database. Now that you have created the essential database objects—tables, queries, forms, and reports—you are ready to maintain and further refine the database.

The Challenge

Mr. Traylor has reviewed your work and knows how carefully you have designed the objects in the Selection, Inc. e-commerce database. He now wants you to further modify it to streamline performance. First, he wants you to make sure the database is as efficient as it can be, and can handle typical data maintenance tasks such as adding and deleting records. Second, he is concerned about security. The security needs are not a significant issue at this point, but he wants to know if there is an easy method for protecting the database with a password. Third, he wants you to develop some sort of a menu system so users do not have to use the Database window to open the forms and reports they will be using. Finally, he wants you to set up the database so that the main menu appears automatically any time the database is opened.

The Solution

You can easily complete each modification to the Selections database that Mr. Traylor has requested. There are three things you can do to verify the efficiency of the database. First, you can check the join properties of each relationship to make sure the proper records are related. Second, you can set the Cascade Update and Cascade Delete options so if an order record is deleted, every related order detail record is deleted as well. Third, you can run the Performance Analyzer to verify that the database is working at an optimum performance level.

To keep the database secure you can set a database password. The password you choose will be required anytime a user opens the database.

Many custom databases have a menu system for opening forms and printing reports. To create the menu Mr. Traylor specified, you can use the Access Switchboard Manager to create a series of switchboards, or menus. Finally, you can specify that the menu will appear every time a user opens the database by modifying the startup properties. The switchboard you will create is shown in Figure 7.1.

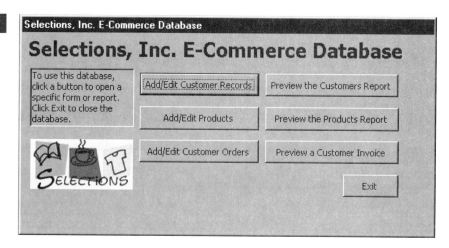

FIGURE 7.1

The Setup

To customize the database as specified above, launch Microsoft Access, open the *Selections, Inc.* database you modified in Project 6, and make sure that you select the settings listed in Table 7.1. If you need additional assistance setting these options, refer to Figure 1.1 through 1.3 of Project 1. This will ensure that your screen matches the illustrations and that the tasks in this project function as described.

Table 7.1   Access Settings

Location	Make these settings:
Office Shortcut Bar	If the Office Shortcut bar is visible, close it by right-clicking the Office icon on the shortcut bar and choosing Exit.
Office Assistant	Hide the Office Assistant.
Tools, Customize	Click the Toolbars tab and display the Database toolbar and the Menu Bar, as shown in Figure 1.1 of Project 1, if they are not currently visible.
Tools, Customize	Click the Options tab, and make sure the check box to display recently used menu commands first is deselected, as shown in Figure 1.2 of Project 1.
Tools, Options	Click the View tab and display Status bar, Startup dialog box, New object shortcuts, and Windows in Taskbar, as shown in Figure 1.3 of Project 1.

Specifying Join Properties in Relationships

When you establish relationships using the Relationships window, Access automatically displays join lines when you add related tables in Query Design view. When you established the relationships in this database, you enforced referential integrity. When referential integrity is enforced, Access displays a 1 above the join line to show which table is on the "one" side of a one-to-many relationship and an infinity symbol to show which table is on the "many" side.

By default, Access created an **_inner join_**, which is a join where records from two tables are combined and added to a query's results only if the values of the joined fields meet a specified condition. For example, when you designed the Customer Orders query, Access created an inner join between tables that select records from both tables only if the values of the joined fields are equal. If one of the tables does not have a matching record in the corresponding table, neither record appears in the query record set.

There might be times when you need to verify the join properties, or change them. In the next task you will learn how to review and modify the join properties.

TASK 1: To View and Modify Join Properties

1 Click the Relationships button ⊞ on the Database toolbar.

2 Right-click the join line between the Customers and Orders tables and choose Edit Relationship, as shown in Figure 7.2.

FIGURE 7.2

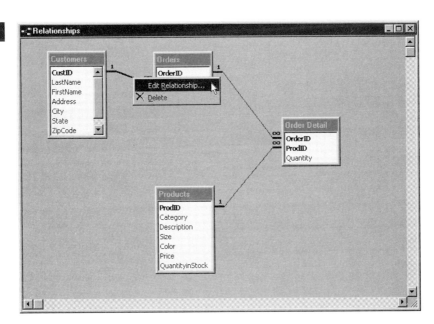

3 The Edit Relationships dialog box will appear. Click Join Type, as shown in Figure 7.3.

FIGURE 7.3

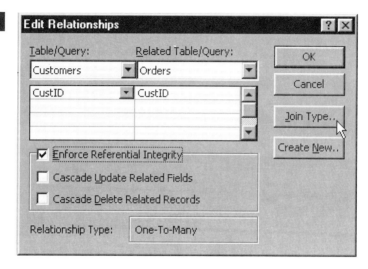

4 The Join Properties dialog box will appear (see Figure 7.4). The first option is selected by default. This is an inner join.

FIGURE 7.4

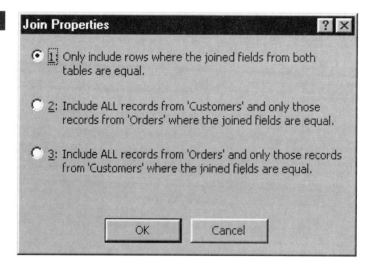

In this case, the inner join is the setting you want, because a query combining data from both tables should return a record set containing records where the order number is the same in both tables.

5 Click OK to close the Join Properties dialog box.

6 Click OK or Cancel to close the Edit Relationships dialog box.

TIP For the many-to-many relationship, the join type for the two one-to-many relationships with the junction table should also be an inner join.

Web Tip

For more information about the join types in relational databases, visit http://msdn.microsoft.com/library/psdk/sql/8_qd_09_1.htm.

Setting Cascade Update and Cascade Delete Options

When you created the relationships between tables in the Selections, Inc. database, you established referential integrity. You will recall that referential integrity specifies the rules that prevent you from adding records to a related table when there is no associated record in the primary table, changing values in the primary table that would result in orphan records in a related table, and deleting records from the primary table when there are matching related records in a related table. There are two additional settings you must consider when specifying referential integrity. Setting the **Cascade Update** option will cause Access to update the key value in a related table if you change the primary key in the parent table. Access will automatically update the primary key to the new value in all related records in the child table. For example, if you change a customer's ID in the Customers table, the CustomerID field in the Orders table is automatically updated for every one of that customer's orders so that the relationship isn't broken. In this case, Access cascades updates without displaying any message.

If you select the **Cascade Delete** check box when defining a relationship, Access automatically deletes related records in the child table any time you delete records in the parent table. Thus, if you delete a customer record from the Customers table, all the customer's orders are automatically deleted from the Orders table (this includes records in the Order Details table related to the Orders records). When you delete records from a form or datasheet with the Cascade Delete Related Records check box selected, Access warns you that related records may also be deleted.

> **TIP** If the primary key in the parent table is an AutoNumber field, setting the Cascade Update Related Fields check box will have no effect because you can't change the value in an AutoNumber field. Because the Customers table and the Orders table each contain a primary key that is an AutoNumber data type, the only setting you can change is the relationship between the Order Detail table and the Products table.

TASK 2: To Set Cascade Update and Cascade Delete Options

1 Right-click the join line between the Order Detail table and the Products table.

2 Choose Edit Relationships.

3 Click the Cascade Update Related Records option.

Check Point

Why do you not want to select the Cascade Delete Related Records check box?

4 When your settings match Figure 7.5, click OK.

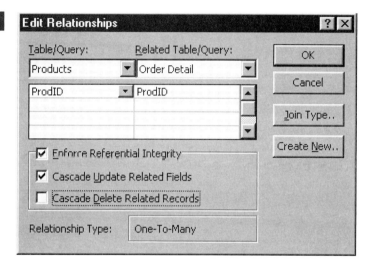

FIGURE 7.5

Now if you update the primary key field for one or more products, the key field in the Order Detail table for each record will also be updated.

5 Close the Relationships window.

Using the Database Performance Analyzer

Mr. Traylor wants to make sure the Selections, Inc. e-commerce database runs at optimum performance. How will you know? If you want to optimize the performance of an Access database, consider running the **Performance Analyzer** first. This Access tool will analyze the database and make recommendations as to how it can be modified for optimization. You can use the Performance Analyzer to analyze a whole database, or just selected objects in a database. The Performance Analyzer can also make changes for you, if you want.

TROUBLESHOOTING To complete the next task, you must have the Performance Analyzer add-in installed on your computer.

TASK 3: To Run the Performance Analyzer

1 Choose Tools, Analyze, and choose Performance, as shown in Figure 7.6.

FIGURE 7.6

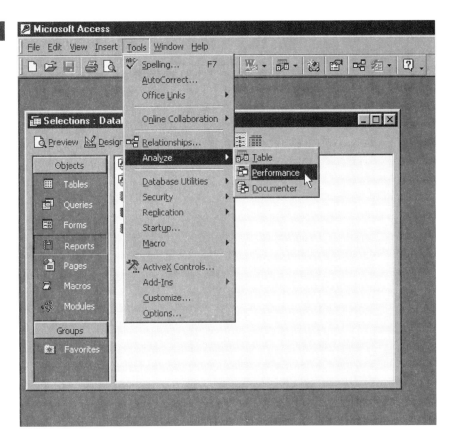

2 The Performance Analyzer dialog box will appear. Click the All Object Types tab to analyze the performance of all the database objects and then click Select All, as shown in Figure 7.7.

FIGURE 7.7

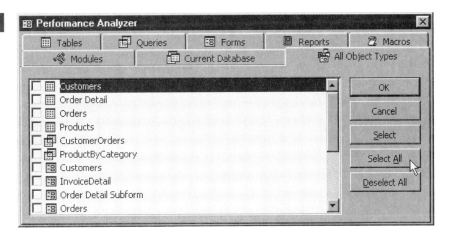

3 Click OK. The Performance Analyzer will display the status of the analysis as each object is being analyzed. After a moment, the Results dialog box shown in Figure 7.8 will appear.

FIGURE 7.8

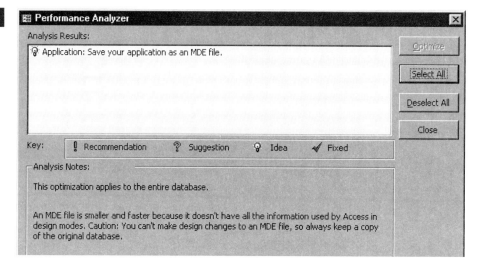

Access will make one recommendation: saving the database as an MDE file. Because you will continue to modify the database throughout the remainder of the projects in this module, you will ignore this recommendation for the time being.

4 Click the Close button.

Setting and Modifying a Database Password

You will recall that Mr. Traylor is concerned with the security of the prototype e-commerce database. In Access, you have different options for establishing database security. If you set a **database password**, all users must enter that password before they are allowed to open the database. Adding a database password is an easy way to prevent unwanted users from opening your database; however, once a database is open, there are no other security measures in place unless you have also defined user-level security. By setting user-level security definitions, you can prevent users from modifying specific database objects, or from changing the database password.

TIP Defining user-level security is a better option for protecting a database. In this case, the database administrator or an object's owner can grant specific permissions to individual users and groups of users on the tables, queries, forms, reports, and macros in the database. However, data access pages and modules are not protected by user-level security.

TASK 4: To Set a Database Password

1 Choose File, Close to close the *Selections.mdb* database.

> **TROUBLESHOOTING** To set a database password, you must first close the database and then open it for exclusive use. Make sure you close the database, and not Access.

2 Choose File, Open.

3 Locate the *Selections.mdb* database file on your floppy disk.

4 Select the file and click the drop-down arrow next to the Open button in the Open dialog box, as shown in Figure 7.9. Choose Open Exclusive from the menu.

FIGURE 7.9

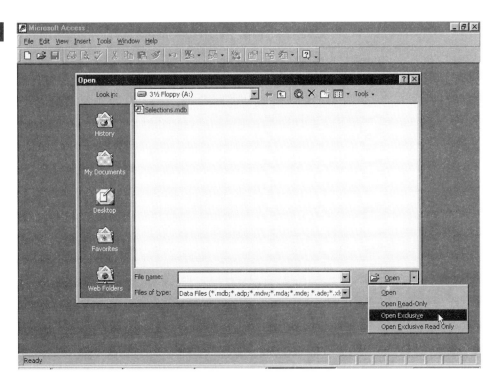

5 Choose Tools, Security, and click Set Database Password, as shown in Figure 7.10.

FIGURE 7.10

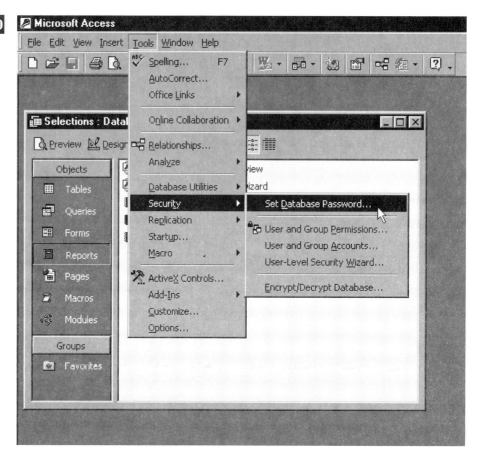

6 Type **1234** as the database password. Note that as you enter the password, asterisks appear in the dialog box for security.

7 Press TAB once. Type **1234** in the Verify textbox.

8 Click OK (see Figure 7.11).

FIGURE 7.11

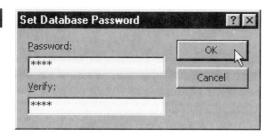

Access adds the password to the database.

TIP Write down this password and store it in a safe place. If you forget the password, you will not be able to open the database.

9 Close the database, and then reopen it. Access displays the Password Required dialog box shown in Figure 7.12.

FIGURE 7.12

10 Type **1111** and click OK. Because this password is incorrect, Access displays the warning shown in Figure 7.13.

FIGURE 7.13

11 Click OK.

12 Type **1234** and then click OK. The database now opens.

 Check Point

Why should you write down the password and store it in a safe place?

After you have established a database password, you can easily unset it. You would unset a password if security was no longer an issue, or if you wanted to change the password. To change a password, you would first remove the existing password and then assign a new one to the database.

 TASK 5: To Remove a Database Password

1 Choose Tools, Security, and click Unset Password, as shown in Figure 7.14.

2 Type **1234** to open the database. Access has now removed the database password.

FIGURE 7.14

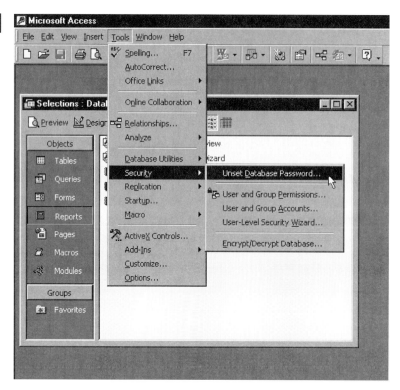

Web Tip

There are other considerations when assigning a database password. Visit http://msdn.microsoft.com/library/officedev/odeopg/ deovrimportantconsiderationswhenusingdatabasepassword.htm for more information.

Break Point

If necessary, you can exit Access and continue this project later.

Creating a Switchboard

If you create a database by using the Database Wizard, Access automatically creates a switchboard that helps you to navigate within the database. A *switchboard* is a form that contains buttons used to open forms and reports, or to exit the database. A switchboard can also display other switchboards that open additional forms and reports in a more complex database. You have two methods for creating a switchboard. You can use the Switchboard Manager to create a switchboard similar to one created by the Database Wizard. This option is useful if you want to quickly add functionality to the database without using Design view. If you want to create a custom switchboard with a specific look, you can create a switchboard form using Form Design view.

Because a switchboard is a form, you can modify the switchboard using Form Design view. If you create a switchboard using the Switchboard Manager, Access creates a Switchboard Items table that describes what the buttons on the form display and what actions each button performs. If you make changes to the switchboard form later in Form Design view, the application might not work. If you expect to customize your switchboard form after creating it, it is best to create the form from scratch and then specify it as the startup form. In the next task you will create a switchboard form using Form Design view.

TASK 6: <u>To Create a Switchboard Using Form Design View</u>

1 Launch Access if it is not currently running, and open the *Selections.mdb* database if necessary.

2 Click the Forms button in the Database window.

3 Click the New button ![New] on the Database toolbar to create a new form. Specify Design view, but do not base the form on a table or query. When your settings match those shown in Figure 7.15, click OK.

FIGURE 7.15

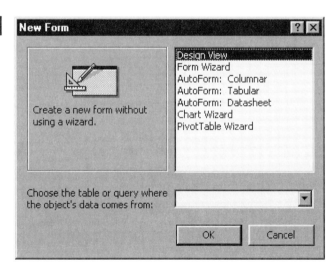

4 Click the Toolbox button ![Toolbox] on the Report Design toolbar to display the Toolbox. Reposition the Toolbox so that it appears at the right of the Report Design window.

5 Add a label control at the top of the form. Type **Selections, Inc. E-Commerce Database** as the label caption, change the font to Tahoma, 18 point, bold, and change the font color to blue. Resize the control as necessary. The label should look similar to the one displayed in Figure 7.16.

FIGURE 7.16

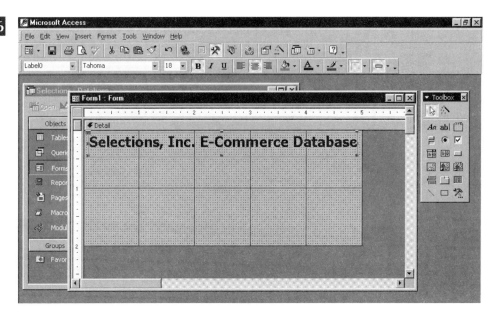

6 Add an image control to the lower left corner of the form. When the Insert Picture dialog box appears, navigate to your floppy disk, select the Selections Logo.bmp file, and click OK, as shown in Figure 7.17.

Web Tip

If you do not have a copy of this image file, you can download it from the Select Web site at http://www.prenhall.com/selectadvanced

FIGURE 7.17

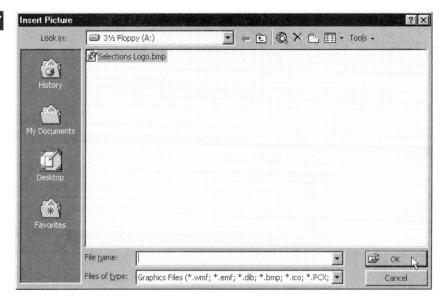

7 Add a label control between the label appearing at the top of the form and the image appearing at the bottom of the form. Type the following text as the label caption: **To use this database, click a button to open a specific form or report. Click Exit to close the database.**

8 Resize the label so its width matches the width of the image appearing on the form.

9 Right-click the label and choose Special Effect. Choose the last option in the first row, which is the sunken effect.

10 Click the View button to switch to Form view. Your form should look similar to the form displayed in Figure 7.18.

FIGURE 7.18

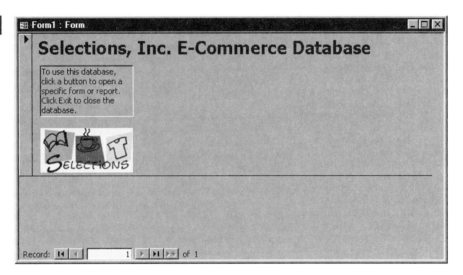

11 Return to Form Design view. Right-click the area in the form appearing below the Detail section and choose Properties from the shortcut menu.

12 Click the Format tab in the Form Properties dialog box. Set the properties for the form listed in Table 7.2.

Table 7.2   Form Property Settings

Property	Setting
Caption	Selections, Inc. E-Commerce Database
Scroll Bars	Neither
Record Selectors	No
Navigation Buttons	No
Border Style	Dialog
Dividing Lines	No
Auto Resize	No
Control Box	No

The Properties dialog box will now appear as shown in Figure 7.19.

FIGURE 7.19

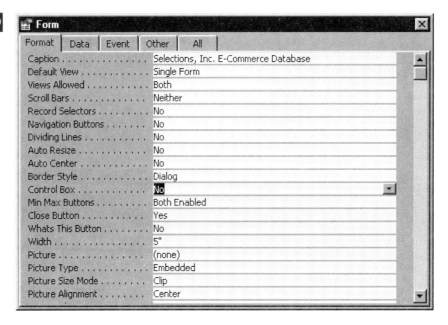

13 Close the Properties dialog box.

14 Save the form as **Startup**.

15 Click the View button to exhibit the form in Form view. Your form should look similar to the form shown in Figure 7.20.

FIGURE 7.20

Adding Command Buttons to the Switchboard

You are now ready to add command buttons to the switchboard form. A ***command button*** is a control that will add functionality to the switchboard. When a user selects a command button appearing on the switchboard, the specified form or report will be displayed. When you add each command button to the switchboard form, Access will prompt you to specify an action which the button will perform. After you have added the appropriate command buttons to the switchboard, you can resize the form.

TASK 7: <u>To Add a Command Button to the Switchboard Form</u>

1 Display the form in Design view.

2 Click the Command Button tool in the Toolbox.

3 Click the Control Wizards button in the Toolbox. This will enable the Control Wizards, which will assist you in adding functionality to the command buttons you will create.

4 Add a command button control to the form, as shown in Figure 7.21.

FIGURE 7.21

5 The Command Button Wizard will appear. Select Form Operations in the Categories: list, and Open form in the Actions: list. When your settings match those shown in Figure 7.22, click Next.

FIGURE 7.22

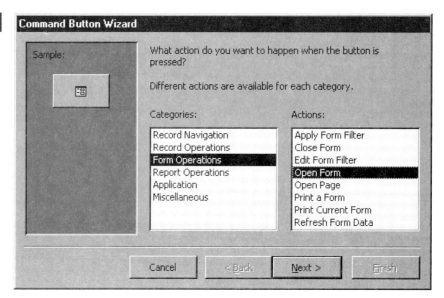

6. In the next step of the Command Button Wizard, Access will select the Customers form by default. Accept the default and click Next.

7. Next, Access will ask you to select an option for displaying the records. The default setting is to open the form and display all records. Accept the default and click Next.

8. Access will ask you to specify how the button will appear. Click the Text option button and select Add/Edit Customer Records as the caption for the button, as shown in Figure 7.23. Click Next.

FIGURE 7.23

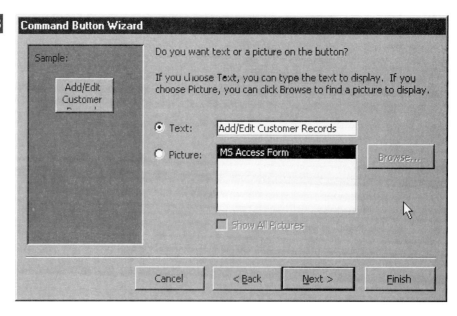

9 In the last step of the Command Button Wizard, you will be prompted to name the command button. Type **cmdOpenCustomersForm** as the name for the command button and click Finish (see Figure 7.24).

FIGURE 7.24

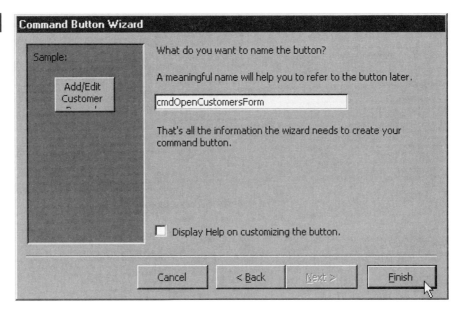

TIP The name you are assigning to the form follows Visual Basic naming conventions. You will learn more about the naming conventions for controls in Project 9.

10 Save your changes to the form.

TASK 8: To Add Additional Command Buttons to the Customers Form

1 Create another command button control immediately to the right of the command button you just added to the switchboard.

FIGURE 7.25

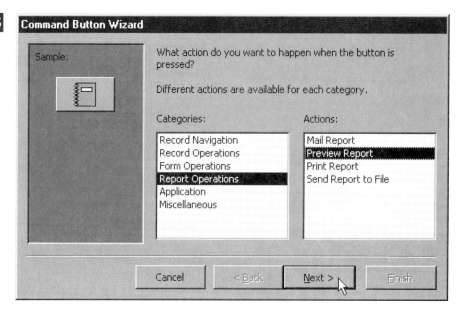

Choose the Customers report and click Next.

Set the display of the command button to Text. Type **Preview the Customers Report** as the caption for the button and click Next (see Figure 7.26).

FIGURE 7.26

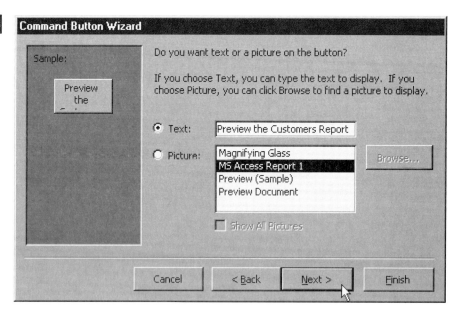

Type **cmdPreviewCustomersReport** as the name for the command button, and then click Finish.

Add five additional buttons to the switchboard, using the specifications listed in Table 7.3

Table 7.3

Operation	Action	Datbase Object	Caption	Specification	Name
Form	Open form	Products form	Add/Edit Products	All records	cmdOpenProducts Form
Report	Preview Report	Product List report	Preview the Products Report	N/A	cmdPreview ProductListReport
Form	Open form	Orders form	Add/Edit Customer Orders	All Records	cmdOpenOrders Form
Report	Preview Report	Customer Invoice	Preview a Customer Invoice	N/A	cmdPreview CustomerInvoice Report
Application	Quit Application		Exit	N/A	CmdExit

TIP Add the command buttons in the order listed in Table 7.3. If you do, users will be able to tab through the buttons in an orderly sequence.

7 Reposition and size the command buttons as appropriate. Resize the form to the size shown in Figure 7.27.

FIGURE 7.27

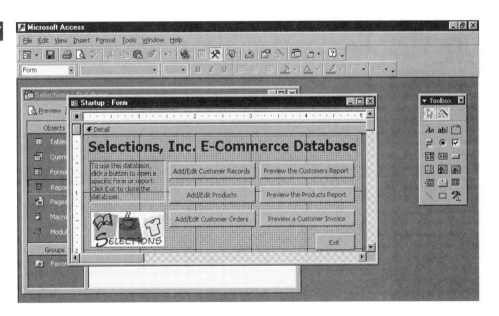

8 Save the form.

9 View the form in Form view. Your form should look similar to the switchboard form displayed in Figure 7.28.

> **TROUBLESHOOTING** Do not select any of the command buttons at this time!

FIGURE 7.28

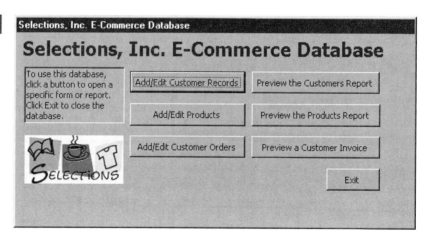

Selections, Inc. E-Commerce Database

Selections, Inc. E-Commerce Database

To use this database, click a button to open a specific form or report. Click Exit to close the database.

SELECTIONS

Add/Edit Customer Records	Preview the Customers Report
Add/Edit Products	Preview the Products Report
Add/Edit Customer Orders	Preview a Customer Invoice
	Exit

10 Click the Design button to return to Form Design view.

11 Close the form.

Check Point

Why must you switch to Form Design view to close the form?

Setting Database Startup Options

You are almost finished with your modifications to the database. Your last task is to set the startup options for the database so that the switchboard form will display. In addition, you will hide the Database window, because the users will use the switchboard for opening the appropriate forms and reports.

TASK 9: To Set the Database Startup Options

1 Choose Tools, Startup. The Startup dialog box will appear.

2 Type **Selections, Inc. E-Commerce Database** as the database title.

3 Click the drop-down list arrow next to Display Form/Page and select the Startup form.

4 Deselect the option to display the Database window. When your settings match those shown in Figure 7.29, click OK.

FIGURE 7.29

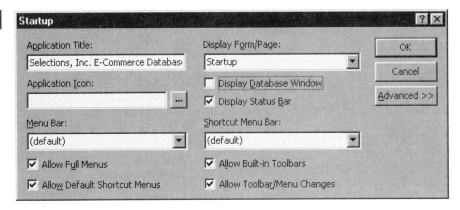

5 Close the database.

6 Open the database. Access will display a new database title, show the Startup form, and hide the Database window, as shown in Figure 7.30.

FIGURE 7.30

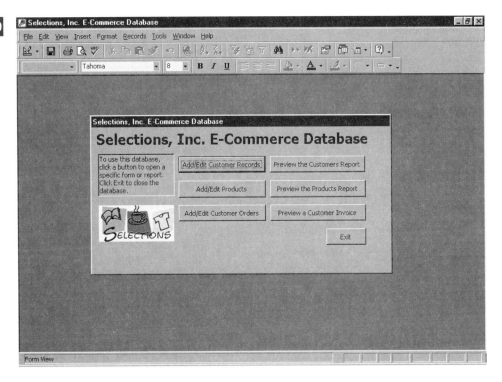

7 Click each button on the switchboard that opens a form or report to verify the database functionality. After you open each object, close it without adding any data to the database.

> **TIP** To display the Database window, choose Window, Unhide, select the *Selections: Database* option in the list, and click OK.

8 Click the Exit button to close the database and exit Access. You are now ready to show Mr. Traylor the enhancements you have made to the database.

Summary and Exercises

Summary

- To change the records returned by a query based on related tables, you can change the join properties in the table relationship.
- Set Cascade Update and Cascade Delete options.
- To verify that a database is running in an optimized state, run the Database Performance Analyzer.
- To prevent specific users from opening a database, assign a database password.
- You can create a switchboard for navigating within a database using Form Design view.
- Command buttons add functionality to a database switchboard.
- To automatically display a switchboard when a database opens, change the startup options.

Key Terms and Operations

Key Terms

Cascade Delete
Cascade Update
command button
database password
inner join
Performance Analyzer
switchboard

Operations

add command buttons to a switchboard form
create a switchboard using Form Design view
remove a database password
run the Performance Analyzer
set a database password
set Cascade Update settings
set database Startup options
verify join properties

Study Questions

Multiple Choice

1. Which Access setting specifies that related records in a child table are deleted when the associated record in the parent table is deleted?
   a. Inner join
   b. Cascade Update
   c. Outer join
   d. Cascade Delete
   e. Referential Integrity

2. When you add a password to a database file, a user must supply the correct password to open:
   a. tables.
   b. queries.
   c. forms.
   d. reports.
   e. the database.

3. A switchboard is what kind of database object?
   a. A table
   b. A query
   c. A form
   d. A sub form
   e. A report

4. Which Access settings specify how a database appears when it is first opened?
   a. Join type
   b. Startup Options
   c. Referential Integrity
   d. Security
   e. Cascade Update

5. Which Access feature will verify that a database is optimized?
   a. Switchboard Manager
   b. Cascade Update setting
   c. Performance Analyzer
   d. Referential Integrity setting
   e. Join Properties dialog box

6. Which Access setting specifies that related records in a child table are deleted when the associated record in the parent table is deleted?
   a. Inner join
   b. Cascade Update
   c. Outer join
   d. Cascade Delete
   e. Referential Integrity

7. To show the Database window after it has been hidden, choose:
   a. file.
   b. edit.
   c. view.
   d. tools.
   e. window.

8. Which of the following cannot be set using the database Startup options?
   a. Application title
   b. Startup form or page
   c. Visible setting of the Database Window
   d. Menu specifications
   e. Relationships window

9. A switchboard typically uses which kind of control to open the forms and reports in a database?
   a. Label
   b. Image
   c. Text box
   d. Command button
   e. Subform/subreport

10. Which Access feature or view do you use to create a form for navigating within a database?
   a. Performance Analyzer
   b. Database Startup dialog box
   c. Switchboard Manager
   d. Table Design view
   e. Relationships window

Short Answer

1. Which Access tool will check a database to make sure it is running at optimum performance?

2. What does the Cascade Delete referential integrity setting do?

3. How do you hide the Database window when a database opens?

4. How can you create a switchboard automatically?

5. What kind of control usually appears on a switchboard?

6. Which Access tool in the Toolbox must be activated if you want assistance specifying an action for a command button?

7. What is a join line?

8. How do you protect an Access database from an unauthorized user?

9. If you know that you need to significantly modify a switchboard, how should you create it?

10. What kind of join is the default in relationships enforcing referential integrity?

Fill in the Blank

1. You can use the _____ _____ Add-in to check the performance of an Access database.

2. The _____ _____ setting for referential integrity will cause related fields in the child table to be changed if the primary key entries are changed in the parent table.

3. The _____ _____ setting for referential integrity will cause related fields in the child table to be deleted if one or more records in the parent table are deleted.

4. A database switchboard consists of one or more _____.

5. To display a form as a switchboard, you must change the _____ _____ of the database.

6. The _____ _____ of a relationship determine exactly how related records are returned by a query.

7. By default, Access creates a(n) _____ join when a relationship is established that enforces referential integrity.

8. A database _____ protects a database from unauthorized access.

9. If you anticipate making extensive changes to a switchboard, consider creating the switchboard using _____ _____.

10. The _____ _____ is an Access tool for creating a database switchboard.

For Discussion

1. Why is it important to consider how the Cascade Update and Cascade Delete options are set in table relationships?

2. What are join properties, and why might you consider changing the join property of a relationship?

3. What options do you have for adding security to an Access database?

4. What happens if you assign a database password and then later forget it?

5. When should you consider creating a switchboard using Form Design view as opposed to using the Switchboard Manager?

Hands-On Exercises

1. Encrypting and Decrypting a Database

In this project you learned how to protect a database using a password. You can also protect a database from being viewed by other applications by encrypting it. Encrypting a database compacts the database file, and makes it indecipherable by a utility program or word processor. Decrypting a database reverses the encryption. For this exercise, make a copy of the *Products.mdb* database file you modified in the end of chapter exercises for Project 6. Name the copy **Copy of Products.mdb**. If you do not have a copy of this file, ask your instructor where you can obtain it.

To Encrypt a Database:

1. Launch Access without opening a database.

2. Choose Tools, Security, and choose Encrypt/Decrypt Database.

3. Navigate to your floppy disk, select the *Copy of Products.mdb* database file, and click OK, as shown in Figure 7.31.

FIGURE 7.31

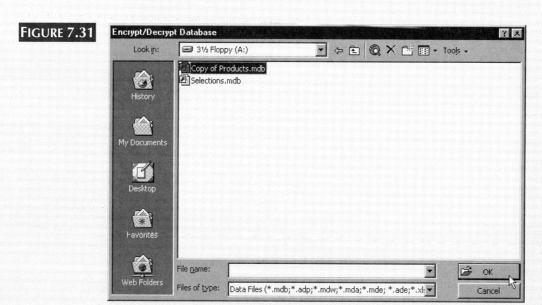

4. Access will request the name and location of the encrypted database. Type **Products – Encrypted.mdb** and click Save, as shown in Figure 7.32.

FIGURE 7.32

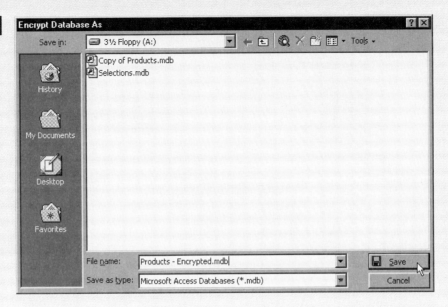

5. Access compacts, encrypts, and saves the database.

> **TIP** To decrypt a database, follow the same procedure.

6. Close the database.

2. Using the Database Splitter

In this project you used the Performance Analyzer to verify the optimization status of the database. Access also includes the Database Splitter, another useful add-in for improving performance. When you split a database, Access converts the database to two files: one that contains the tables, and one that contains all other database objects. After splitting a database, users who need to access the data can customize their own forms, reports, pages, and other objects while maintaining a single source of data tables on the network.

To Split a Database:

1. Open the *Products – Encrypted.mdb* Database.

2. Choose Tools, Database Utilities, and click Database Splitter, as shown in Figure 7.33.

FIGURE 7.33

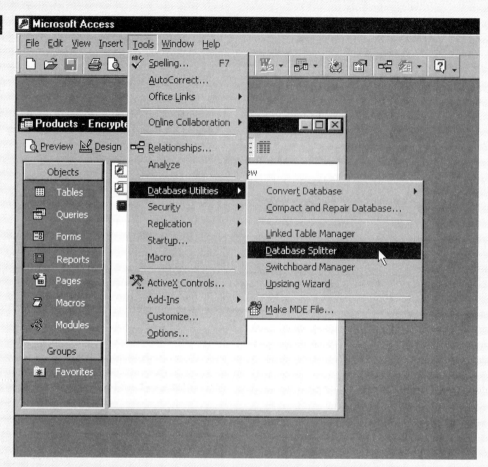

3. The Database Splitter Wizard will appear. Click Split Database.

4. Access will prompt you for a name for the back end file. Accept the default shown in Figure 7.34 and click Split.

FIGURE 7.34

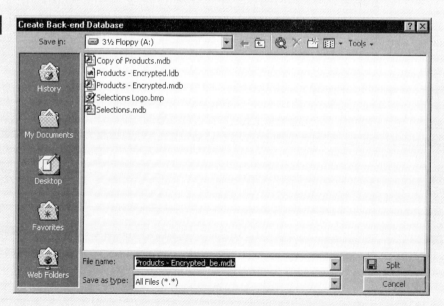

5. Access will split the database, and, if the procedure is successful, the message shown in Figure 7.35 will appear.

FIGURE 7.35

6. Click OK.

7. Open the *Products – Encrypted* database. Access has added the arrow next to the Products table, as shown in Figure 7.36. This indicates that the database is split, and the data appears in a back end file.

FIGURE 7.36

8. Close the database.

On Your Own Exercises

1. Optimizing Data Type Usage

There might be times when you will want to change the data type for fields in a database to make the data storage more efficient. Launch Access, open the Office Assistant, and search for the help topic entitled *What data type should I use for a field in my table?* Select the *Summary of Field Data Types* link, and review the list displayed in Figure 7.37.

FIGURE 7.37

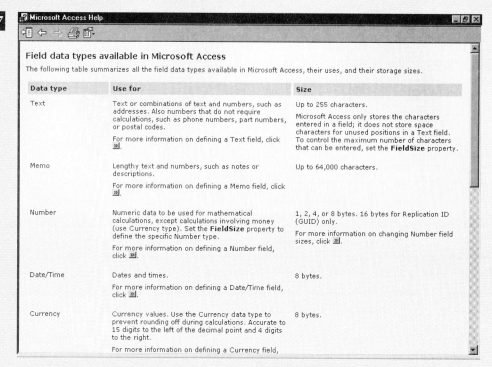

Close the Office Assistant when you are finished reviewing how to optimize data types.

2. Replicating a Database

There might be times when you will need to create a copy of a database for a mobile user. By replicating an Access database, you can share it with other users, and even synchronize the copies of the database.

1. Open the *Web Sites.mdb* database.

2. Choose Tools, Replication, and click Create Replica.

3. Access will inform you that the database will be closed and the replica created.

4. Click Yes. Access will recommend that you back up the database.

5. Click Yes to automatically create a backup copy.

6. Accept the default name for the replicated copy.

7. Access will display a message when the replication is finished. Note that changes to the database structure can be made only in the master copy.

8. Click OK and close the database.

3. Creating a Switchboard Using the Switchboard Manager

In this project you learned how to create a switchboard in Form Design view. In this exercise you will create a switchboard using the Switchboard Manager.

Open the *Web Sites.mdb* database. This is the master copy of the replicated database. Choose Tools, Database Utilities, and select Switchboard Manager. Access will inform you that a valid switchboard does not exist. Select the option to create one. When Access displays a list of the switchboards it created, select the main switchboard and click the Edit button. Add at least one action to the switchboard. Save your changes, and view the switchboard. Close the database when you are finished.

Displaying Access Data on the World Wide Web

All applications in Microsoft Office 2000 include new features for integrating data on the Web. One feature included in Access 2000 is the database engine. Access 2000 now uses the Microsoft Database Engine (MSDE), which enables you to build solutions that are compatible with Microsoft's SQL Server. The MSDE is a client/server data engine. Access 97 featured the Jet database engine, which does not support true client/server applications. A second enhancement is the introduction of a new database object, the data access page.

In Access you can create both static and dynamic Web solutions. Static web pages are those with content that does not frequently change. Dynamic web content will change, based on changes in an underlying database. In this project you will learn how to use the World Wide Web as a resource for displaying and changing Access data.

Objectives

After completing this project, you will be able to:

➤ Describe three strategies for using Access data on the World Wide Web

➤ Create a static HTML page from Access data

➤ Create dynamic data access pages

➤ Add hyperlinks to Access objects

➤ Create a grouped data access page

Running Case

Access 2000 includes Web integration features that will enable business efforts such as the Selections, Inc. e-commerce initiative to thrive.
The new version of this popular database management system includes new features for displaying database information on the Web. In this project, you will create a number of Web resources for Mr. Traylor.

The Challenge

After Mr. Traylor reviewed the changes you last made to the database, he determined that you are ready to begin developing resources for interacting with the database through the World Wide Web. He knows that Access includes features for data entry and data display using a Web browser, and he anticipates that not all Selections, Inc. employees who need to work with the e-commerce database will have Access installed on their computers. There are four Web resources that he wants you to create. First, he wants to make the Selections, Inc. e-commerce product list available to anyone with access to the World Wide Web. This resource can be a simple page listing the product numbers, descriptions, sizes, colors, and prices. This list will be available to all current and prospective customers, and will be posted on the company's Website. It appears as shown in Figure 8.1.

FIGURE 8.1

ProdID	Description	Size	Color	Price
RCX2001100	Team Ritchey - Yahoo! T-Shirt	Child	White	$12.95
RCX2001110	Team Ritchey - Yahoo! T-Shirt	Medium	White	$16.95
RCX2001120	Team Ritchey - Yahoo! T-Shirt	Large	White	$16.95
RCX2001130	Team Ritchey - Yahoo! T-Shirt	Extra Large	White	$16.95
RCX3052110	Team Ritchey Competition Jersey, Short Sleeve	Medium	Team Colors	$49.95
RCX3052120	Team Ritchey Competition Jersey, Short Sleeve	Large	Team Colors	$49.95
RCX3052130	Team Ritchey Competition Jersey, Short Sleeve	Extra Large	Team Colors	$49.95
RCX3082110	Team Ritchey Competition Jersey, Long Sleeve	Medium	Team Colors	$69.95
RCX3082120	Team Ritchey Competition Jersey, Long Sleeve	Large	Team Colors	$69.95
RCX3082130	Team Ritchey Competition Jersey, Long Sleeve	Extra Large	Team Colors	$69.95
RCX5007210	Team Ritchey Bicycle Shorts	Small	Black	$29.95
RCX5007220	Team Ritchey Bicycle Shorts	Medium	Black	$29.95
RCX5007230	Team Ritchey Bicycle Shorts	Large	Black	$29.95
RCX5007240	Team Ritchey Bicycle Shorts	Extra Large	Black	$29.95
RLA1001110	Team Ritchey Water Bottle	Small	White	$4.95
RLA1001120	Team Ritchey Water Bottle	Large	White	$4.95
RLA1001210	Team Ritchey Water Bottle	Small	Clear	$4.95
RLA1001220	Team Ritchey Water Bottle	Large	White	$4.95
RLA2007350	CPR-4 Multi-Purpose Tool	Standard	Silver Anodized	$2.95

Second, he wants you to create two Web pages that employees can use to enter and edit database records. One page will enable employees to enter and edit product information, and the other page will enable employees to modify the Customers list. These will be posted on the company intranet for internal use. Figure 8.2 shows how the Product information page will appear in Microsoft's Internet Explorer. Figure 8.3 shows how the Customers page will appear.

FIGURE 8.2

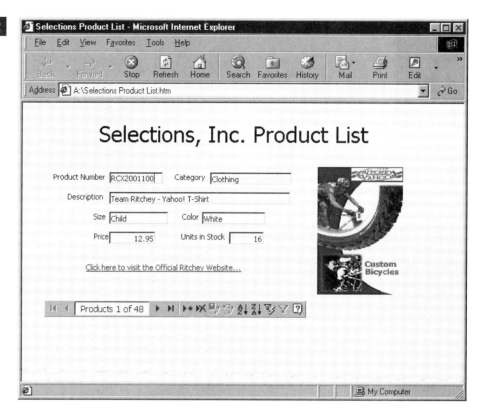

FIGURE 8.3

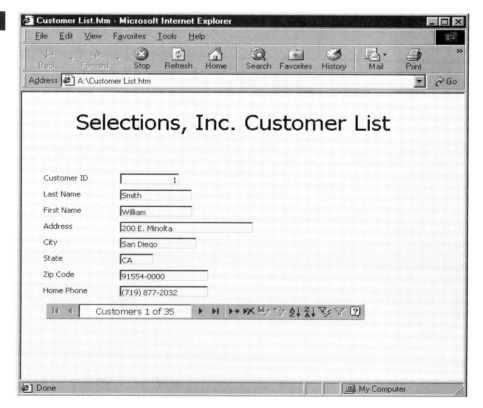

Finally, Mr. Traylor wants to provide a page to the Sales and Marketing Department that lists current inventory status. This page will display a summary of all inventory quantities in stock and the value of the inventory by individual item and product category. This page is also for internal use only, and will be posted on the corporate intranet. Figure 8.4 shows how the inventory report displays when the page is first opened. Figure 8.5 shows the inventory detail for the first inventory item in the Clothing category.

FIGURE 8.4

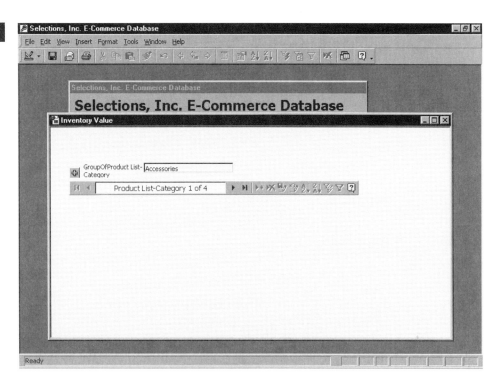

FIGURE 8.5

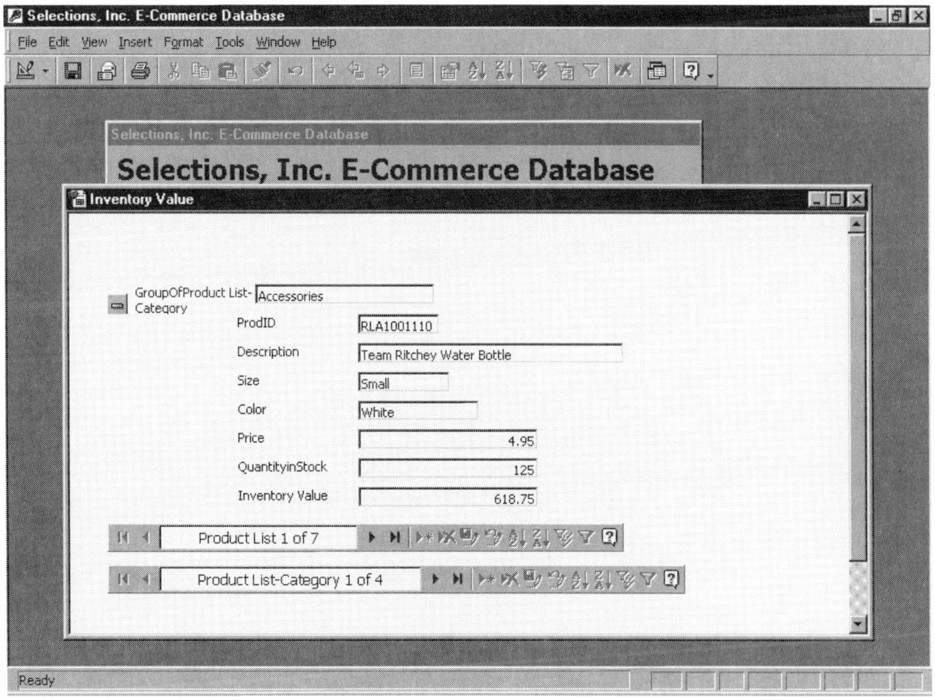

The Solution

For the product listing, you will create a static HTML document, as customers and potential customers do not need to modify or otherwise interact with this information. As with other Office applications, you can save database objects such as tables and queries as a Web page. Once you have created the HTML page, you can post it to an Internet Web server.

To create the two pages linked to the Products and the Customers tables, you can use a new feature in Access 2000, the data access page. A data access page is bound to a database object, enabling users to add, modify, and delete table data using a Web page interface. Because both of these pages are for use by Selections, Inc. employees only, you can post them to the intranet Web server once you have created them.

The final object you will create is a data access page that will group the list by product category, and sort the inventory data by inventory value. As you will see, a grouped data access page enables the user to expand and collapse the list, thereby interacting with the data in different ways.

The Setup

To design the Web components described above, launch Microsoft Access, open the *Selections, Inc.* database you modified in Project 7, and make sure that you select the settings listed in Table 8.1. If you need additional assistance setting these options, refer to Figure 1.1 through 1.3 of Project 1. This will ensure that your screen matches the illustrations and the tasks in this project function as described.

Table 8.1 Access Settings

Location	Make these settings:
Office Shortcut Bar	If the Office Shortcut bar is visible, close it by right-clicking the Office icon on the shortcut bar and choosing Exit.
Office Assistant	Hide the Office Assistant.
Tools, Customize	Click the Toolbars tab and display the Database toolbar and the Menu Bar, as shown in Figure 1.1 of Project 1, if they are not currently visible.
Tools, Customize	Click the Options tab, and make sure the check box to display recently used menu commands first is deselected, as shown in Figure 1.2 of Project 1.
Tools, Options	Click the View tab and display Status bar, Startup dialog box, New object shortcuts, and Windows in Taskbar, as shown in Figure 1.3 of Project 1.

Access 2000 and the World Wide Web

With Access 2000 you can create both static and dynamic resources for the Internet. A **static resource** is a listing of records from your database that represent the state of the database at a specific point in time. Static resources are appropriate for information, such as price lists that may change infrequently. Static data is not bound to the database. A **dynamic resource**, on the other hand, represents data that changes frequently, and therefore must be refreshed. Dynamic resources are bound to the database, so any changes on the data are reflected in the Web resource. HTML documents saved from the database are static resources. Data access pages are dynamic resources. In this project you will create both static and dynamic resources.

Creating Static HTML Pages from Access Data

You can save Access data as static HTML files from tables, queries, forms, and reports. When you view the saved data in a Web browser, the reports will display in a report format; tables, queries, and forms will display as a datasheet. You can use static HTML files if you want the information to be visible in any Web browser.

> **TIP** The Web browser must support HTML version 3.2 or later.

Remember that any HTML files you create represent the data at the time you published them. If your data changes, you will need to export your files again to be able to view any updates. In this task you will create a query displaying the product information you want to display, and then publish the list to a static HTML file.

TASK 1: To Publish the Products Table as a Static HTML File

1. Click Window, Unhide. The Unhide Window dialog box will appear.

Check Point

Why do you need to unhide the Database window?

2. Accept the default shown in Figure 8.6 and click OK.

FIGURE 8.6

3 Click the Queries tab. Create a query in Design view based on the Products table. Include the ProdID, Description, Size, Color, and Price fields.

4 Format the Price field as currency.

 Check Point

How do you format a field in a query?

5 Save the query as **Product List**. The query design should appear as shown in Figure 8.7.

FIGURE 8.7

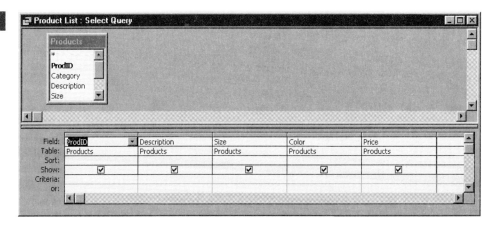

6 Close the query.

7 In the Queries page of the Database window, right-click the Product List query and choose Export, as shown in Figure 8.8.

FIGURE 8.8

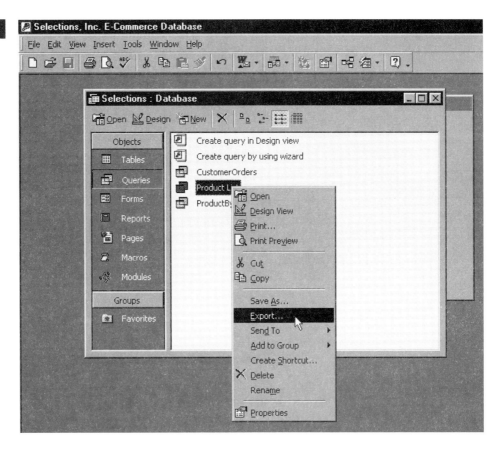

8 The Export Query dialog box will appear. Navigate to your floppy disk as the storage location, specify HTML documents as the document type, and check the option to save the list as formatted. When your settings match those shown in Figure 8.9, click Save.

FIGURE 8.9

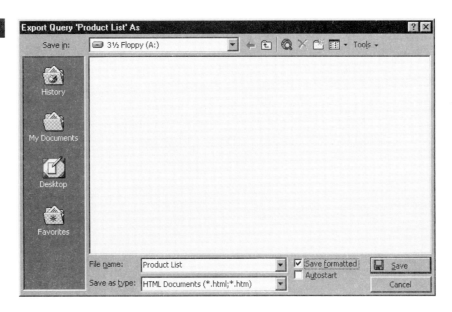

9 The HTML Output Options dialog box will appear. Because you have not defined any templates, click OK.

> **TIP** An HTML template is a set of formatting options that will cause a page to display using prespecified elements such as headings, graphics, and themes. Companies will often define HTML templates so all company documents have a consistent "look and feel."

10 Access saves the datasheet as an HTML file. Because the HTML file is external to Access and must therefore be viewed using a Web Browser, it is not currently displayed.

11 Minimize Access and use My Computer to navigate to your floppy disk.

12 Double-click the Product List.html file. The Product List will open in your registered Web Browser. Figure 8.10 shows how the list will appear in Microsoft Internet Explorer.

FIGURE 8.10

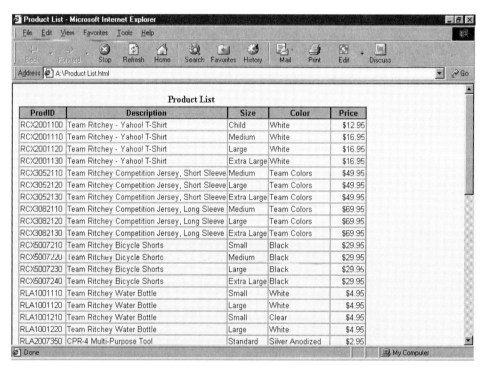

13 Close your Web browser.

14 Restore Access.

Creating Dynamic Data Access Pages

When you create a *data access page*, you create a special Access database object that is connected directly to the database. You save this page as a file, external to the Access database, for posting on a Web server. When you display the data access page in Microsoft Internet Explorer, you view your own copy of the page. Any filtering, sorting, or other changes you make to the way the data is displayed will impact only your page. Any changes, however, to the record data, such as adding records, deleting records, or changing records, are stored in the underlying database.

You can create different kinds of data access pages. Because Mr. Traylor wants users to be able to edit customer and product data using a Web browser, you can think of the data access pages you will create as a database form available in Microsoft Internet Explorer. In the next two tasks, you will create two data access pages. You will first create a Customers data access page using a wizard, and then create a data access page using Design view.

> **TIP** To view and work with the data access page on the Internet or an intranet, users need Microsoft Internet Explorer 5 and a Microsoft Office 2000 license.

TASK 2: To Create a Data Access Page Using the Wizard

1 Click the Pages button in the Database window.

2 Click the New button `New`.

3 In the New Data Access Page dialog box, click Page Wizard and base the page on the Customers table, as shown in Figure 8.11. Click OK.

FIGURE 8.11

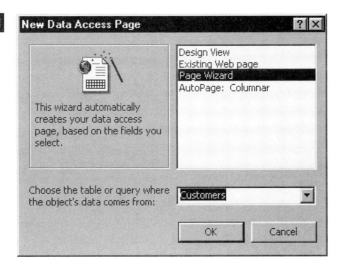

New Data Access Page

Design View
Existing Web page
Page Wizard
AutoPage: Columnar

This wizard automatically creates your data access page, based on the fields you select.

Choose the table or query where the object's data comes from: Customers

OK   Cancel

4 Click the double arrow button ▸▸ to move all fields from the Available Field list to the Selected Field list. When your settings match Figure 8.12, click Next.

FIGURE 8.12

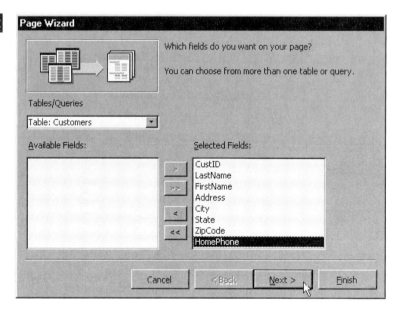

FIGURE 8.12

5 You are now prompted to add grouping levels. Accept the default settings shown in Figure 8.13 and click Next.

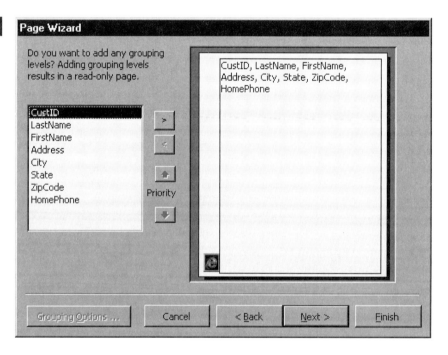

FIGURE 8.13

6 Next, you are prompted to specify the sort order. Click Next.

7 In the final step of the Page Wizard, Access will recommend Customers as the name for this page. Choose the option to open the page and click Finish (see 8.14).

FIGURE 8.14

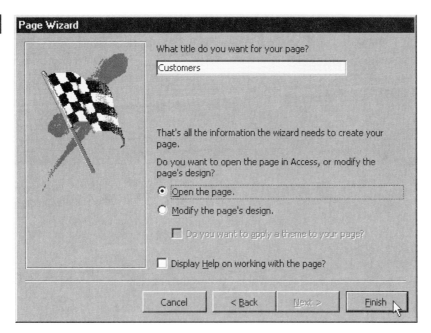

8 Access displays the page as shown in Figure 8.15.

FIGURE 8.15

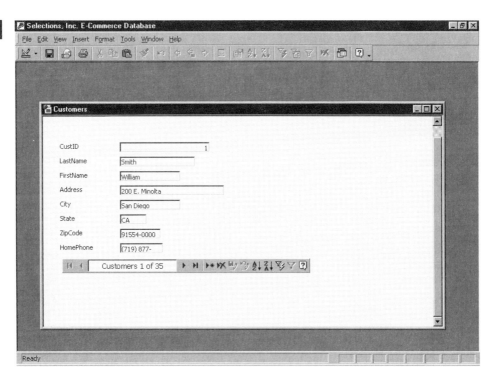

TROUBLESHOOTING If your page does not display any record data, switch to Design view and then back to Page view.

9 You will notice that some of the fields are truncated, and that no title appears above the Customer list.

10 Switch to Design view, and resize the fields as appropriate. When you are finished, the fields should appear similar to the ones shown in Figure 8.16.

FIGURE 8.16

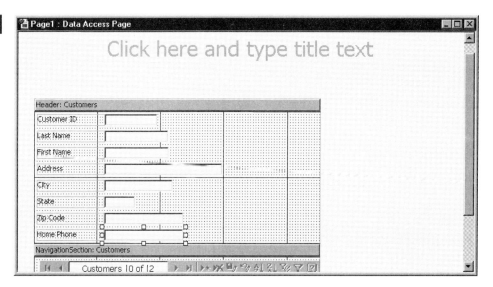

11 Click the label at the top of the page and type **Selections, Inc. Customer List**.

12 At this point you have defined the data access page, but you have not saved it. Choose File, Save. The Save As Data Access Page dialog box will appear.

13 Save the page to your floppy disk as **Customer List**. Notice that the default file type is Page. When your settings match Figure 8.17, click Save.

FIGURE 8.17

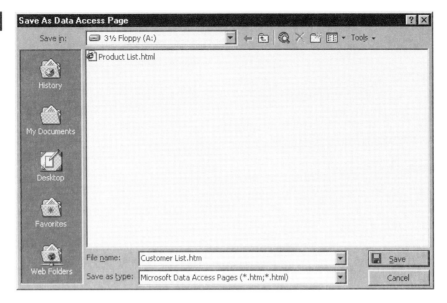

14 Open the Customer List data access page in Microsoft Internet Explorer, as shown in Figure 8.18.

FIGURE 8.18

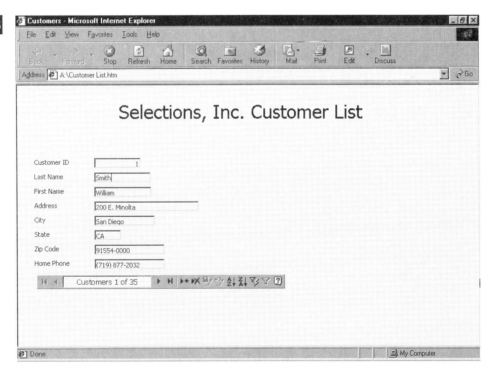

15 Close Microsoft Internet Explorer, and close the Customer List page in Access.

TIP The data access page you created is bound to the database when you save it. You can make changes to the design of the page in Access, but if you do, you will need to save it again to the location of the Web server on your network.

Creating a Data Access Page Using Design View

Now that you have created a data access page using a wizard, you are ready to create a page in Design view.

TASK 3: <u>To Create a Data Access Page Using Design View</u>

1 Click the New button. The New Data Access Page dialog box will appear.

2 Select Design View and base the page on the Products table. When your settings match Figure 8.19, click OK.

FIGURE 8.19

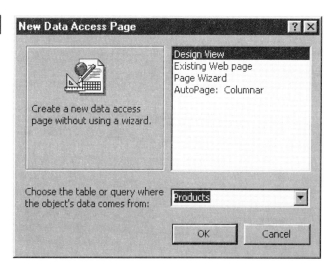

3 Access will display a blank page in Page Design view.

4 Click the Add button in the Field List dialog box to add all the fields from the Products table to the page, as shown in Figure 8.20.

FIGURE 8.20

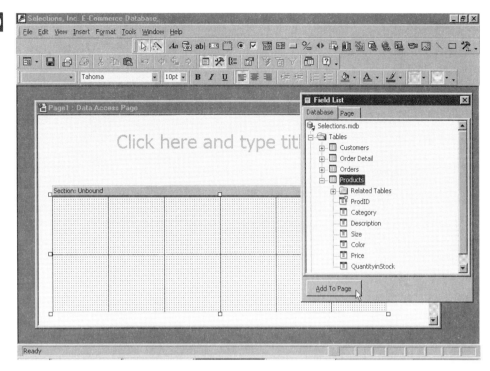

5 The Layout Wizard dialog box, shown in Figure 8.21, will appear. Accept the default option to display individual controls and click OK.

FIGURE 8.21

6 Access will add a control representing each field in the table to the page section, as shown in Figure 8.22.

FIGURE 8.22

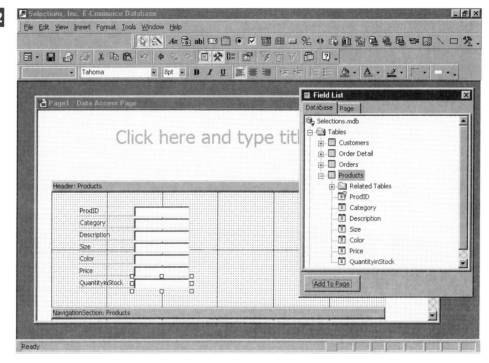

TIP When you add the field controls to the page section, notice that it is no longer unbound, as indicated by the name of the section.

Check Point

What does it mean that the section is bound?

7 Close the Field List dialog box.

8 Select the title for the page and type **Selections, Inc. Product List** as the page title.

9 Reposition the controls and rename the associated labels (see Figure 8.23). Change the alignment of each label associated with a bound field to right aligned.

FIGURE 8.23

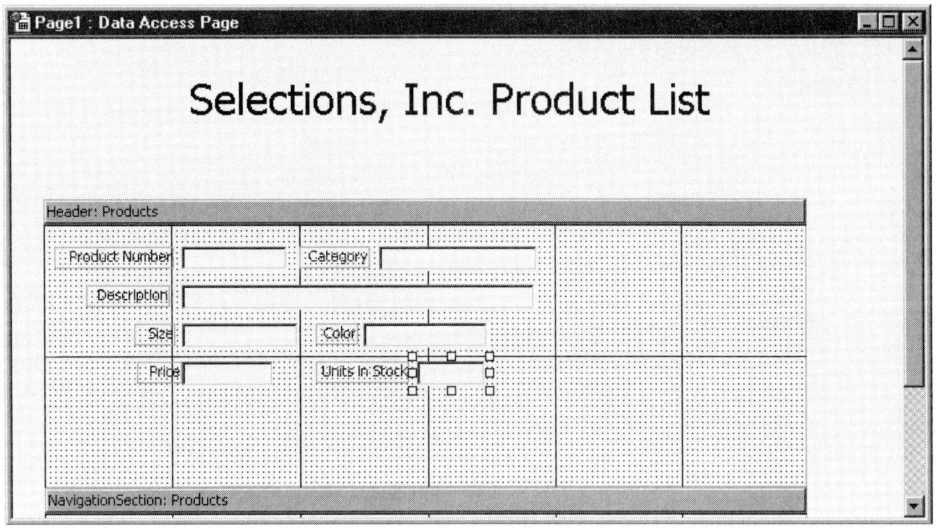

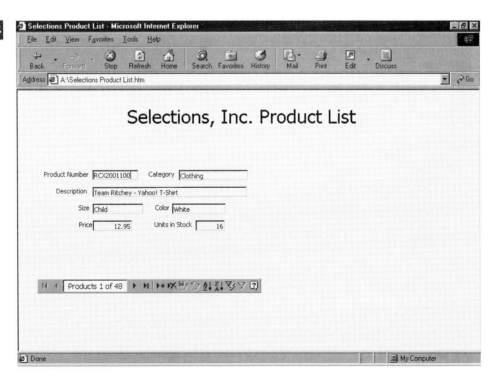

10 Save the Page to your floppy disk as **Selections Product List**.

11 Close the page in Access.

12 Open the page in Microsoft Internet Explorer. It will appear as shown in Figure 8.24.

FIGURE 8.24

13 Close Microsoft Internet Explorer when you are finished viewing the page.

Break Point

If necessary, you can exit Access now and continue this project later.

Adding Hyperlinks to Access Objects

Access 2000, like all core applications in the Office 2000 suite, enables you to add hyperlinks to tables, forms, and reports. A **hyperlink** is either colored and underlined text, or a graphic that you select to jump to a file, a location in a file, an HTML page on the World Wide Web, or an HTML page on an intranet.

> **TIP** Office hyperlinks can also jump to Gopher, Telnet, newsgroup, and FTP sites.

If you have completed the end of chapter exercises in this book, you have worked with the **hyperlink data type**, which is a special Access database field for storing hyperlinks in tables. You can also add text, label, or image controls to forms, data access pages, and reports, and specify a hyperlink for the object.

The Selections, Inc. database contains products from the Ritchey Bicycle Company. In this next task, you will add a hyperlink to the official Ritchey Website to two database objects: the Products form, and the Selections Product List data access page.

TASK 4: To Add a Hyperlink to the Products Form

1 Launch Access if it is not running, and open the *Selections.mdb* database if necessary.

2 Unhide the Database window.

3 Open the Products form in Design view and display the Toolbox, if it is not visible.

4 Choose Insert, Hyperlink.

5 In the Insert Hyperlink dialog box, type **Click here to visit the Official Ritchey Website** as the text to display, and **http://www.ritcheylogic.com** as the Web page name. When your settings match those shown in Figure 8.25, click OK.

> **TROUBLESHOOTING** If you have visited other Web pages, the URLs may appear in the recent files or browsed pages list.

FIGURE 8.25

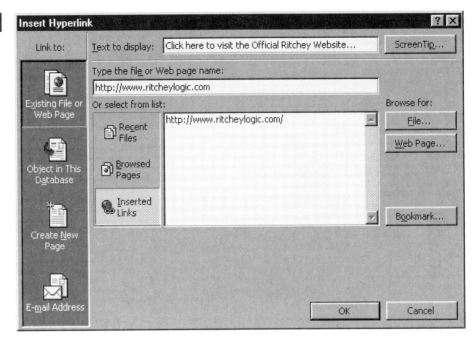

6 Move the link to the bottom of the form and save the form. Switch to Form view. Move the mouse pointer over the hyperlink, as shown in Figure 8.26.

FIGURE 8.26

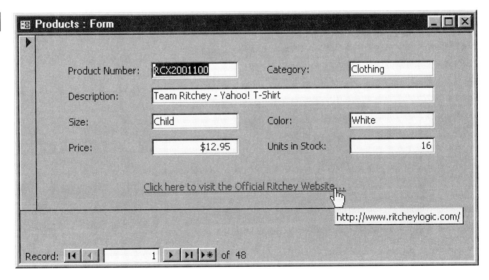

7 Click the hyperlink. If you are currently connected to the Internet, the Ritchey Website will appear, as shown in Figure 8.27.

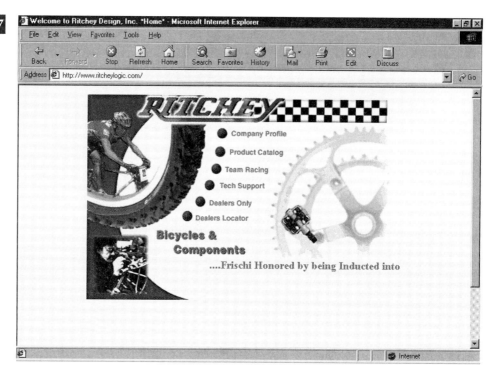

FIGURE 8.27

8 Close your Web browser when you are finished viewing the Ritchey Web site.

9 Close the Products form.

Now that you have added a hyperlink to the Products form, you are ready to add a hyperlink to a data access page.

TASK 5: To Add a Hyperlink to the Selection Product List Data Access Page

1 Open the *Selections Product List* data access page in Design view.

2 Click the section of the page containing the bound controls to select it.

3 Choose Insert, Hyperlink. Add the same specifications for this hyperlink as you added in Step 7 of the previous task.

4 Move the hyperlink control to the bottom of the form. The hyperlink will appear on the page in Design view, as shown in Figure 8.28.

FIGURE 8.28

Selections Product List : Data Access Page

Selections, Inc. Product List

Header: Products

Product Number [   ]   Category [   ]

Description [   ]

Size [   ]   Color [   ]

Price [   ]   Units In Stock [   ]

Click here to visit the Official Ritchey Website...

NavigationSection: Products

|◄ ◄ Products |0 of |2 ► ►| ►* ►X ... |

---

5 Save the data access page, and switch to Page view. Test the hyperlink by selecting it. As before, your Web browser will display the Ritchey Web site.

6 Close your Web browser.

7 Close the Selections Product List data access page.

Creating a Grouped Data Access Page

You are almost finished creating each Web resource Mr. Traylor requested. You will recall that he asked you to create a data access page that lists the total product inventory, and its value, by category. You can create a grouped data access page to accomplish this. A **grouped data access page** creates a hierarchy of grouped records similar to what you might see in an Access report. A grouped data access page has the advantage of interactivity: users can expand the listing and filter records.

To create the grouped data access page, you will first need to modify the Product List query you created earlier in this project. Then you will use the Page Wizard to create the grouped data access page.

TASK 6: To Modify the Product List Query

1 Open the Product List query in Design view.

2 Add the Category and QuantityinStock fields to the Query Design grid.

3 Click the field row of the next available column. Type **Inventory Value: [Price]*[QuantityinStock]** as the expression for this row.

Check Point

This is a calculated expression. What value will it return for each record?

4 Right-click the field row and choose Properties. Set the format of the calculated field to currency.

5 Save and close the query.

TASK 7: To Create a Grouped Data Access Page

1 Click the Pages button in the Database window.

2 Click New. Create a page using the Page Wizard, based on the Product List query, as shown in Figure 8.29. Click OK.

FIGURE 8.29

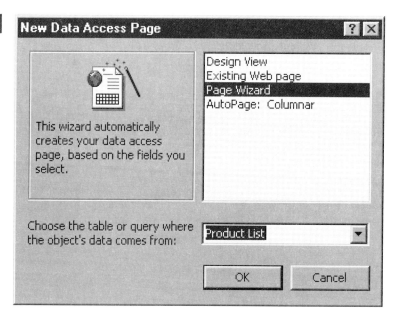

3 Add all of the available fields to the Selected Fields list and click Next, as shown in Figure 8.30.

FIGURE 8.30

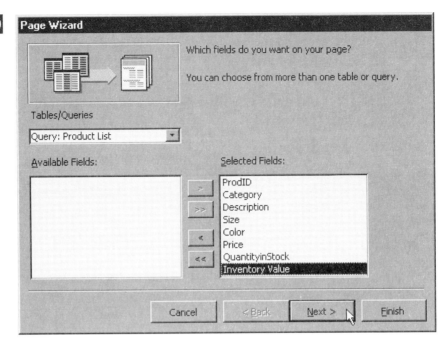

4   Set Category as a grouping level and click Next (see Figure 8.31).

FIGURE 8.31

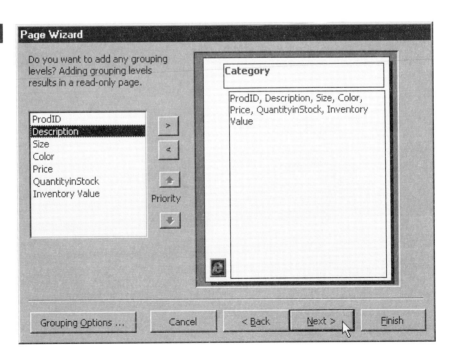

5   Select ProdID as the sort field and click Next, as shown in Figure 8.32.

FIGURE 8.32

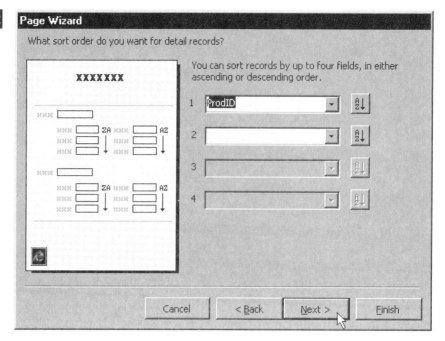

6 In the last step of the Page Wizard, type **Inventory Value** as the name of the page, select the option to display the page, and click Finish (see Figure 8.33).

FIGURE 8.33

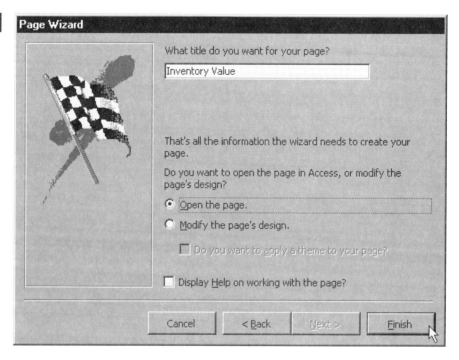

7 Access will create the page and display it. Click the Expand button next to the Category label, as shown in Figure 8.34.

FIGURE 8.34

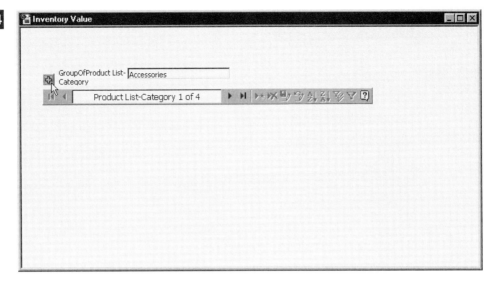

8 Access expands the Category grouping to display the first item in the grouping, as shown in Figure 8.35. Notice that the page also displays the total inventory value for this item.

TROUBLESHOOTING If Access does not display record data in the page, switch to Design View, save the page, and return to Page view.

FIGURE 8.35

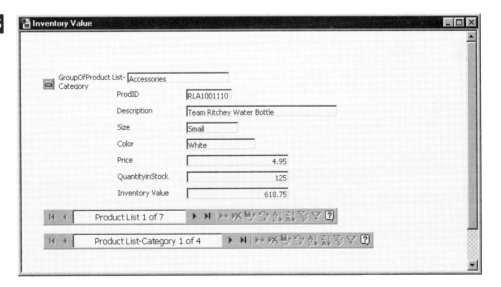

Experiment with the navigation controls for moving among records in a given category, or to display a new category.

9 Click Save, and type **Inventory Value** as the name of the page. Close the page.

10 Close the Selections, Inc. database.

Summary and Exercises

Summary

- Access supports multiple methods of working with Access data on the World Wide Web.

- If you save an Access record set as an HTML file, you will create a static Web resource.

- Data access pages are the new database object class in Access 2000 for creating dynamic Web resources.

- You can add hyperlinks to a variety of Access objects.

- A grouped data access page is an interactive method for displaying database records that can be viewed and edited on the Web.

Key Terms and Operations

Key Terms

data access page
dynamic resource
grouped data access page
hyperlink
hyperlink data type
static resource

Operations

add a hyperlink to the Products form
add a hyperlink to the Selections Product List data access page
create a data access page using a wizard
create a data access page using Design view
create a grouped data access page
modify the Product List query
publish the Products table as a static html file

Study Questions

Multiple Choice

1. Which Access database object enables users to dynamically interact with data using a Web browser?
   a. Table
   b. Form
   c. Query
   d. Page
   e. Report

2. A hyperlink on an Access form can refer to which of the following?
   a. A Website on the Internet
   b. An HTML page on a corporate intranet
   c. A Word document on a network server
   d. A data access page
   e. All of the above.

3. Which term describes the relationship between a data access page and an Access database?
   a. The page is bound to the database.
   b. The page is a static snapshot of the database at a point in time.
   c. A data access page is more flexible than an Access report for viewing the data, because a page is interactive and a report is static.
   d. Both a and b.
   e. Both a and c.

4. Which view do you use to add a hyperlink to an Access page?
   a. Table Design view
   b. Table Datasheet view
   c. Query Datasheet view
   d. Page Design view
   e. Page view

5. A data access page can contain which of the following?
   a. Hyperlinks
   b. Labels
   c. Fields
   d. All of the above.
   e. Both b and c.

6. To filter data on a data access page, you:
   a. create a query from the page and apply a filter.
   b. select the field to filter by and select the Filter button.
   c. replicate the object on which the page is bound and filter the record set.
   d. Both a and b.
   e. All of the above.

7. How can you expand and collapse data on a data access page?
   a. Export a table as a static HTML file.
   b. Link the data access page to a static HTML file.
   c. Create a grouped data page.
   d. Both a and b.
   e. Both a and c.

8. How do you create a static Web resource from an Access table?
   a. Export the table as a data access page.
   b. Export the table as HTML.
   c. Create a query based on the table and export the query as HTML.
   d. Create a report based on the table and export the report as a data access page.
   e. All of the above.

9. What happens if you modify records in a database that has a bound data access page, but modify the records in Table Datasheet view?
   a. The updates are displayed when the data access page is opened or refreshed.
   b. The data access page does not reflect the most recent updates to the database, because a data access page is a static resource.
   c. The records are not updated in the table because the table was modified independently of the data access page.
   d. All of the above.
   e. None of the above.

10. A data access page can be based on all of the following database objects except a:
   a. table.
   b. query.
   c. form.
   d. report.
   e. None of the above.

Short Answer

1. What is a data access page?

2. What is a static Web resource?

3. What is a hyperlink?

4. What is a grouped data access page?

5. Give an example of a static Web resource.

6. Which view do you use to add a hyperlink to a form?

7. What is a grouped data access page?

8. Is a data access page a static or dynamic Web resource?

9. Give an example of a dynamic Web resource.

10. How do you add a hyperlink to a data access page?

Fill in the Blank

1. A(n) _____ _____ _____ is a new database object in Access 2000.

2. A(n) _____ is colored text that, when clicked, jumps to a location in a document or on the Web.

3. A(n) _____ Web resource is not updated automatically when a database is changed.

4. To view a data access page on the Web, you must have _____ _____ Version 5 or greater installed on your computer.

5. To add a hyperlink to a form, use _____ _____ view.

6. You can _____ a table, query, or report as a static HTML document.

7. A(n) _____ data access page enables you to view data interactively on the Web.

8. A(n) _____ Web resource is linked to an Access database object.

9. You view records on a data access page in Access using _____ view.

10. A data access page is a(n) _____ Web resource.

For Discussion

1. How does a static Web resource differ from a dynamic Web resource?

2. What are the requirements for working with data access pages using a Web browser?

3. How do you add a hyperlink to a data access page?

4. How do you create a data access page in Page Design view?

5. How does a grouped data access page differ from a hierarchical report?

Hands-On Exercises

1. Adding an Image to a Data Access Page

In Projects 5 and 6, you learned how to enhance the appearance of forms and reports by adding images to them. You can also add images to data access pages. In this exercise, you will learn how to add an image to a data access page. Complete the following steps:

1. Open the *Selections.mdb* database.

2. Choose Window, Unhide, and unhide the database.

3. Open the Selections Product List page in Design view.

4. Display the Toolbox if it is not visible.

5. Add an image control to the right side of the form.

6. Access will prompt you to select an image. Navigate to your floppy disk, select the Ritchey Logo.bmp file, and click Insert.

Web Tip

If you do not have a copy of this file, you can download it from the Select Website at http://www.prenhall.com/selectadvanced.

7. Resize the image on the page so it appears as shown in Figure 8.36.

FIGURE 8.36

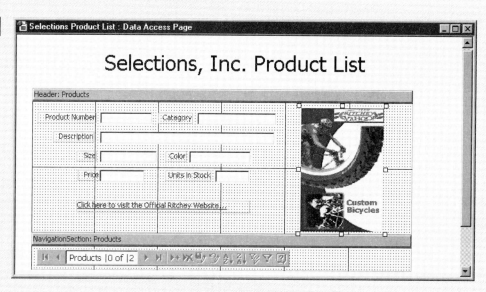

8. Save and close the Data Access Page.

2. Filtering Data in a Data Access Page Using Microsoft Internet Explorer

One advantage of using data access pages to view data from a bound Access database is how easily you can interact with the data in Microsoft Internet Explorer. In this exercise, you will learn how to filter data in a data access page on the Web. Complete the following steps:

1. Navigate to your floppy disk and open the *Selections Product List.htm* file in Microsoft Internet Explorer. Notice that the database includes 48 records.

 **Web Tip**

To complete this exercise, you need to have Microsoft Internet Explorer installed on your computer. Visit http://www.microsoft.com for information about downloading and installing Internet Explorer.

2. Select the Clothing field, and then select the Filter button, as shown in Figure 8.37.

FIGURE 8.37

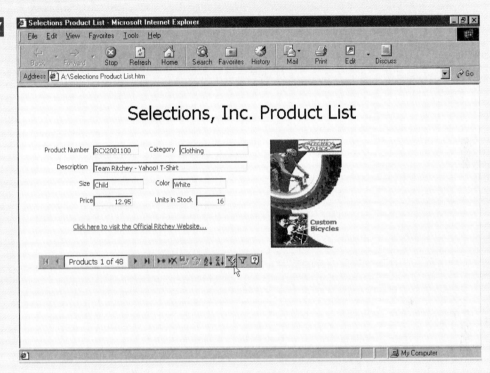

3. Access filters the database to display only the 14 records in the Clothing category, as shown in Figure 8.38.

FIGURE 8.38

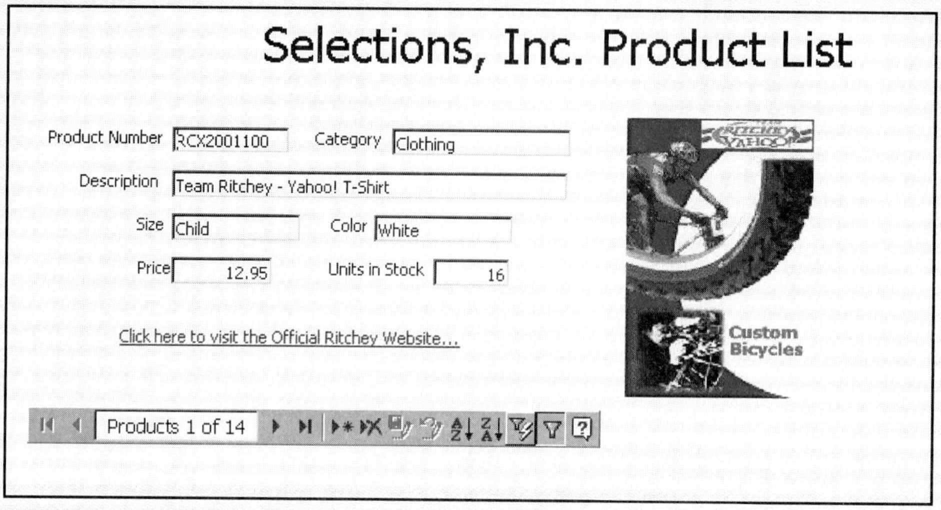

Selections, Inc. Product List

Product Number RCX2001100   Category Clothing

Description Team Ritchey - Yahoo! T-Shirt

Size Child   Color White

Price 12.95   Units in Stock 16

Click here to visit the Official Ritchey Website...

Products 1 of 14

4. Use the navigation controls to view additional records in the table. Close Internet Explorer when you are finished viewing the inventory data.

On Your Own Exercises

1. Creating a Data Access Page for a Table With a Hyperlink Field

In this project you learned how to add hyperlinks to database objects. You will recall that some tables might already contain the hyperlink data type. Open the *Web Sites.mdb* database you created earlier. Use the Page Wizard to create a data access page based on the Sites table. Do not add any grouping or sorting levels. Save the page as **Sites**. The page will appear as shown in Figure 8.39. Notice that the hyperlinks are not active in Access. Close the database when you are finished viewing the page in Access.

FIGURE 8.39

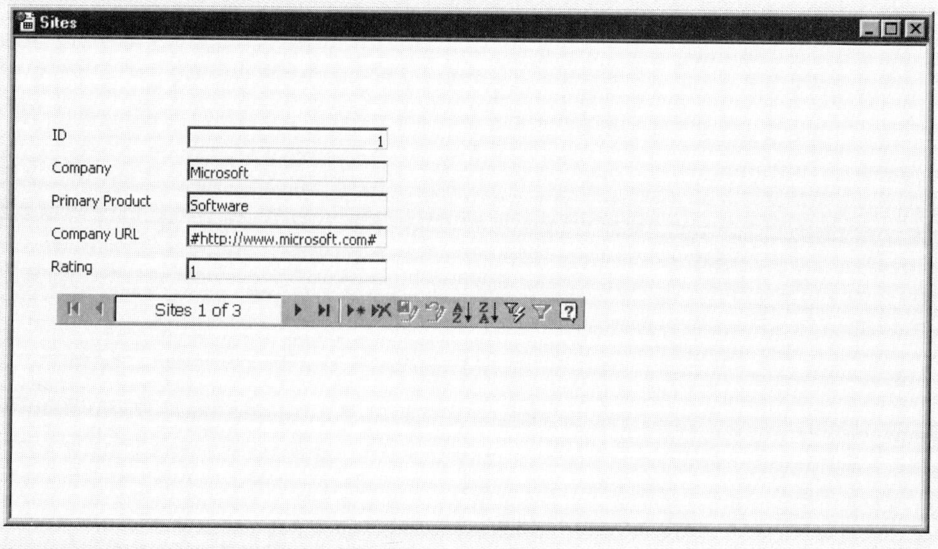

Sites

ID   1

Company   Microsoft

Primary Product   Software

Company URL   #http://www.microsoft.com#

Rating   1

Sites 1 of 3

2. Publishing a Report as an HTML Document

As you know, you can create static Web resources from a variety of Access objects. In this exercise you will create a static Web page from the Inventory report in the Products database. Open the *Products.mdb* database you last modified in Project 6. Open the Inventory report. Export the report as an HTML document, using **Inventory.html** as the filename. Open the report in your Web browser. Close your browser when you are finished.

 Web Tip

In this project you have learned how to create Web resources in Access. To make data access pages available to anyone, the pages need to be published to a Web server. To learn about publishing data access pages to a Web server, visit http://msdn.microsoft.com/library/officedev/off2000/achowPublishDataPageToWebServer.htm

Customizing Access Using Macros and Visual Basic for Applications (VBA)

As an Access database developer, you will want to customize your Access database solutions to make data entry and data maintenance as simple as possible for those who will use the database. You can use macros to automate repetitive or detailed tasks, and for even more power, you can use Microsoft's *Visual Basic for Applications (VBA)* programming language. VBA is a powerful, shared development environment that enables you to accomplish a wide range of programmatic results within any Office application. Based on Microsoft's latest version of Visual Basic, VBA uses a consistent development interface that you can apply to any Office application. As a subset of Microsoft Visual Basic, VBA is a full-fledged programming environment for creating applications and solutions.

You can think of VBA as the "glue" that provides functionality within Microsoft Office. Visual Basic and VBA are event-driven environments as opposed to traditional, structured programming environments. In traditional, structured programming environments, the program controls how the code executes. The program runs starting with the first line of code and follows a predefined path through the application, calling procedures as needed.

In an *event-driven* application, the code doesn't follow a predetermined path, but rather executes different code sections in response to an *event*. Events include user actions (such as choosing a menu), or messages from the application (such as an event that leads to an error and then displays an error message). The sequence of these events determines the sequence in which the code executes; thus, the path through the application's code differs each time the program runs.

Once you understand the difference between structured programming and event-driven programming, you will see why VBA is such a powerful tool for customizing and automating Access. This project assumes no prior programming experience, but we will scratch the surface in terms of what VBA can do.

Objectives

After completing this project, you will be able to:

➤ Use the Macro Builder to create macros

➤ Assign macros to command buttons

➤ Modify an SQL query underlying a form

➤ Use VBA to automatically enter data into a field

➤ Add statements to sub procedures using the Visual Basic Editor

➤ Use VBA to prompt the user for input

Running Case

Mr. Traylor knows that Microsoft Office contains a powerful programming feature for customizing and automating Access. He is interested in how these features can assist the e-commerce department in automating redundant tasks as they work with the Selections, Inc. database.

The Challenge

Mr. Traylor wants you to customize the Selections, Inc. database in the following ways. First, although the Orders form prompts users to select a valid customer number, there is no provision for entering new customer records from this form. He wants you to add a button to the Orders form that displays the Customers form. He wants you to further modify the Customers form so that its user can easily search for a specific customer.

He also wants you to change the Orders form so that it automatically displays the current date each time a new order is initiated. The data in this field must be protected so that users cannot inadvertently change the date for an order. He also wants the Orders form to prompt the user for an item quantity as each item is added to the order. When you are finished customizing the database, he will meet with you to review the changes you have made.

The Solution

Access has the tools you need to create the custom solution Mr. Traylor has requested. First, you can use the Macro window to create two macros: The first macro will open the Customers form and create a new record, the second macro will open the find dialog box so users can search for customer records by either name or customer number. Once you have created these macros, you can assign each one to a command button. Both buttons will appear on the Customers form.

To enter the data automatically each time a new order is initiated, you can create a VBA procedure that responds to a specific event on the Orders form. You will use the Visual Basic Editor to create the procedure. After you create the procedure, you can add code to protect the order date so it cannot be changed. The code you will create is shown in Figure 9.1.

FIGURE 9.1

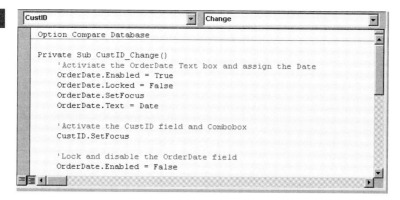

You can write a VBA procedure to prompt the user for an item quantity while an order is being processed, as well. You can use an inputbox to accept user input, and then assign this value to the Quantity field on the form. The inputbox will appear as shown in Figure 9.2.

FIGURE 9.2

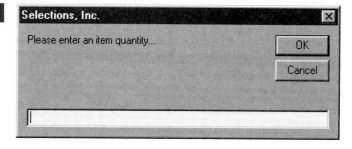

The Setup

To create macros and use Visual Basic for Applications to automate tasks in Access, launch Microsoft Access, open the *Selections, Inc.* database you modified in Project 8, and make sure that you select the settings listed in Table 9.1. If you need additional assistance setting these options, refer to Figure 1.1 through 1.3 of Project 1. This will ensure that your screen matches the illustrations and the tasks in this project function as described.

Table 9.1   Access Settings

Location	Make these settings:
Office Shortcut Bar	If the Office Shortcut bar is visible, close it by right-clicking the Office icon on the shortcut bar and choosing Exit.
Office Assistant	Hide the Office Assistant.
Tools, Customize	Click the Toolbars tab and display the Database toolbar and the Menu Bar, as shown in Figure 1.1 of Project 1, if they are not currently visible.
Tools, Customize	Click the Options tab, and make sure the check box to display recently used menu commands first is deselected, as shown in Figure 1.2 of Project 1.
Tools, Options	Click the View tab and display Status bar, Startup dialog box, New object shortcuts, and Windows in Taskbar, as shown in Figure 1.3 of Project 1.

Creating Macros Using the Macro Builder

In Access, a **macro** is a set of one or more automated actions. Each of these actions performs a particular operation, such as opening a form or printing a report. Macros can help you to automate common tasks.

In Access, you have three methods for automating tasks: building an expression (as you did when you created calculated fields), writing a macro, or creating a Visual Basic procedure. Macros in Access differ from macros in other Office 2000 applications because you create Access macros using the Macro Builder. The **Macro Builder** is a visual workspace that assists you in creating macros. You can open the Macro Builder either by selecting the Macros page in the Database window, or by selecting the Build Event menu for any control.

As you build a macro, it is a good idea to document which actions each line in the macro will perform. The upper pane of the Macro Builder consists of two columns—one for specifying actions, and one for adding documentation comments. In the two tasks that follow, you will build two macros using the Macro Builder. The first macro will select the LastName field in the Customers form, and then display the Find dialog box so users can search for specific records. The second macro will navigate to a new record to the Customers form.

TASK 1: To Build a Macro that Displays the Find Dialog Box

1 Click the Macros button in the Database window.

> **TIP** You may need to unhide the Database window.

2 Click the New button ⏫ New . The Macro Builder will appear, as shown in Figure 9.3.

FIGURE 9.3

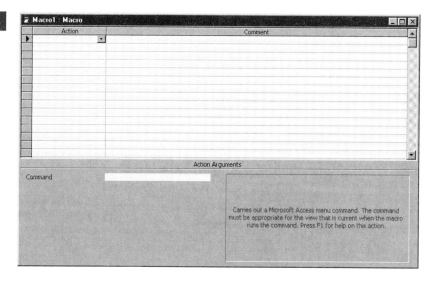

3 Click the drop-down arrow next to the first row in the Action column of the Macro Builder. Scroll the list and choose GoToControl, as shown in Figure 9.4.

FIGURE 9.4

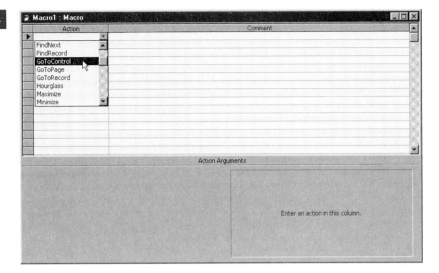

4 Press TAB once to move to the Comment column. Type **Select the LastName field** as the documentation for this action.

5 Click the Control Name row in the lower pane of the Macro Builder. Type **LastName**. The first action in the Macro Builder will appear (see Figure 9.5).

FIGURE 9.5

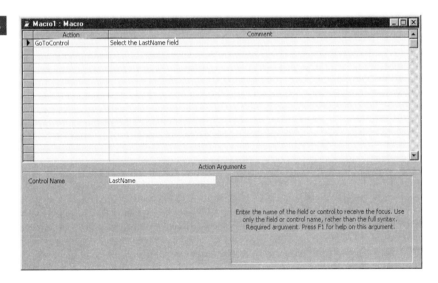

6 Click the next row in the Action list. Choose the RunCommand action, as shown in Figure 9.6.

FIGURE 9.6

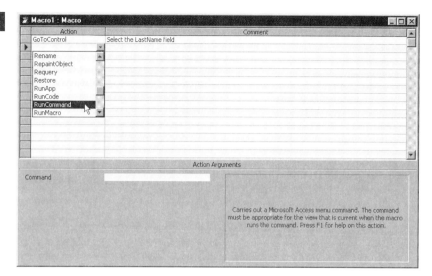

7 Press (TAB) once, and select **Run the Find** command as documentation for this action.

8 Click the Command row in the Action Arguments pane. Choose Find in the list, as shown in Figure 9.7.

FIGURE 9.7

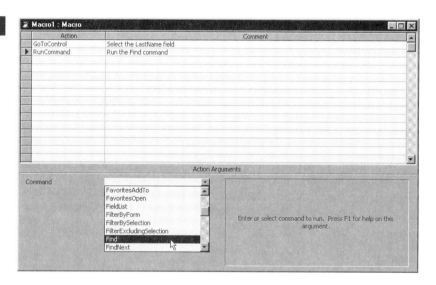

9 Click Save. Type **FindCustomerRecord** as the name for this macro (see Figure 9.8). Click OK.

FIGURE 9.8

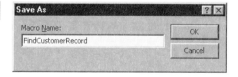

10 Close the Macro Builder. The macro you just created will now appear in the Macros page of the Database window.

Now that you have created a macro to locate a customer record, you are ready to create a macro that automates the task of creating a new, blank record.

TASK 2: To Build a Macro that Navigates to a New Record

1 Click the New button in the Macros page of the Database window, as shown in Figure 9.9.

FIGURE 9.9

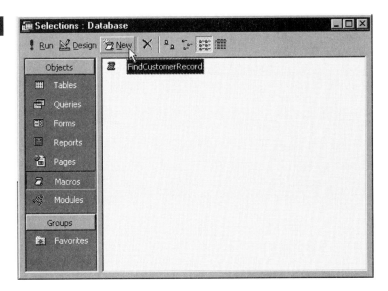

2 Choose GoToRecord as the first action for the macro.

3 Press ⌨TAB, and type **Navigate to a New Record** as the documentation for this step.

4 Click the Object Type row in the Action Arguments pane. Choose Form from the list.

5 Click the Object Name row and choose Customers.

6 Click the Record row and choose New, as shown in Figure 9.10.

FIGURE 9.10

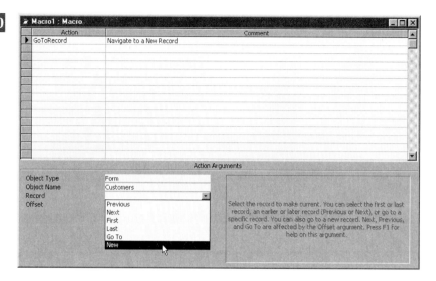

Save the macro as **AddCustomerRecord**.

Close the Macro Builder.

Check Point

Why are the two macros you have created specific to the Customers form?

Running Macros from Command Button Controls

Now that you have created the two macros the database requires, you are ready to assign each macro to a command button control that you will add to the Customers form. In Project 8 you learned how to use the Control Wizards tool to create a command button control, and then assign an action to a new command button. In the next two tasks, you will add two command buttons to the Customers form for each macro, and then assign a macro to each of the command buttons.

TASK 3: To Assign the FindCustomerRecord Macro to a Command Button

Click the Forms button in the Database window.

Open the *Customers* form in Design view and maximize the form.

Activate the Toolbox if it is not currently visible, and make sure the Control Wizards tool is activated.

Check Point

What does the Command Button Wizard do?

4 Create a command button control in the lower left corner of the Detail section of the form. The Command Button Wizard will appear.

5 Choose Miscellaneous in the Categories column, and Run Macro in the Actions list. When your settings match those shown in Figure 9.11, click Next.

FIGURE 9.11

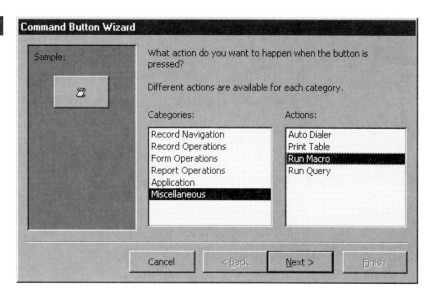

6 The Command Button Wizard will prompt you to select a macro to assign to the command button. Choose *FindCustomerRecord* and then click Next, as shown in Figure 9.12.

FIGURE 9.12

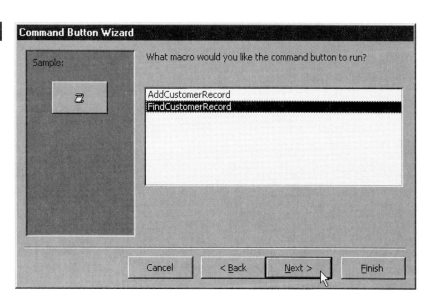

7 You will be prompted to specify text or an image as the caption for the command button. Click the Show All Pictures check box and choose the Binoculars1 image. Click Next, as shown in Figure 9.13.

FIGURE 9.13

8 The last step of the Command Button Wizard will prompt you to name the command button. Type **cmdFindCustomerRecord** in the text box (see Figure 9.14). Click Finish.

FIGURE 9.14

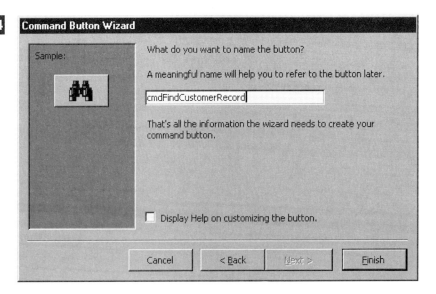

9 Save the form and switch to Form view.

10 Click the command button on the form. Access will display the Find and Replace dialog box, as shown in Figure 9.15.

FIGURE 9.15

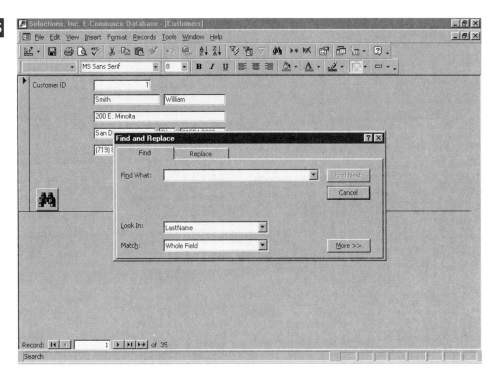

TIP You will notice two things about the form. First, it is still maximized, because you maximized it when you opened it in Design view. Second, the Find and Replace dialog box will search the last name field because you specified this field in the macro.

11 Click Cancel in the Find and Replace dialog box.

12 Close the form.

TASK 4: To Assign the AddCustomerRecord Macro to a Command Button

1 Create a command button control on the form, immediately to the right of the command button you created in the previous task.

2 In the first step of the Command Button Wizard, choose Miscellaneous in the Categories list and Run Macro in the Actions list, as shown in Figure 9.16. Click Next.

FIGURE 9.16

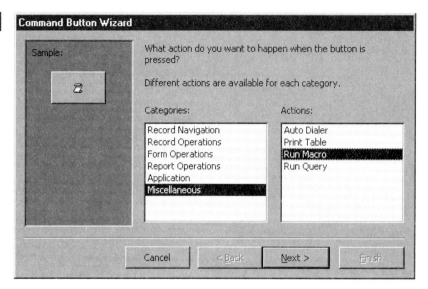

3 Choose the Goto New 2 image for the button, as shown in Figure 9.17. Click Next.

TIP Users familiar with Access will recognize this icon as representing the procedure of adding a new record to the database. Notice that it uses the same familiar icon that appears on the navigation control at the bottom of the form.

FIGURE 9.17

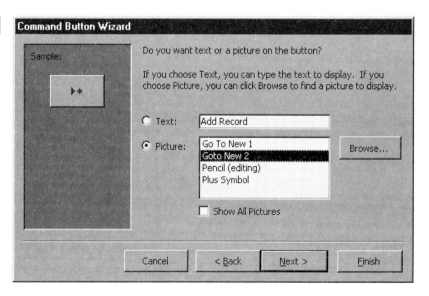

4 Type **cmdAddCustomerRecord** as the name for the button. Click Finish.

5 Restore the form.

6 Save the form.

7 Display the form in Form view. If necessary, resize the form so it shows the command buttons you added to the form.

8 Click the Find button. Type **Tepley** as the name to search for and press (ENTER).

9 Close the Find and Replace dialog box. Access shows the fifth record in the table, as shown in Figure 9.18.

FIGURE 9.18

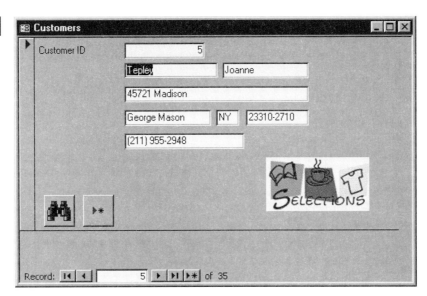

10 Save the form and close it.

Break Point

If necessary, you can exit Access and continue this project later.

Using Visual Basic for Applications to Customize Access

When you're looking for a level of power and control over your database that goes beyond what you can accomplish using macros or expressions, VBA is the place to find it. Visual Basic for Applications (VBA) is the programming language for Microsoft Office and its associated applications. You use it for the same reason you use macros: to tie the database objects in your application together into a coherent system. The difference is that VBA provides more power and a finer degree of control than you get by using macros or expressions alone. As a subset of Visual Basic, VBA procedures cannot run independently of their host application. Thus, the custom VBA solutions you create in Access require Access to run them.

How do you learn VBA? There are two approaches. One is to exhaustively cover the fundamentals of the Visual Basic environment, and learn how to build Access applications from the ground up. Obviously, this approach is beyond the scope of this module. A second approach is to identify specific elements in the current database that need customization, and to learn the specific Visual Basic properties and methods that apply to customizing those elements. We will take the second approach.

 **Web Tip**

Need assistance with Visual Basic for applications? Visit the Microsoft Developers VBA Website at http://msdn.microsoft.com/vba.

As mentioned previously, you have three options for building events in Access: the Expression Builder, the Macro Builder, and the Code Builder. The **Code Builder** is a tool in Access for writing Visual Basic procedures.

When you choose to build an event using the Code Builder, Access will open the **Visual Basic Editor**, which is the interface for working with VBA. The Editor contains a number of windows that display different components of the VBE environment. The **Visual Basic Window** displays the program code you create to customize Access. The program steps you define in this project will consist of three sub procedures. A **sub procedure** is a series of Visual Basic statements, enclosed by the *Sub* and *End Sub* statements, that performs actions but doesn't return a value. Sub procedures are a series of program statements that relate to a specific object, such as a text box. A **statement** is an explicit instruction that usually occupies one line of code. In each statement, the name of an object, method, or property is separated from other elements in the statement with a period. When you run the event specified by the sub procedure, Access will execute each line of Visual Basic code.

> **TIP** Visual Basic statements can also appear in code modules, which makes the statements available to all objects in an application.

In Visual Basic, an object represents an element of an application, such as a table, form, field, text box, report, and so on. In Visual Basic code, you must identify an object before you can change the value of a property or apply a method. Individual controls such as command buttons have properties and methods. **Properties** are settings such as the caption of a button, and **methods** are specific actions related to an object, such as the Close method to close a form.

There are specific actions that Mr. Traylor wants you to implement in the database. You will recall that he wants the current data to appear automatically on the Orders form each time a new order is initiated. Before writing a Visual Basic sub procedure to accomplish this task, you will need to modify the query underlying the Orders form. The SQL query underlying the Orders form does not contain the OrderDate field. Before you assign a date to this field, it must be available to the form. You can make it available by adding it to the SQL query.

TASK 5: To Add the Orderdate Field to the SQL
Query Underlying the Orders Form

1 Launch Access if it is not currently running, and open the *Selections.mdb* database, if necessary.

2 Open the Orders form in Design view.

3 Choose View, Properties to display the Properties for the form.

4 Click the Data tab, and then click the Event button (the ellipsis) for the Data Source Row, as shown in Figure 9.19.

FIGURE 9.19

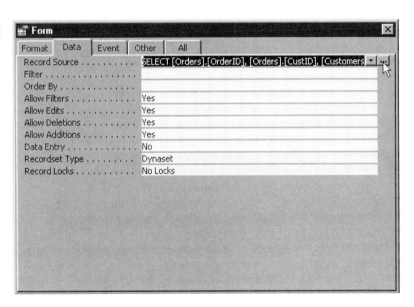

5 Drag the OrderDate field to any column in the Query Design grid.

Check Point

Do you remember the definition of a relation in the First Normal Form (1NF)? A relation is in the 1NF if it is does not contain any multi-valued attributes. In Codd's relational model, the order of attributes in a relation is inconsequential. Therefore, you can add the OrderDate field to any column in the SQL query.

6 Close the query, using the Close button for the Query Design window.

7 When you are prompted to update the SQL query click Yes, as shown in Figure 9.20.

FIGURE 9.20

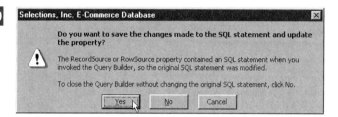

8 Close the Properties dialog box.

9 Choose View, Field List. A dialog box displaying the field available to the query will appear. Position this dialog box on the screen so that the upper portion of the form is visible.

10 Drag the OrderDate field from the Field List to the form, as shown in Figure 9.21.

FIGURE 9.21

Drag the OrderDate field to here

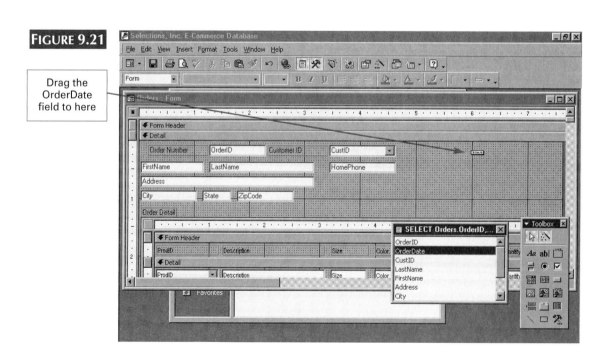

11 Close the Toolbox and the Field List.

12 Change the label caption for the associated label to **Date of Order:**, and position the label and text box as shown in Figure 9.22.

FIGURE 9.22

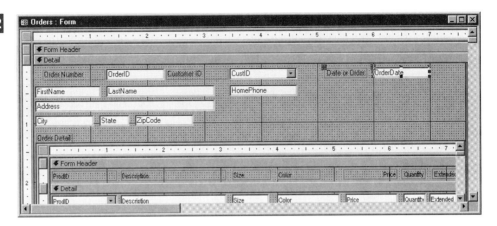

13 Save these changes to the form.

Using VBA to Automatically Enter Data into a Field

You are now ready to create your first Visual Basic sub procedure. You will recall that Visual Basic is an **event-driven** environment, meaning that program statements are activated in response to a specific event. When you think of automatically entering the date into the form, you need to decide which event should trigger adding the date. If you remember how the Orders form works, each time a new order is placed, the form appears. If you select the New Record button in the Navigation controls, the form shows a blank record. No data appears in the form, however, until you select the Customer ID list and choose a customer. At this point, Access updates the Orders table by adding a customer number as the foreign key value, and sets an AutoNumber value for the OrderID field.

Thus, you may want to consider adding the date to the form after the CustomerID field is changed. You will want the date to be entered automatically, with no further action by the user.

TASK 6: ## To Write a Visual Basic Event to Automatically Enter the Order Date

1 Right-click the CustID combo box on the form and choose Properties.

2 Click the Event tab in the Properties dialog box.

3 Place the insertion point in the On Change row then click the Build button, as shown in Figure 9.23.

FIGURE 9.23

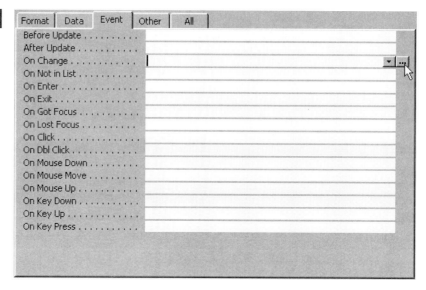

4 The Choose Builder dialog box will appear. Choose Code Builder and click OK, as shown in Figure 9.24.

FIGURE 9.24

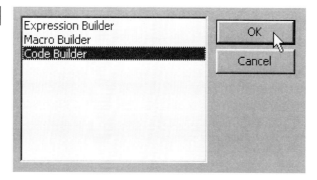

5 The Visual Basic Editor will open, as shown in Figure 9.25. The upper right pane contains the code for the sub procedure, which currently only includes two statements.

FIGURE 9.25

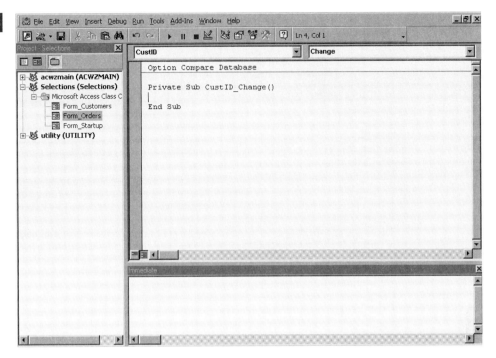

6 Type the following statements at the Insertion point. Press (ENTER) at the end of each line:

'Activate the OrderDate Text box and assign the Date
   OrderDate.Enabled = True
   OrderDate.Locked = False
   OrderDate.SetFocus
   OrderDate.Text = Date
   'Activate the CustID field and Combobox
   CustID.SetFocus

   'Lock and disable the OrderDate field
   OrderDate.Enabled = False
   OrderDate.Locked = True

7 When you are finished, the code will appear as shown in Figure 9.26.

FIGURE 9.26

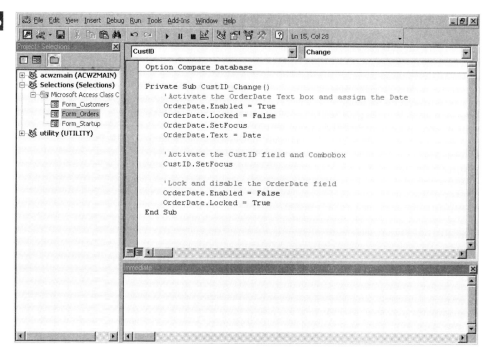

```
Option Compare Database

Private Sub CustID_Change()
    'Activate the OrderDate Text box and assign the Date
    OrderDate.Enabled = True
    OrderDate.Locked = False
    OrderDate.SetFocus
    OrderDate.Text = Date

    'Activate the CustID field and Combobox
    CustID.SetFocus

    'Lock and disable the OrderDate field
    OrderDate.Enabled = False
    OrderDate.Locked = True
End Sub
```

TROUBLESHOOTING Make sure the statements appear exactly as shown here, or the procedure may generate an error when you try to run it.

Let's review what these statements do. Private Sub Cust_ID Change () specifies the event associated with the CustID field that will run the code. The next two statements enable the OrderDate control, and unlock it. Both of these properties are required before the control can accept input. The next statement activates the control using the SetFocus method. The final statement in this group assigns the current date from the system click to the text property of the control.

The next lines of code lock and disable the OrderDate control, so that once a date is entered, it cannot be changed using the form. This prevents users from accidentally changing the order date. The next statement sets the focus to the CustID control, so the application will return to the condition it was in after the user selected a customer record.

TIP Some of the code appears as green text, and some as blue text. Any text in a code statement that is preceded with an apostrophe character (') is a comment line, and will appear in green. It is always a good idea to add statements that document a specific procedure. The text appearing in blue are key words. The Sub and End Sub statements define the starting and ending points of the procedure. The terms True and False are property settings for the specified controls. If your code contains any errors, the line containing the error will appear in Red.

8 Click the Save button.

9 Close the Visual Basic window.

10 Close the Orders form.

TIP You will not see how the procedure runs until after you have created the next procedure. To use the code you have written to add a new customer to the database and process an order, complete Hands-On Exercise 1 at the end of this project.

Creating a VBA Procedure that Prompts the User for Input

You are almost finished customizing the Selections, Inc. e-commerce database! Remember that Mr. Traylor wants the database to prompt the user for the item quantity once an item has been added to the order. As with the previous procedure, you will need to determine which event should trigger the sub procedure. Once a user has selected an item, they should then be prompted to enter the item quantity. You can use the Visual Basic **Inputbox function** to accept input from a user. When you implement this function, a dialog box appears with instructions for entering data in the associated text box.

Check Point

Which control and which event will contain the sub procedure?

TASK 7: To Prompt the User for Input Using the Inputbox Function

1 Open the *Order Detail Subform* in Design view.

2 Right-click the ProdID Combo box and click Properties.

3 Click the Event tab.

4 Click the On Change row and click the Build button. Choose the Code Builder.

5 Enter the following statements in the Code window:

```
'Declare variables for the input box title and prompt
    Dim Prompt, Title
    Prompt = "Please enter an item quantity..."
    Title = "Selections, Inc."

'Activate the Order textbox
 Quantity.SetFocus

'Prompt the user for a value
'Assign the value to the text property of the Order control
 Quantity.Text = InputBox(Prompt, Title)
```

'Set the focus to the ProdID combo box
ProdID.SetFocus

The code will appear as shown in Figure 9.27.

FIGURE 9.27

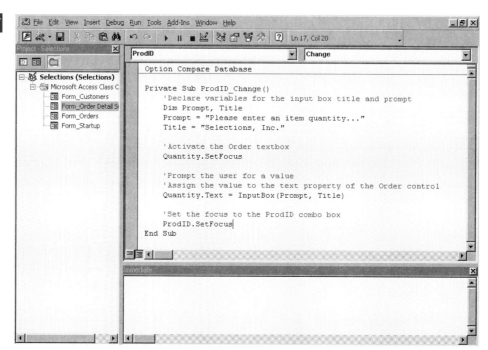

 Check Point

Explain what each line of the code appearing in this procedure will do when
the procedure is run.

6 Click the Save button.

7 Close the Visual Basic Editor.

8 Close the form.

Adding a Command Button to the Orders Form

You have one remaining task. When users are in the process of adding orders, they might need to open the Customers form to either search for a customer, or add a new customer to the database. You have added these capabilities to the Customers form, but now you need to add a command button
to the Orders form that will open the Customers form. You can do this by
simply using the Control Wizard.

TASK 8: To Add a Command Button to the Orders
Form and Specify an Action for the Button

1 Open the Orders form in Design view.

2 Activate the Toolbox. Add a command button in the area of the form below the Home Phone field.

3 Specify Form Operations, and open a form in the first step of the Command Button Wizard. Click Next.

4 Specify the Customers form. Click Next.

5 Specify that the form should show all records. Click Next.

6 Click the option button to add text to the button and type **View Customers** as a caption. Click Next.

7 In the last step of the Command Button Wizard, name the command button **cmdOpenCustomersForm**. Click Finish.

Web Tip

Are you confused by these Visual Basic naming conventions? Visit http://support.microsoft.com/support/kb/articles/Q110/2/64.asp for more information about the conventions for naming objects in Visual Basic.

8 Reposition the button as necessary.

9 Save the form.

You have now customized the database exactly as Mr. Traylor requested. He is looking forward to meeting with you and reviewing your work. To test the procedure you have written, complete the Hands-On Exercises at the end of this project.

Web Tip

Do you need more information on using Visual Basic for Applications? Visit http://officeupdate.microsoft.com/2000/awfeedback/P40243.htm.

Summary and Exercises

Summary

- You can use the Macro Builder to automate repetitive tasks.
- The Command Button Wizard will assist you in assigning a macro to a command button on a form.
- Visual Basic for Applications (VBA) is the programming environment you use to create sophisticated solutions in Access.
- You can use the Code Builder to create VBA sub routines associated with specific controls and events.
- The Inputbox function prompts the user for input.

Key Terms and Operations

Key Terms

Code Builder
event
event-driven
Inputbox function
macro
Macro Builder
method
property
statement
sub procedure
Visual Basic Editor
Visual Basic for Applications (VBA)
Visual Basic Window

Operations

assign a macro to a command button
build a macro that displays the Find dialog box
build a macro that navigates to a new record
modify the SQL query that underlies the Orders form
write a sub procedure using the Inputbox function
write a Visual Basic procedure to automatically enter the order date

Study Questions

Multiple Choice

1. To create a VBA sub procedure, use the:
   a. Expression Builder.
   b. Macro Builder.
   c. Code Builder.
   d. All of the above.
   e. None of the Above.

2. Access records a macro using the:
   a. Macro Builder.
   b. Visual Basic Editor.
   c. Command Button Wizard.
   d. Create Macro property.
   e. Field List.

3. Which tool in Access is the simplest method for creating a calculated field?
   a. Expression Builder
   b. Code Builder
   c. Macro Builder
   d. All of the above.
   e. None of the above.

4. Which of the following is an example of a control in Access?
   a. Table
   b. Form Detail section
   c. The Database window
   d. A Visual Basic sub procedure
   e. A command button

5. Which of the following is a property of a control?
   a. Click
   b. On Update
   c. Sub Cust_ID_Click ()
   d. Text
   e. None of the above.

6. To run a macro easily from a click event, assign it to a:
   a. command button.
   b. form.
   c. custom procedure.
   d. table.
   e. Visual Basic statement.

7. Which of the following refers to an action performed in VBA?
   a. Method
   b. Editor
   c. Window
   d. Property
   e. Object

8. VBA is a subset of:
   a. Microsoft Access.
   b. Microsoft Windows.
   c. Microsoft Office.
   d. Visual Basic.
   e. an Access expression.

9. Remarks in the code window are what color?
   a. Red
   b. Blue
   c. Green
   d. Black
   e. Yellow

10. If a VBA procedure contains an error, it will appear as what color in the visual Basic window?
    a. Red
    b. Blue
    c. Green
    d. Black
    e. Yellow

Short Answer

1. The letters VBA stand for what?

2. When you record a macro, which page of the Database window do you open?

3. Which kind of object should you use to run a macro?

4. Where do you enter VBA statements?

5. What is the Macro Builder?

6. Why do VBA solutions require a host application to run?

7. Quantity.Text is an example of what?

8. What is the Visual Basic Editor?

9. How do you document the actions in a macro?

10. What kinds of information do you specify in the lower pane of the Macro Builder?

Fill in the Blank

1. VBA procedures are dependent on a(n) _____ application.

2. All Visual Basic procedures require a(n) _____ and a(n) _____ statement

3. A(n) _____ contains VBA code statements.

4. You can easily create a macro using the _____.

5. A(n) _____ is an action performed on an object.

6. VBA is a subset of _____.

7. In Access, the _____ _____ will open the Visual Basic Editor so you can write code for an event.

8. In Access, you often assign a macro to a(n) _____ _____ control.

9. You can add comments to a VBA sub procedure using the _____ character.

10. You can use the _____ method to select a specific control on a form.

For Discussion

1. What is a macro? Why are macros useful?

2. Explain three methods for creating events in Access.

3. How does VBA differ from Visual Basic?

4. How do controls, objects, properties, and methods differ?

5. Why might you consider creating a Visual Basic procedure rather than creating a macro to customize an Access database?

Hands-On Exercises

1. Adding a New Customer to the Database and Processing an Order

In this project you learned how to customize an Access database using macros and VBA. In this exercise you will see the results of your work. Assume that you are placing an order for a customer who has never ordered products from Selections, Inc. before. You first search the database for the customer, add a customer record, and then process an order for the customer.

To Add a New Customer to the Database and Process an Order

1. Open the *Selections, Inc.* database.

2. Click the Add/Edit Customer Orders button on the switchboard.

3. Click the View Customer button.

4. Click the Find button on the Customers form. Search for a customer with *Hayward* as a last name.

5. Access does not find any matching records, as shown in Figure 9.28.

FIGURE 9.28

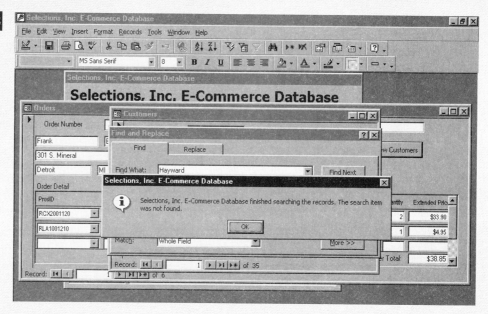

6. Click OK.

7. Close the Find and Replace dialog box.

8. Add the record displayed in Figure 9.29.

FIGURE 9.29

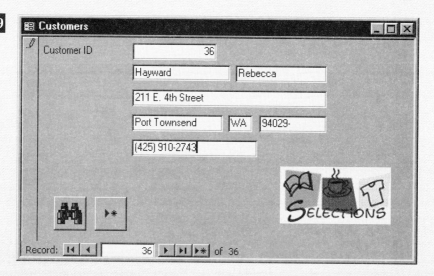

9. Close the Customers form.

10. Click the new record button.

11. Click the Customer ID drop-down list and choose Hayward, as shown in Figure 9.30.

FIGURE 9.30

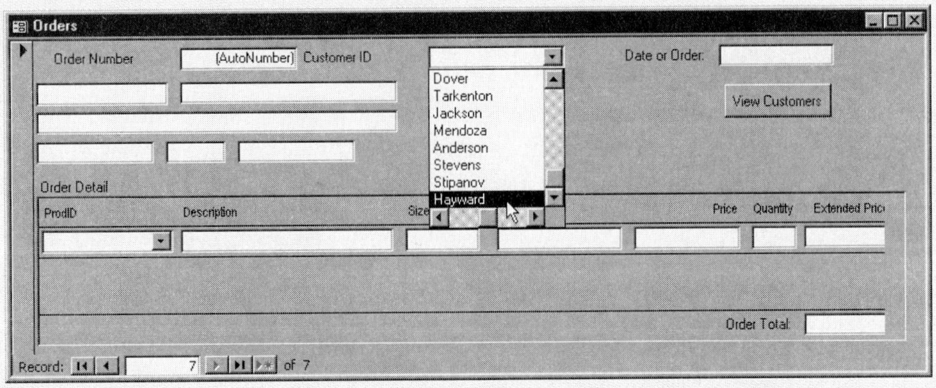

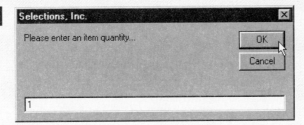

12. The customer information appears on the form, and the date is automatically entered as well.

13. Click the ProdID drop-down list in the Order Detail section. Choose item number RCX2001120.

14. The inputbox for the item quantity will appear. Type **1** and click OK, as shown in Figure 9.31.

FIGURE 9.31

Selections, Inc.

Please enter an item quantity...

OK

Cancel

1

15. Click another control on the form so the order total calculates. The order now appears as shown in figure 9.32.

FIGURE 9.32

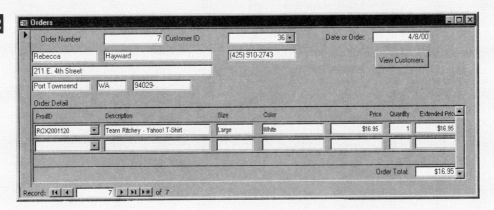

16. Close the form and the database.

2. Changing the Properties of the OrderID Field

If you completed the previous exercise, you might have noticed that the OrderID field appears as a single integer. This is due to the fact that the field uses the AutoNumber data type. The AutoNumber data type is optimized for this field because it is the primary key for the table. As you will recall from reviewing Access data types, an AutoNumber field is assigned automatically by Access and will never contain a duplicate value.

You can change the appearance of this field by changing the Format property of specific database objects. In this next exercise you will change the format property of the field and specific controls bound to those fields.

To Change the Format Property of Specific Database Objects

1. Open the *Selections.mdb* database and unhide the Database window.
2. Open the Orders table in Design view.
3. Set the Format property in the OrderID field to **\SO-0000** ("S", Capital "O", a hyphen, and three zeros). Save and close the table.
4. Open the Orders form in Design view.
5. Select the OrderID text box, right-click, and choose Properties.
6. Type **\SO-0000** as the format for the OrderID text box.
7. Save and close the form.

On Your Own Exercises

1. Adding a New Order to the Selections, Inc. Database

Open the *Selections.mdb* database. Click the option in the switchboard to Add/Edit Customer Orders. Add a new order for Kyle Barbour using these products and quantities:

Item:	Quantity:
RMD2001258	**1**
RCX5007230	**1**
RCX2001130	**3**

When you are finished, his order will appear as shown in Figure 9.33. Close the Orders form.

FIGURE 9.33

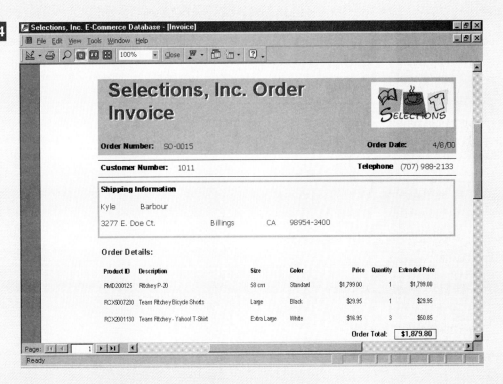

2. Printing a Customer Invoice

Now that you have entered an order for Kyle Barbour, print a copy of his invoice. From the switchboard, select the option to Preview a Customer Invoice. When you are prompted, enter **015** as the order number. The invoice will appear, as shown in Figure 9.34. If you have problems viewing the invoice, close the Print Preview window, and verify the order number.

FIGURE 9.34

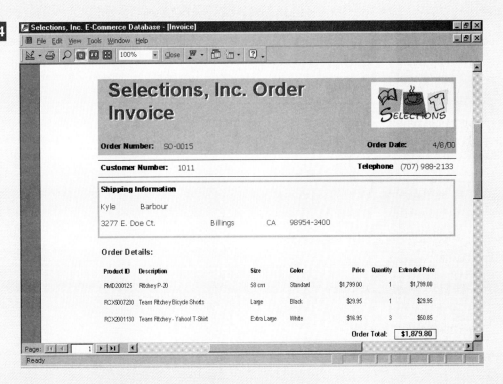

Using Access with Excel and Visual Basic

In this module you have learned to use the advanced features in Access to design and build an efficient database solution. As a member of the Office 2000 Suite, Access 2000 has numerous capabilities for sharing and integrating data with other Office 2000 applications.

There might be times when you will need to share data between Excel and Access for analyzing data. In many environments, Excel is used for certain tasks, and Access for others. It is common, therefore, to integrate data among these applications.

The database application you have created is fully functional within Microsoft Access, but how will you share the database with users who do not have Access installed on their computers? To enable users who do not have Microsoft Access installed on their computer to use the database, you can create a stand-alone application in Visual Basic that uses the Selections, Inc. database.

Objectives

After completing this project, you will be able to:

➤ Link data between an Excel worksheet and an Access table

➤ Create a query from a linked table

➤ Create a report from a query

➤ Add a chart to an Access report using Microsoft Graph

➤ Drag and drop data from Access to Excel

➤ Convert an Access 2000 database to an Access 97 database

➤ Create a Visual Basic front end to an Access database

Running Case

Mr. Traylor has three tasks he wants you to complete. First, the IT department has given him a sample of e-commerce transaction data that he wants you to summarize in an Access report. The report will list the sales summaries for three regions, and he wants the information graphically displayed in a pie chart. Second, the Marketing Department is getting ready to electronically publish a list of Selections, Inc. products, but some of their users do not have Access on their computers. They have requested a product list as an Excel workbook.

Finally, some Selections employees who need to work with the Customer database do not have Access or a Web browser installed on the computers they are using. Mr. Traylor wants to know if there is any way of creating a custom application for them that will integrate with the existing Selections, Inc. database.

The Challenge

Mr. Traylor has a few projects he wants you to complete. First, he received an Excel workbook from the marketing department that contains sample transaction data. The worksheet lists customer and purchase information by sales region. Because not all Selections, Inc. departments use Microsoft Access, he wants you to integrate the Excel spreadsheet data with an Access database. He can then determine the feasibility of using both applications in the future. The marketing department has also requested the product list. Unfortunately, not all members of the marketing department have Internet access, so they are not able to open the data access pages and static HTML documents you created previously. He wants to know if you are able to deliver this information to them using Microsoft Excel. He also wants you to create a chart that summarizes the total sales by region.

Second, some Selections employees who need to work with the Customer database do not have Access or a Web browser installed on the computers they are using. Mr. Traylor wants to know if there is any way of creating a custom application for them that will integrate with the existing Selections, Inc. database.

The Solution

Access has all the features and capabilities you need to meet Mr. Traylor's request. You can link an Excel workbook to an Access data table. Once the link is established, you can create additional database objects using the linked Excel data. You can maintain the data independent of Access, yet also use the features in Access to query and report the data. To create the chart, you can use Microsoft Graph to add a custom chart to an Access report. Figure 10.1 displays the summary report with a graph.

FIGURE 10.1

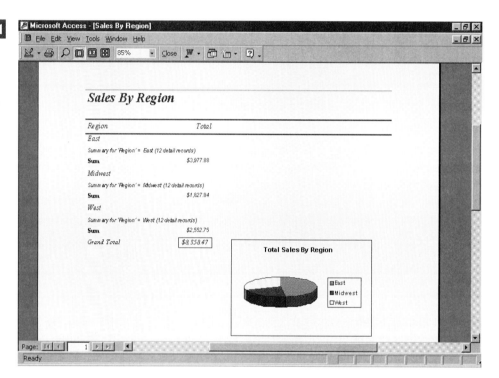

To provide the marketing department with the product list, you can use drag-and-drop technology to generate a product list for them in Excel. Figure 10.2 shows how unformatted data from Access will appear.

FIGURE 10.2

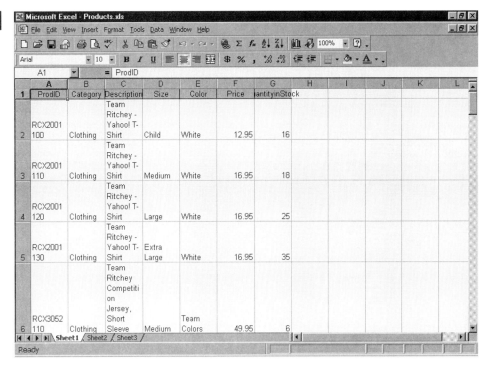

You can create a custom application in Visual Basic to enable users without Access or a Web browser to edit and modify customer records in a shared copy of the Selections, Inc. database. The Visual Basic application, as shown in Figure 10.3, is bound to the Access database.

FIGURE 10.3

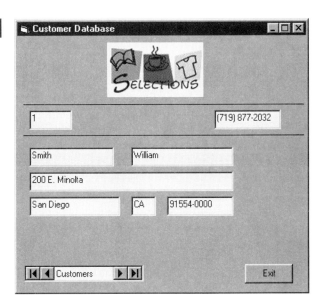

The Setup

To integrate data between Access and other applications, launch Microsoft Access and open the database named *Sales Analysis.mdb* that is on your floppy disk.

 ## Web Tip

If you do not have a copy of this file, you can download it from the Select Web Site at http://www.prenhall.com/selectadvanced

Make sure that you select the settings listed in Table 10.1. If you need additional assistance setting these options, refer to Figure 1.1 through 1.3 of Project 1. This will ensure that your screen matches the illustrations and the tasks in this project function as described.

Table 10.1   Access Settings

Location	Make these settings:
Office Shortcut Bar	If the Office Shortcut bar is visible, close it by right-clicking the Office icon on the shortcut bar and choosing Exit.
Office Assistant	Hide the Office Assistant.
Tools, Customize	Click the Toolbars tab and display the Database toolbar and the Menu Bar, as shown in Figure 1.1 of Project 1, if they are not currently visible.
Tools, Customize	Click the Options tab, and make sure the check box to display recently used menu commands first is deselected, as shown in Figure 1.2 of Project 1.
Tools, Options	Click the View tab and display Status bar, Startup dialog box, New object shortcuts, and Windows in Taskbar, as shown in Figure 1.3 of Project 1.

Linking Excel Data to an Access Database

You can envision many situations where you might want to link an Access table with an external data source, such as an address list in Excel that you want to query in Access. In an Access database, **linking** data enables you to read data from an external source and update the external data source without importing. The format of the data in the external source is not altered so that you can continue to use the file with the program that originally created it. However, since you have established a link, you can add, delete, and edit its data by using Microsoft Access.

In this case, Mr. Traylor wants you to link an Access database to an Excel data source. In the next task, you will link an Access table to an Excel workbook. You will then create a query based on the linked data.

TASK 1:   To Link an Access Table to an Excel Workbook

1   Click File, Get External Data, Link Tables, as shown in Figure 10.4.

FIGURE 10.4

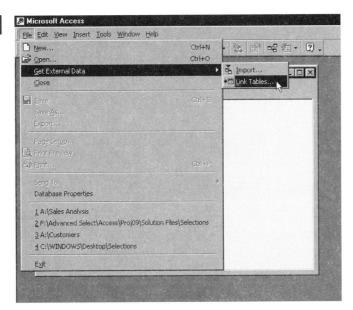

2   In the Link dialog box, navigate to your floppy disk, and change the files of type list to show Microsoft Excel workbooks. *Sales Analysis.xls* will be selected by default, unless you have other workbooks on your disk. Click Link, as shown in Figure 10.5.

FIGURE 10.5

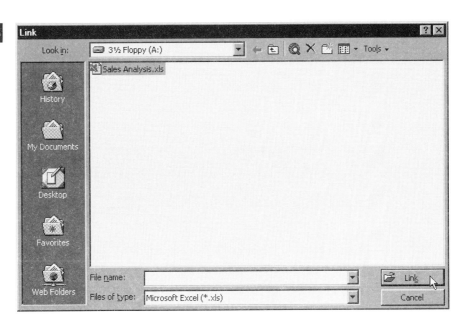

3 The Link Spreadsheet Wizard will appear. Because there is only one worksheet in the workbook, click Next (see Figure 10.6).

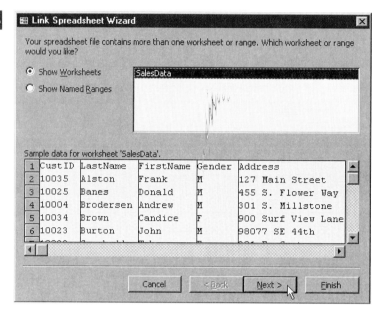

FIGURE 10.6

4 As you can see from the sample data, the first row of the worksheet contains headings. These will become the field names in the linked Access table. Make sure the check box for the first row heading is checked, and click Next, as shown in Figure 10.7.

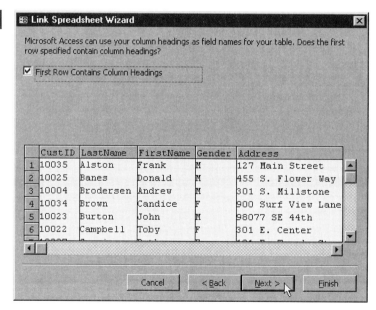

FIGURE 10.7

5 In the final step of the Link Spreadsheet Wizard, Access recommends naming the table *SalesData*. Click Finish, as shown in Figure 10.8.

FIGURE 10.8

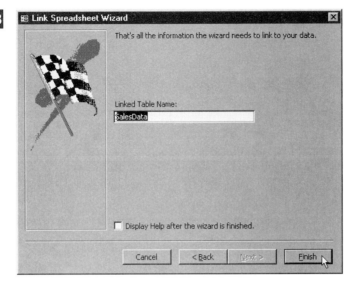

6 When Access successfully completes the link, the dialog box shown in Figure 10.9 will appear. Click OK.

FIGURE 10.9

7 Access adds a table name to the Tables page of the Database window, as shown in Figure 10.10. Notice the icon representing the link.

FIGURE 10.10

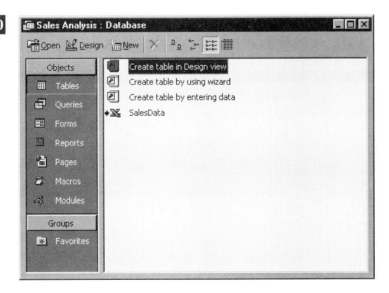

Check Point

Want can you tell about the linked data source from this icon?

Creating a Query from a Linked Table

Now that you have created a linked table, you can create any database objects based on the linked table as you would if the table data was stored in Access rather than an external file. The only limitation is that you will not be able to change the properties of the linked table, since the data is external to Access. You can, however, create a report based on the linked table.

Remember that Mr. Traylor wants you to create a chart that summarizes the sales by region. The SalesData table contains price and quantity data for individual sales, but it does not contain a calculated total. To create a report that summarizes total sales by region, you must first calculate this total.

Check Point

In Access, what object must you use to create a calculated field?

Although you could create a calculated control in a report, your best option will be to create a calculated field in a query. First, create a query based on the table. After you create the query with a calculated total, you can then create a report that summarizes sales data by region. You can use Microsoft Graph to add a chart based on the summaries to the report.

TASK 2: <u>To Create a Query from a Linked Table</u>

1 Click the Queries button in the Database window.

2 Click New [New].

3 Create the query using Design view. Add the SalesData table to the Query Design window, and close the Add Tables dialog box.

4 Add the Region, Quantity, and Price fields to the query.

5 Save the query as **SaleByRegion**. The query will now appear as shown in Figure 10.11.

FIGURE 10.11

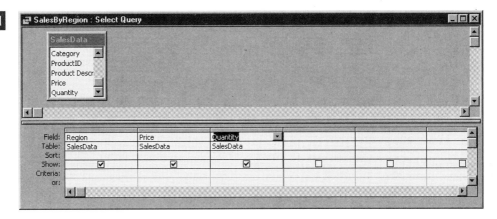

6 Select the field row of the next available column in the Query Design Grid. Type **Total: [Price]*[Quantity]** as the expression for the calculated field. Format the field as currency.

7 Save and close the query.

Creating a Report from a Query

Now that you have created a query with a calculated field, you can create the report that will summarize the regional sales data. You will group the report by region, and summarize the data in the report.

TASK 3: To Create a Report Based on a Query

1 Click the Reports button in the Database window.

2 Click New [New].

3 In the New Report dialog box click Report Wizard, and base the report on the SalesByRegion query, as shown in Figure 10.12. Click OK.

FIGURE 10.12

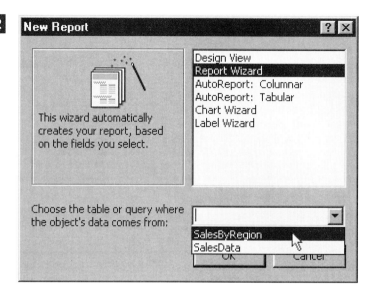

4 Add the Region and Total fields to the report. Click Next, as shown in Figure 10.13.

FIGURE 10.13

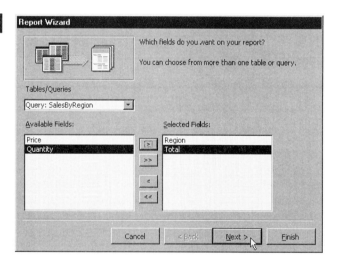

5 Add **Region** as a grouping level. Click Next, as shown in Figure 10.14.

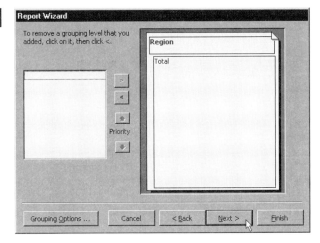

FIGURE 10.14

6 Click the Summary Options button. Check the box to sum the field, check the option to display the summary only, and click OK, as shown in Figure 10.15.

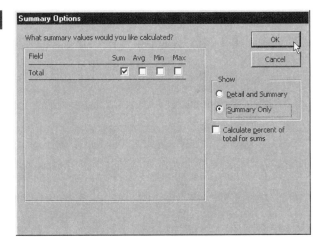

FIGURE 10.15

7 Click Next. Accept the default layout options and click Next.

8 Click Corporate as the report style and click Next.

9 Change the name of the report to **Sales By Region**, and then click Finish.

10 Maximize the report in the Preview window. The report will appear as shown in Figure 10.16. If necessary, resize the controls so the numbers display correctly.

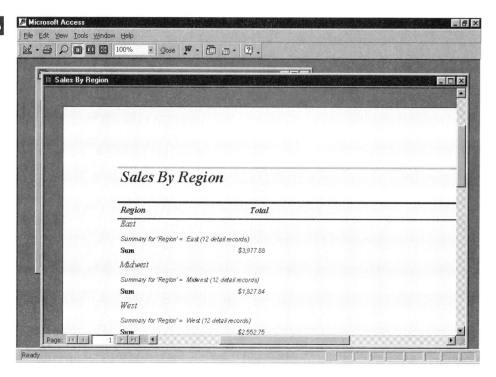

FIGURE 10.16

Adding a Chart to an Access Report Using Microsoft Graph

When you add a chart to an Access 2000 report using the Chart Wizard, Access uses Microsoft Graph 2000 to create the chart. ***Microsoft Graph 2000*** is an Office add-in that provides charting functionality in all Office applications. In this next task you will use the Chart Wizard to add the chart Mr. Traylor requested to the Sales By Region report.

TASK 4: To Add a Chart to an Access Report Using Microsoft Graph

1 Click the View button in the Print Preview window to switch to Report Design view.

2 Select Insert, Chart, as shown in Figure 10.17.

FIGURE 10.17

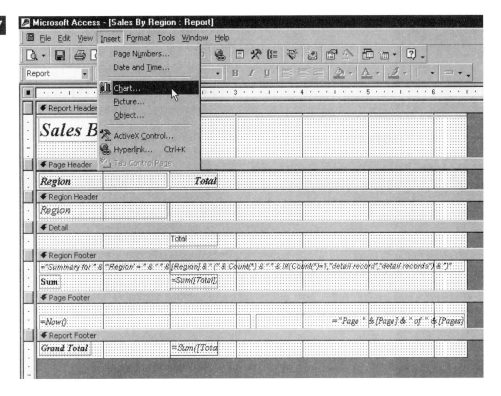

③ Move the insertion point to the Report Footer section and draw a graph in the position shown in Figure 10.18.

FIGURE 10.18

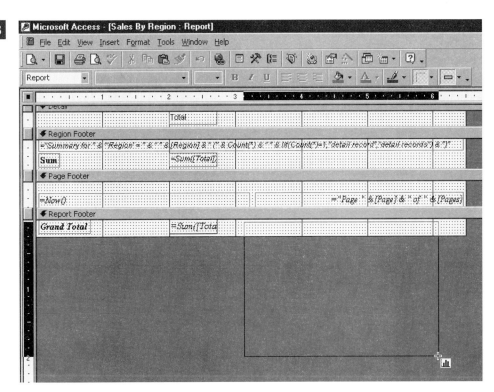

4 Select the option to view queries, select the SalesByRegion query, and click Next, as shown in Figure 10.19.

FIGURE 10.19

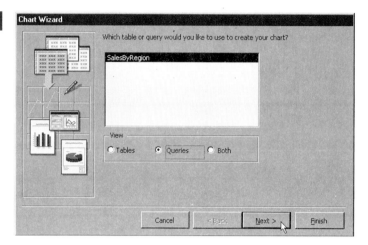

5 Specify the fields to add to the chart. Add Region and Total and click Next.

6 Select the 3-D pie chart option, as shown in Figure 10.20. Click Next.

FIGURE 10.20

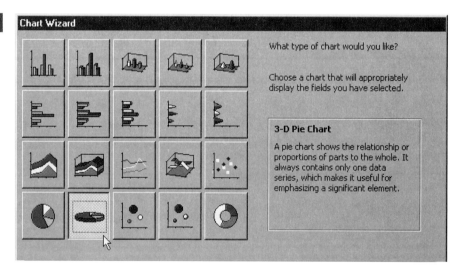

7 You can specify how to lay out the data in the chart. Do not change the settings, and your screen should match Figure 10.21. Click Next.

FIGURE 10.21

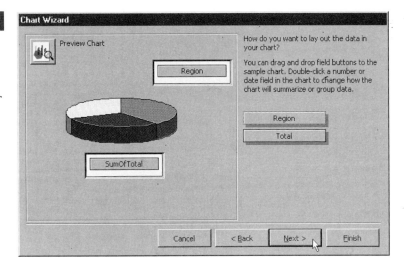

8 Specify whether the chart should change from record to record. If the fields appearing in both the report fields and the chart Fields columns contain any field names, highlight the name and delete it. When your settings match Figure 10.22, click Next.

FIGURE 10.22

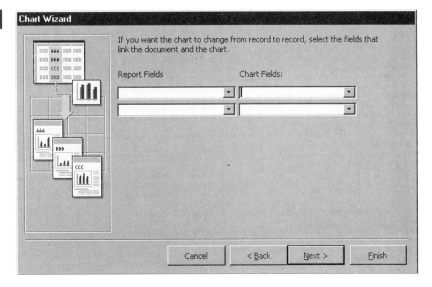

9 Change the report title to **Total Sales By Region**, accept the default to display a legend, and then click Finish.

10 Access adds a chart to the report. Preview the report at 100% zoom. Scroll down the report until the chart appears. The chart will appear as shown in Figure 10.23.

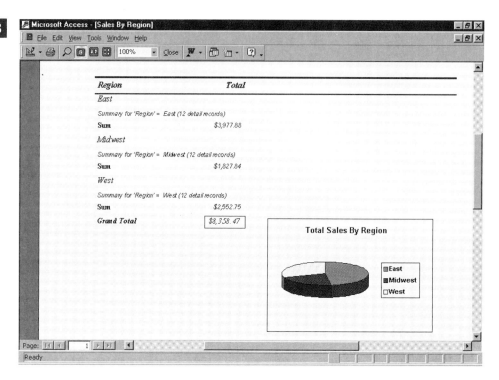

Check Point

The chart is based on the linked table. What will happen if you close Access, modify the data in the Excel workbook, and then preview the chart in Access?

11 Close the Report Preview window.

12 Save and close the report, and close the Sales Analysis database.

Break Point

If necessary, you can exit Access now and continue this project later.

Using Drag-and-Drop to Export Access Data to Excel

You are now ready to create the Product list the marketing department requested. Remember: many of the employees in this department do not have Microsoft Access or a Web browser installed on their computers. They do, however, use Excel extensively. Therefore, you will need to export the Products table to Excel.

In Project 1 you learned how to import and export table data from Access to Excel. In this next task you will see how easily it is to move an entire database object from Access to Excel using drag-and-drop.

TASK 5: To Export a Table from Access to Excel Using Drag-and-Drop

1 Launch Access if it is not currently running.

2 Open the *Product.mdb* database from your floppy disk.

 Web Tip

If you do not have a copy of this file you can download it from the Select Web Site at http://www.prenhall.com/selectadvanced.

3 Launch Excel.

4 Resize Access and Excel on the desktop so both are visible.

5 Click the Products table in the Database window, and while holding down the left mouse button, drag the table to cell A1 of the Excel worksheet, as shown in Figure 10.24.

FIGURE 10.24

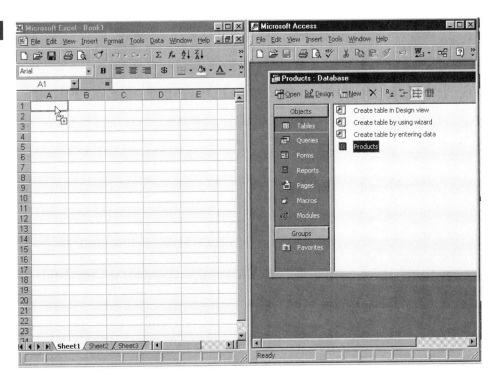

6 Access exports the entire table to Excel. Maximize the Workbook window and select cell A1.

7 Save the workbook to your floppy disk as **Products.xls**. The worksheet in Excel appears as shown in Figure 10.25.

FIGURE 10.25

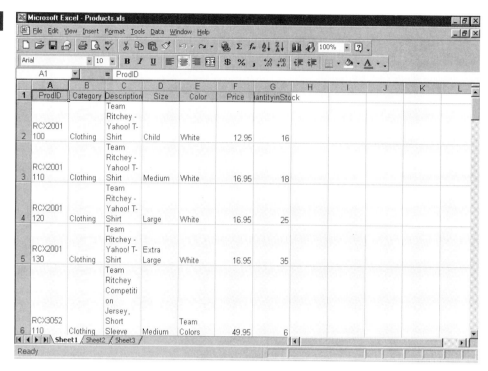

⑧ Close Excel.

Creating a Database Front End with Microsoft Visual Basic

As you learned in Project 9, Microsoft Access and Visual Basic share many of the same components for developing information solutions. Microsoft Access utilizes Visual Basic controls for developing forms, reports, and applications. Visual Basic is a programming environment for developing computer applications for the Microsoft Windows operating system. Visual Basic also supports connectivity between applications and Microsoft Access database objects. You can use Visual Basic to create a front-end application to an Access database. A database **front-end** is an application containing a user interface and methods for interacting with data stored in a table structure. Forms created in Microsoft Access are similar to a front-end, in that they provide a user interface that shields users from database tables and queries. Access forms however, are a part of the Access application. There are two reasons why you might consider developing a database front-end in Visual Basic. First, the application can be used on Windows-based computers that do not have Access installed. Second, because Visual Basic is a full-featured programming environment, more flexibility can be built into the application than when a database application is created using Access.

In Visual Basic there is a distinction between design time and run time. **De-sign time** refers to the work environment used to create the application. You create forms, add controls to forms, and write code in design time. **Run time** refers to the application as it is being executed. In the Visual Basic environment, you can view your application in run time from within design time.

The remaining tasks in this project are devoted to building a stand-alone database application. A **stand-alone application** can be run independent of Microsoft Access. You will build an application that connects to the Customers data table in the *Customers.mdb* database file. Although a working knowledge of Visual Basic version 6 is helpful, many of the concepts and procedures introduced here will be familiar to you. The application you will create is shown in Figure 10.3 at the beginning of this project.

The procedures for building this application are similar to working with forms and reports in Microsoft Access. You will construct a project in Visual Basic that consists of one form. The form will contain various controls, some containing Visual Basic code. The form and project are saved as files that will be used by the Setup Wizard to create a set of disks for installing the application.

You complete five tasks to create your database application. First, you will need to convert the *Customers2000.mdb* database file to an Access 97 database. This is because Visual Basic 6 works with the **Jet Database Engine**, and not the new Microsoft Database Engine. Second, you will create a new Visual Basic project. Third, you will add a data control to your application's form. Fourth, you will add text box, label, and command button controls to the form. Finally, you will write a form load event to specify what will occur when the application is run. If you complete Hands-On Exercise 2 at the end of this project, you will learn how to create a set of installation disks for installing your application.

Converting an Access 2000 Database to a Previous Version

If you need to share an Access database with users who have a prior version of Access installed on their computers, or if you want to use Visual Basic 6 with an Access database, you will need to convert the database to a prior version.

TASK 6: To Convert an Access 2000 Database to an Access 97 Version

1 Create a folder on your floppy disk named **VB**.

2 Open the *Customers2000.mdb* database from your floppy disk.

Web Tip

If you do not have a copy of this database, you can download it from the Select Web Site at http://www.prenhall.com/selectadvanced.

3 Choose Tools, Database Utilities, Convert Database, To Prior Access Database Version, as shown in Figure 10.26.

FIGURE 10.26

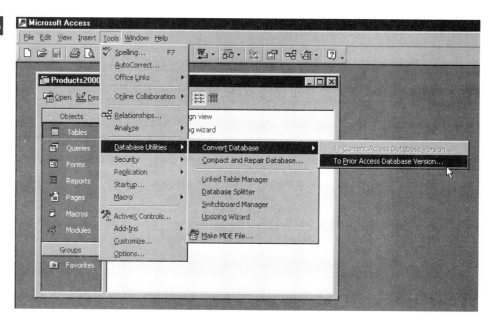

4 Type **Customers97.mdb** as the database name in the Convert Database Into dialog box and click Save, as shown in Figure 10.27.

FIGURE 10.27

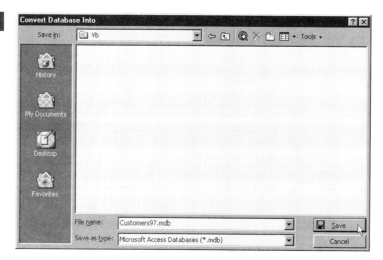

5 Access will convert the database. Close the database when you are finished converting it, and exit Access.

Creating a New Visual Basic Project

Now that you have converted the database to a version that Visual Basic 6 can use, you are ready to build the database front-end application.

TIP To complete the remaining tasks in this project, you must have Visual Basic Version 5 or 6 installed on your computer. If you complete Hands On Exercise 2, you will need Visual Basic Version 6.

TASK 7: To Create a New Visual Basic Project

1 Launch Visual Basic Version 5 or 6.

TROUBLESHOOTING If you do not know how to launch Visual Basic, ask your instructor for assistance.

2 In the New Project dialog box, choose Standard Exe as the project type and click Open, as shown in Figure 10.28.

FIGURE 10.28

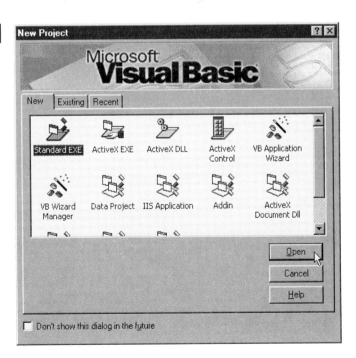

3 Click Form 1 and resize it to about the same size as the form that is shown in Figure 10.29.

TIP Notice that Project 1 is maximized, and the Properties pane is visible.

FIGURE 10.29

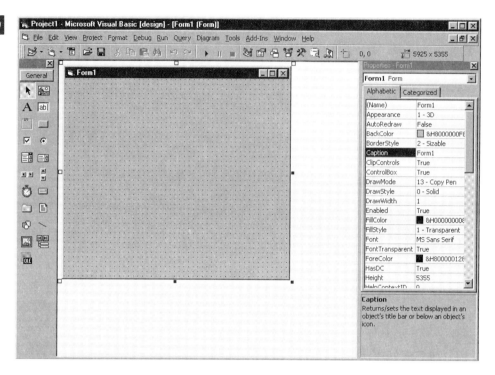

4 Using the Toolbox, create an image label control in the upper center of Form 1.

5 In the Properties window, choose the Picture property for the control you just created, and click the small button with the ellipsis, as shown in Figure 10.30.

FIGURE 10.30

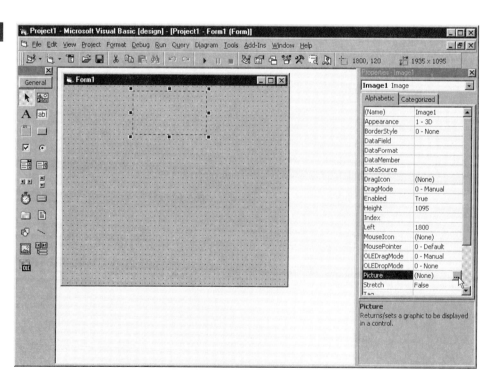

6 Select the *Selections Logo.bmp* file that is on your floppy disk and click Open. The image will appear in the image control.

7 Select the form. The title bar in the Properties window will change to Form 1. Type **Customer Database** as the caption property. Choose Save Project from the File menu. The Save File As dialog box will appear.

8 Save the form as **frmCustomers.frm** to the VB folder on your floppy disk, as shown in Figure 10.31. Click Save.

FIGURE 10.31

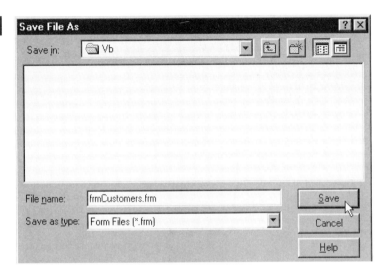

9 Because this is a new project, you will need to save the project file as well. Type **Customers.vbp** as the name of the project and click Save, as shown in Figure 10.32.

FIGURE 10.32

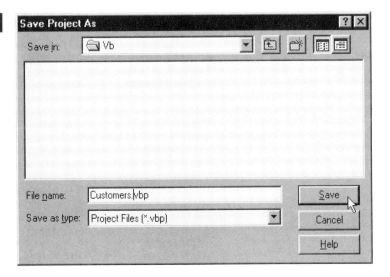

You have now successfully created a Visual Basic form and saved your Visual Basic project file.

Visual Basic Naming Conventions

Visual Basic programmers usually name Visual Basic objects in a consistent manner. Each control is given a three character identifier that specifies the control type, followed by a descriptive name explaining what the control does. The descriptive name usually consists of one or more words and must begin with a capital letter. Avoid using spaces and special characters. Table 10.2 lists the three character identifier for certain objects.

Table 10.2   Visual Basic Naming Conventions

Object	Three Character Identifier
Form	Frm
Text Box	Txt
Label	Lbl
Command Button	Cmd
Data Control	Dat

Web Tip

For more information on naming Visual Basic objects, visit http://msdn.microsoft.com/library/devprods/vs6/vbasic/vbcon98/vbconobjectnamingconventions.htm.

Using the Visual Basic Data Control

To display Microsoft Access data in a Visual Basic application, you must first establish a connection between the data source (the Access database table) and the application. You can do this easily by adding a data control to your Visual Basic form. The **data control** enables you to move from record to record, and to display and manipulate data from the records in bound controls. After adding a data control to the form, you can then bind controls to the data control.

TASK 8:   To Add a Data Control to Your Form

1 Click the Data Control tool in the Toolbox, as shown in Figure 10.33.

FIGURE 10.33

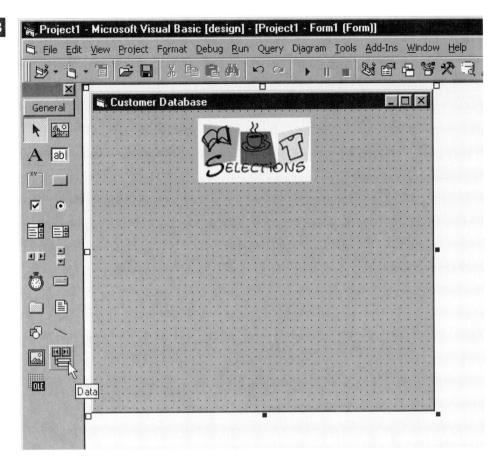

2 Draw a data control near the lower left of the form.

3 Click the data control you just created to display its default properties in the Properties window.

4 Type **datCustomers** as the Name property, and **Customers** as the Caption property for this control.

5 Click inside the DatabaseName row and click the ellipsis button. Click *Customers97.mdb* on your floppy disk as the database and click Open, as shown in Figure 10.34.

FIGURE 10.34

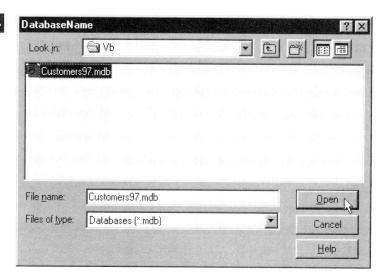

6 Scroll down in the Properties window to access the Record Source property. You will use this to specify a database object to which the database will be bound.

7 Click inside the RecordSource row and click the drop-down list icon. Choose Customers in the list, as shown in Figure 10.35.

FIGURE 10.35

8 Choose Save from the File menu to save your project.

Adding Controls to a Visual Basic Form

Now that you have established a connection between the Access database object and your Customers application, you can add controls to the top the form. Earlier in this module you learned the difference between bound and unbound controls. You will bind the text box controls to the data control, and add line and command button unbound controls to the form to enhance its appearance and functionality.

TASK 9: To Add Controls to the Visual Basic Form

1 Click the Line Control tool in the Toolbox and add a line control immediately below the image control. Extend the control across the entire form to within a small margin of the left and right edges of the form.

2 Create an additional line about 1/2 inch below the existing line.

3 Click the Text Box tool in the Toolbox and draw a text box control between the two lines, near the left side of the form.

4 Notice that the properties for the control appear in the Properties window. Enter **txtCustID** as the name property, **datCustomers** as the DataSource property (choose this from the drop-down list), **CustID** as the DataField property (choose this from the drop-down list), and **Cust ID** as the Text property.

5 Create seven additional text box controls to the form. Position and size the controls on the form as shown in Figure 10.36.

FIGURE 10.36

Customer Database

SELECTIONS

| CustID | | Text1 |

| Text2 | Text3 |

| Text4 |

| Text5 | Text6 | Text7 |

|◄ ◄ Customers ► ►|

6 Using the values displayed in Table 10.3, change the Name, DataField, DataSource (use datCustomers), and Text properties of each control. Reference Figure 10.37, if necessary.

Table 10.3

Control Name	Control DataField	Control Text
txtPhone	HomePhone	Phone
txtLastname	LastName	Last
txtFirstname	FirstName	First
txtAddress	Address	Address
txtCity	City	City
txtState	State	State
txtZipCode	ZipCode	Zip Code

FIGURE 10.37

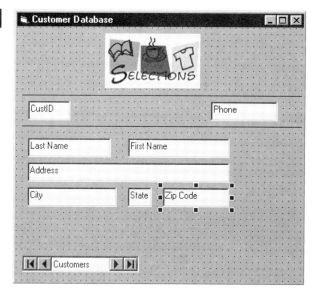

7 Using the Command Button Control, create a command button in the lower right side of the form.

8 Set the Name property to **cmdExit** and the Caption property to **Exit**.

9 Place the insertion point over the command button and right-click to display a shortcut menu. Select View Code as shown in Figure 10.38 to open the Code window.

FIGURE 10.38

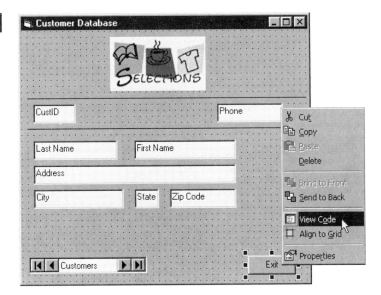

10 Choose cmdExit as the control in the left drop down list in the Code window, as shown in Figure 10.39. This is the control that will contain code to exit the application when the button is clicked.

FIGURE 10.39

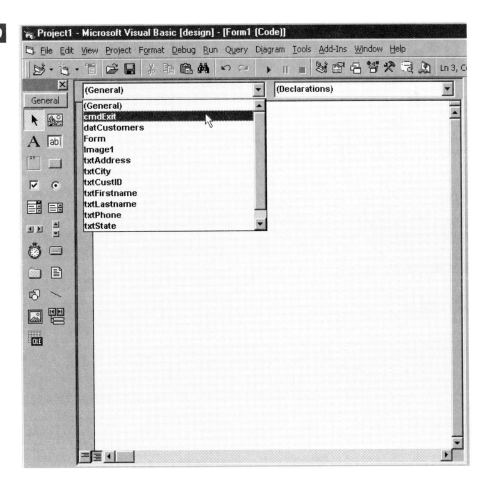

11 Type **End** between the Private Sub and End Sub statements, as shown in Figure 10.40. This code specifies that the command button control will close the application in response to a button click event.

FIGURE 10.40

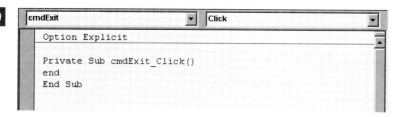

```
cmdExit                          ▼    Click                          ▼
    Option Explicit

    Private Sub cmdExit_Click()
    end
    End Sub
```

12 Close the Code window and save your project.

13 Click Run, and click Start. Visual Basic will display the form in Run time. It will appear as shown in Figure 10.41.

FIGURE 10.41

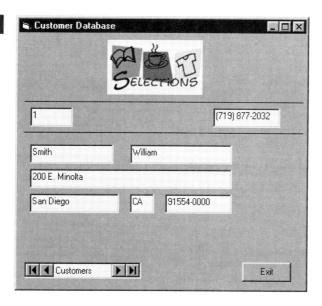

14 Use the navigation buttons on the data control to move among records in the database. When you are finished, click Exit.

15 Close Visual Basic.

There are many enhancements you can make to the front-end application, including adding command buttons to add and delete records. In this project you have learned how to use Visual Basic to connect to an Access database. If you complete the Hands-On Exercises that follow, you will learn how to prepare your application for distribution.

You have completed each task Mr. Traylor assigned to you. As you can see, you have many options for integrating Access data with other Windows applications.

Summary and Exercises

Summary

- You can use the Link Tables feature to connect an Access database with an external data source.
- Once you have created a linked table, you can add a calculated field by creating a query based on the linked table object.
- To display sales summary data, create a report that is based on a query that returns the sales summary information.
- You can use Microsoft Graph to display charts in Access reports.
- You can export data from Access to Excel using drag-and-drop.
- You can convert an Access 2000 database to a prior Access version using the Database Utilities in Access.
- You can create a custom front-end to an Access database using Visual Basic.

Key Terms and Operations

Key Terms

data control
design time
front-end
Jet Database Engine
linking
Microsoft Graph 2000
path-independent
run time
stand-alone application

Operations

add a chart to an Access report using Microsoft Graph 2000
add a data control to a Visual Basic form
add controls to a Visual Basic form
convert an Access 2000 database to an Access 97 version
create a new Visual Basic project
create a query from a linked table
create a report based on a query
export a table from Access to Excel using drag-and-drop
link an Access table to an Excel workbook

Study Questions

Multiple Choice

1. Which option do you use to bind an Access database to an external data source?
   a. Export
   b. Import
   c. Link Tables
   d. Open
   e. Open As

2. Which Microsoft Office add-in application enables you to add charts to Access reports?
   a. Chart Wizard
   b. Visual Basic for Applications
   c. Microsoft Graph 2000
   d. Import Wizard
   e. Both a and c.

3. Which chart option is good for displaying the parts of a whole?
   a. Line
   b. Bar
   c. Pie
   d. X Y
   e. Scatter

4. Which of the following is a bound control?
   a. Command button control
   b. Image control
   c. Line control
   d. Label control
   e. Data control

5. When you create a Visual Basic front-end for an Access database, which control binds the application to the record source?
   a. Label
   b. Text Box
   c. Line
   d. Image
   e. Data

6. Assume you have a linked table in an Access database. Which database object do you use to create a calculated field for the table data?
   a. Table
   b. Query
   c. Form
   d. Report
   e. None of the above.

7. Which control is used to display a bitmap on a Visual Basic form?
   a. Text box
   b. Data control
   c. Line control
   d. Image control
   e. Form control

8. A front-end application usually provides an interface to:
   a. a web browser.
   b. an HTML document.
   c. a Visual Basic application.
   d. a text editor.
   e. a database.

9. Which three characters will precede the name of a data control name if you are following Visual Basic naming conventions?
   a. dat
   b. dta
   c. dll
   d. dbc
   e. drl

10. Visual Basic is which category of software?
    a. Web browser
    b. database file
    c. programming environment
    d. text editor
    e. database management system

Short Answer

1. Which Office Add-in will add charts to an Access report?

2. What is a linked table?

3. How do you convert an Access 2000 database to a previous Access version?

4. What is a database front-end?

5. How do you run a Visual Basic application?

6. What is a bound control?

7. How do you add an image to a Visual Basic form?

8. How do you use drag-and-drop to export tables and queries from Access to Excel?

9. What is design time?

10. What is the Visual Basic data control?

Fill in the Blank

1. The _____ control will display a bitmapped graphic on a Visual Basic form.

2. A(n) _____ table gets its data from an external data source.

3. You can use _____ and _____ to export a table from Access to another Office application, such as Excel.

4. Database field information appears in a Visual Basic application using a(n) _____ control.

5. A line control is _____.

6. A Visual Basic project has at least one _____.

7. Controls are added to a Visual Basic application in _____.

8. To convert an Access 2000 database to a previous version, use the _____ menu.

9. A(n) _____ control is used to bind data on a Visual Basic form to an external database file.

10. Both Microsoft Access 97 and Visual Basic 6 use the _____ to work with database information.

For Discussion

1. How do you link an Access table to an external data source? What are the advantages and disadvantages of a linked table?

2. What is Microsoft Graph 2000? How can you use MS Graph 2000 to enhance Access 2000 reports?

3. What is Visual Basic? How do you connect a Visual Basic application to an Access database?

4. What is a Visual Basic form? How does a VB form differ from a form in Access?

5. Describe two circumstances where you might need to convert an Access 2000 database to a previous Access version.

Hands-On Exercises

1. Preparing a Visual Basic Database Front-End Application for Distribution

When you set the properties for the data control in the front-end application you created in this project, you specified the name and path for the database as a property for the data control. Since the DatabaseName property of the data control contains both the names of the database file and the path, the application will always look for the database file on a floppy disk. This will cause a run time error if the application is installed on a user's hard drive.

You can set the path for the database file so that Visual Basic looks for the database in the directory where the executable file resides. As long as the database file is located in the same directory, an error will not occur. The code to set the path can be added to the event of the form being loaded into memory when the application is run. In this way, the database application is *path-independent*, meaning that the data control will look for the database in the path for the application, itself.

To Make the Database Path-Independent

1. Open the Visual Basic project you completed earlier.

2. Choose the datCustomer data control, select the DatabaseName property, and delete it. When deleted, the cell should be blank.

3. Place the insertion point somewhere over Form 1, but not on a specific control, and right-click.

4. Choose View Code from the shortcut menu.

5. Choose Form from the drop-down list located in the left side of the Code window.

6. The code in the Code window should appear as shown in Figure 10.42. The insertion point should be between the Private Sub Form_Load()and End Sub statements.

FIGURE 10.42

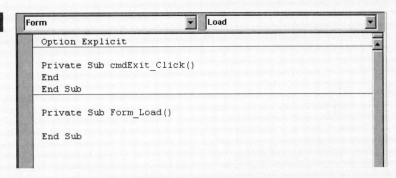

```
Form                          ▼   Load                              ▼

    Option Explicit

    Private Sub cmdExit_Click()
    End
    End Sub

    Private Sub Form_Load()

    End Sub
```

7. Type **datCustomers.DatabaseName = App.Path &** **"\Customers97.mdb"** and press ENTER.

8. Type **datCustomers.Refresh**.

9. The code should now look like Figure 10.43.

FIGURE 10.43

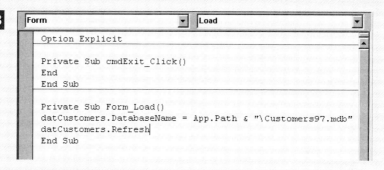

```
Form                          ▼   Load                    ▼

    Option Explicit

    Private Sub cmdExit_Click()
    End
    End Sub


    Private Sub Form_Load()
    datCustomers.DatabaseName = App.Path & "\Customers97.mdb"
    datCustomers.Refresh
    End Sub
```

10. Save the project.

11. Run the project. It should run without errors.

12. Return to Design view.

13. Choose Make Customers.Exe from the File menu as shown in Figure 10.44.

FIGURE 10.44

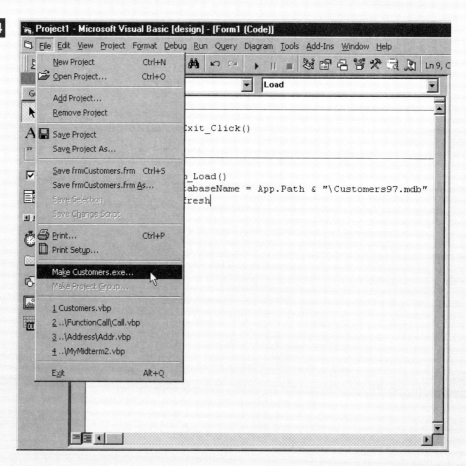

14. Select the default filename of *Customers.exe*, and the default location. Click Save.

15. Exit Visual Basic, saving your most recent changes.

2. Using the Visual Basic Package and Deployment Wizard

To distribute your database front-end, you will need to use the Visual Basic Package and Deployment Wizard, which is a tool accompanying Visual Basic 6.0. This Wizard will walk you through the steps necessary to package your application so it can be installed on any computer running Windows 95, 98, 2000, or NT.

> **TROUBLESHOOTING** To complete this exercise, you must have write privileges to the C: drive, and there must be a minimum of 12 MB free disk space.

To Use the Package and Deployment Wizard

1. Launch the Package and Deployment Wizard.
2. Browse for your project, and select Package, as shown in Figure 10.45.

 FIGURE 10.45

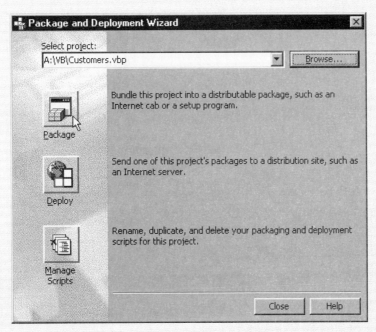

3. In the dialog box that appears on the screen, click No to use the Executable you created.
4. Choose the Standard Setup Package option and click Next.
5. The package files require too much space to store on a floppy disk. Choose the C: drive and select the option to create a new folder. Create a folder named **MyVB**. When your settings are similar to Figure 10.46, click Next.

FIGURE 10.46

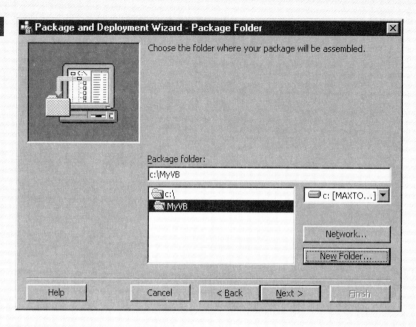

6. Add the ODBC with Jet Workspaces database driver. Click Next.

7. Add the *Customers97.mdb* file to the set. Click Add, locate the file on your disk, and click Open. When the database appears in the list, as shown in Figure 10.47, click Next.

FIGURE 10.47

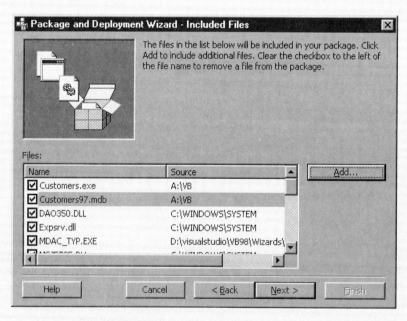

8. You will need to specify the method you will use to install your application. Assume that you will install it over a network. Choose the default option shown in Figure 10.48 and click Next.

FIGURE 10.48

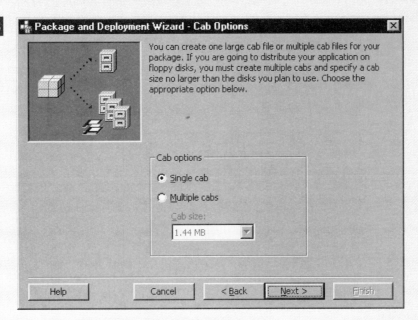

Check Point

How would you create a distribution set on floppy disk?

9. Type **Customers Database** as the title for the application and click Next.

10. Accept the default group settings shown in Figure 10.49. Click Next.

FIGURE 10.49

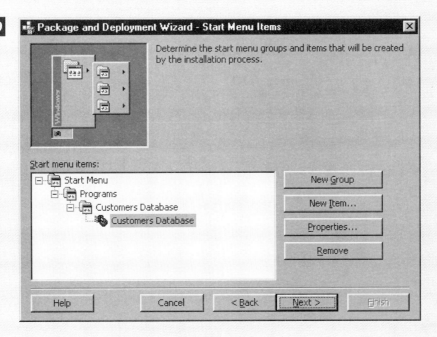

11. Do not modify any of the installation settings. Click Next.

12. Do not set any files as shared programs. Click Next.

13. Accept the default name for the package script and click Finish.

14. The Wizard will display a report of the packaging results. Close the report, and then close the Package and Deployment Wizard.

15. Using My Computer, navigate to the C: drive and open the *MyVB* folder. It contains the files shown in Figure 10.50.

FIGURE 10.50

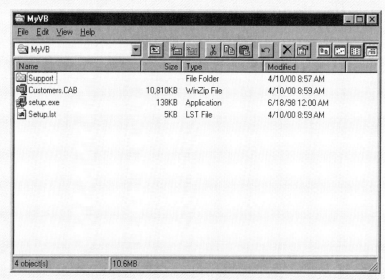

To install the application on remote computers, copy these files to the appropriate network location.

On Your Own Exercises

1. Installing a Visual Basic Application

If you completed the previous exercise, you might want to test your installation. Display and run the Setup.exe file in My Computer. Follow the instructions onscreen. If necessary, remove the application from your computer after you have installed and run it.

2. Using the Link Table Manager

In this project you learned how to link an Access database table to an external data source. Access includes the Link Table Manager, a tool for managing external files. This tool will update links if the external file is moved. Open the *Sales Analysis.mdb* database you modified in this project. Choose Tools, Database Utilities, Linked Table Manager. Check the SalesData table and select Update. Close Access when you are finished.

Working with Access

A s you learned in the Overview section, Access is based on the relational database model. This model assists you in creating powerful applications that can be implemented in a variety of ways. This Appendix will review the data objects available in Microsoft Access 2000, assist you in working with object views and show you how to get help using the Office Assistant.

Microsoft Database Objects

In addition to tables, Access 2000 databases contain other components, each of which is called an object. Access has seven classes of database objects: table, query, form, report, page, macro, and module. The purpose of each object is listed below.

Tables

Tables are an organized collection of rows and columns used to store field data. Tables consist of one or more fields that store data using one of the data types listed in Table A.1.

Table A.1   Access Data Types

Setting	Type of data	Size
Text	Text is the default data type in Access. Contains text or combinations of text and numbers, as well as numbers that don't require calculations, such as phone numbers.	Up to 255 characters or the length set by the FieldSize property, whichever is less. Access does not reserve space for unused portions of a text field.
Memo	Used for lengthy text or combinations of text and numbers.	Up to 65,535 characters
Number	Holds numeric data used in mathematical calculations. For more information on how to set the specific Number type, see the FieldSize property topic.	1, 2, 4, or 8 bytes (16 bytes if the FieldSize property is set to Replication ID)
Date/Time	Stores date and time values for the years 100 through 9999.	8 bytes
Currency	Stores currency values and numeric data used in mathematical calculations involving data with one to four decimal places. Accurate to 15 digits on the left side of the decimal separator and to 4 digits on the right side.	8 bytes

Table A.1   Access Data Types   (continued)

Setting	Type of data	Size
AutoNumber	Assigns a unique sequential (incremented by 1) number or random number assigned by Access whenever a new record is added to a table. AutoNumber fields can't be updated. For more information, see the NewValues property topic.	4 bytes (16 bytes if the FieldSize property is set to Replication ID)
Yes/No	Yes and No values and fields that contain only one of two values (Yes/No, True/False, or On/Off).	1 bit
OLE Object	An object (such as a Microsoft Excel spreadsheet, a Microsoft Word document, graphics, sounds, or other binary data) linked to or embedded in a Microsoft Access table.	Up to 1 gigabyte (limited by available disk space)
Hyperlink	Stores text or combinations of text and numbers stored as text and used as a hyperlink address.	Each part can contain up to 2048 characters.

Tables are basic objects in Access. All other objects (except forms containing unbound controls) require table data. Table records are displayed in a table datasheet.

Query

A query is an object that is used to view, change, or organize data. You can create a query from the data in one or more tables or queries. The most common type of query is a Select query, which returns specific record and field data according to the query specifications. Records returned by a query are displayed in a query datasheet.

Form

A form is a graphical object that displays data from a table or a query in an easy-to-use format. Forms contain controls, which define the user interface for the form. Examples of the kinds of controls you might see on a form are text boxes, labels, image or picture controls, command buttons, lines, and other control objects. In a well-designed database, end users interact with data only through forms.

Report

A report is an object used to present your data in a printed format, primarily for data output. Reports are based upon one or more tables or queries. Reports also contain controls that define where and how record data appears when printed.

Pages

Access 2000 introduced a new data object, the data access page. A data access page is an HTML file designed in Access and formatted to display in a Web browser. Data access pages are bound to specific tables or queries. By creating a data access page, you can make Access record data available for editing on the Web.

Macro

A macro is a set of one or more actions that automate common tasks such as opening a form or printing a report. Macros are often assigned to a command button so users can complete the procedures specified by the macro by clicking a button.

Module

A module is a collection of Visual Basic for Applications programming components that are stored together as a unit. The procedures in a macro can be called from any object in the database. Modules are useful when you are creating complex custom solutions in Access.

Working with Objects: Understanding Object Views

When you create a Microsoft Access database, each object you add to the database is stored in a single database (*.mdb) file. You can display the various database objects using the Database window, which is the graphical interface for choosing among database objects. A page in the Database window represents each object type. The page displays the names of the specific objects you have created. Figure A.1 displays the Tables page in the Database window.

FIGURE A.1

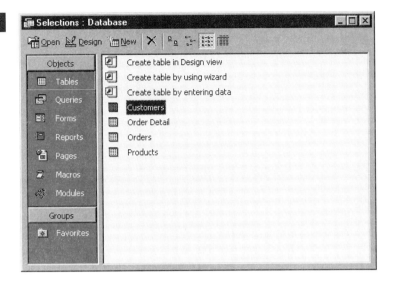

To change the page that is displayed in the Database window, click an object button appearing in the left side of the Database window. The area of the Database window containing the object buttons is called the Database window toolbar.

Object Views

Each object in Access supports two or more views. The current view specifies how the object is displayed. All objects have a Design view, which is the view you use to create or modify the object. You change the view of any object using either the View menu or the View button that appears on the object's toolbar.

> **TIP** In Access, the name of the toolbar appearing on the screen will vary depending on which database object you are currently viewing. For example, when you are working with a table in Design view, the toolbar is called the Table Design toolbar.

Tables

Tables have two views: Design view and Datasheet view. You use Design view to create and modify the structure of a table. You use Datasheet view to view, add, delete, and edit data in a table. Figure A.2 shows Table Design view for a new table. Figure A.3 displays a table in Datasheet view.

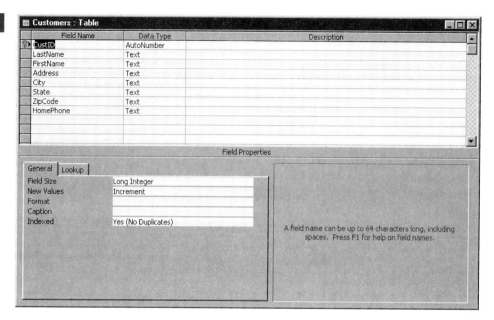

FIGURE A.2

FIGURE A.3

CustID	LastName	FirstName	Address	City	State	ZipCode
1	Smith	William	200 E. Minolta	San Diego	CA	91554-0000
2	Williams	Peter	3401 W. Florida	Lake Hudson	NY	23412-1311
3	Snyder	Patricia	4001 SE Masor	Mission	CA	92144-9243
4	Broadman	Frank	301 S. Mineral	Detroit	MI	45812-0000
5	Tepley	Joanne	45721 Madison	George Mason	NY	23310-2710
6	Mason	Sue	33975 E. Missis	Aurora	IL	61645-3412
7	Cummings	Bethany	101 E. Remingt	Ft. Winchester	CA	98134-6584
8	Masters	Paul	2377 South Old	Redwood	NY	21389-1234
9	Johnston	Pauline	3 Paul Revere L	Boston	MA	01233-7927
10	Miller	Stephen	P.O. Box 3122	Youngstown	MI	57566-2190
11	Barbour	Kyle	3277 E. Doe Ct.	Billings	CA	98954-3400
12	Young	Gwen	105 95th NW	Seattle	WA	98876-0000
13	Williams	Kurt	121 RR 57	Alden	MI	46981-3217
14	Lawson	Barb	9011 Williams D	Miami	OH	21190-9999
15	Jackson	Lawrence	925 S. Bull Run	Amazon	MI	65122-7888
16	Petersen	Ivan	1211 Moscow	Duane	CA	98812-6700
17	Lilley	Warren	P.O. Box 121	Jackson	NY	21198-2111
18	Allison	Fraiser	9001 Tucson Ct	Arizona City	CA	98766-9090
19	Peterson	Janet	12122 S. Marior	Georgian	MI	47812-6755
20	Ward	Sylvia	307 N. Hines	Bridge	MA	10123-0000
21	Rogers	Tasha	4 Courtside #31	Albans	NY	20233-9090

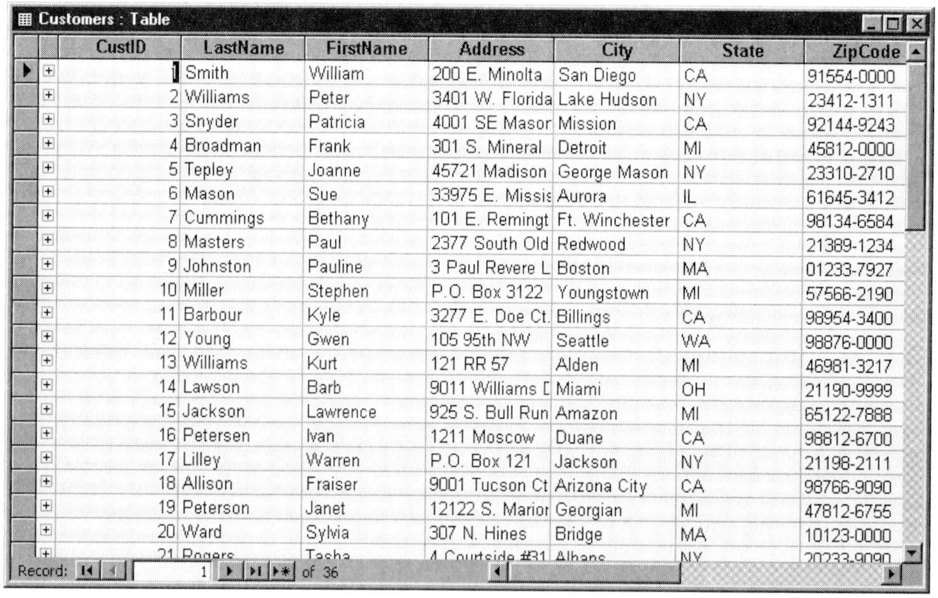

Queries

A query has three views: Design view, Datasheet view, and SQL view. SQL view displays the Structured Query Language (SQL) statement that specifies the data returned by a query. Figure A.4 displays the Query Design window. Figure A.5 shows a query datasheet. Figure A.6 displays the SQL statement underlying a query in SQL view.

FIGURE A.4

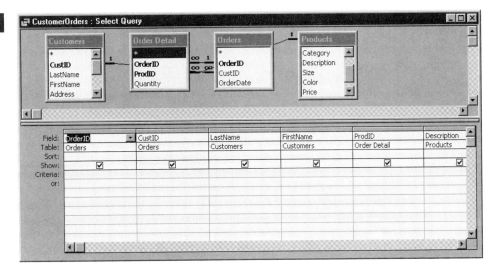

FIGURE A.5

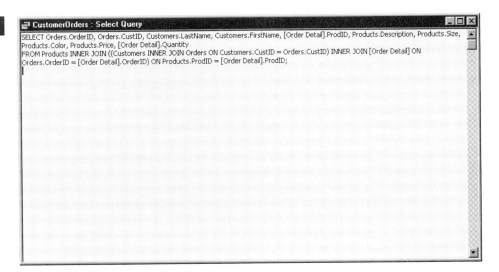

Forms

Forms have three views: Design view, Form view, and Datasheet view. As with tables and queries, forms can display record data in a datasheet. Figure A.7 displays Design view, Figure A.8 shows Form view, and Figure A.9 displays a form in Datasheet view.

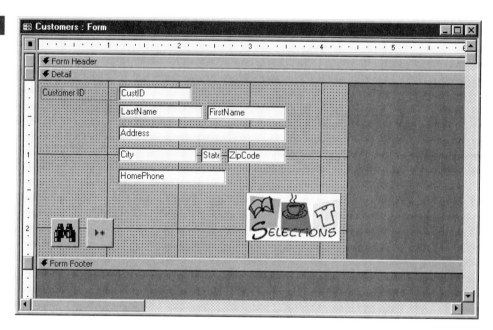

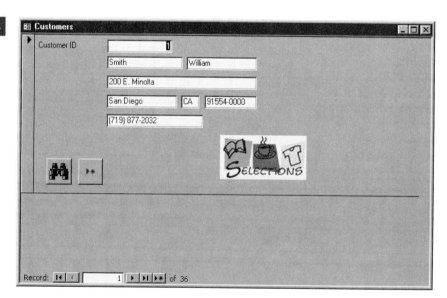

FIGURE A.9

Customers

	Customer ID	LastName	FirstName	Address
▶	1	Smith	William	200 E. Minolta
	2	Williams	Peter	3401 W. Florida Street
	3	Snyder	Patricia	4001 SE Mason
	4	Broadman	Frank	301 S. Mineral
	5	Tepley	Joanne	45721 Madison
	6	Mason	Sue	33975 E. Mississippi
	7	Cummings	Bethany	101 E. Remington
	8	Masters	Paul	2377 South Olde Bridge Parkv
	9	Johnston	Pauline	3 Paul Revere Lane
	10	Miller	Stephen	P.O. Box 3122
	11	Barbour	Kyle	3277 E. Doe Ct.
	12	Young	Gwen	105 95th NW
	13	Williams	Kurt	121 RR 57
	14	Lawson	Barb	9011 Williams Drive
	15	Jackson	Lawrence	925 S. Bull Run
	16	Petersen	Ivan	1211 Moscow
	17	Lilley	Warren	P.O. Box 121
	18	Allison	Fraiser	9001 Tucson Ct.

Record: ◄◄ ◄ 1 ► ►► ►* of 36

Reports

Reports have three views: Design view, Print Preview, and Layout Preview. You use Design view to create a report or change the structure of an existing report, Print Preview to view the report data as it will appear on every page, and Layout Preview to view the report's layout, which includes just a sample of the data in the report. Figure A.10 shows Report Design view. Figure A.11 shows the same report in Print Preview.

FIGURE A.10

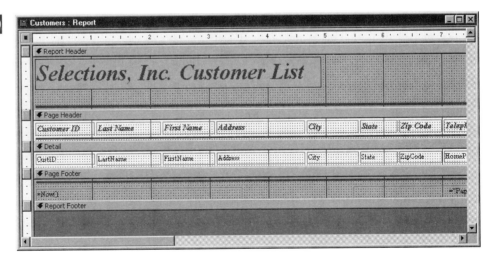

FIGURE A.11

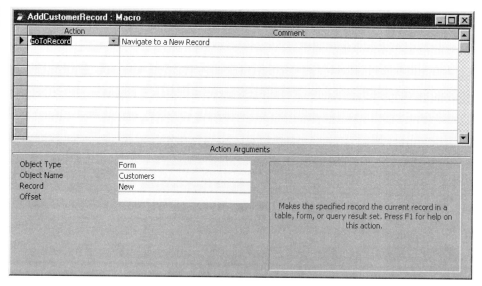

Selections, Inc. Customer List

Customer ID	Last Name	First Name	Address	City	State	Zip Code	Tele
1001	Smith	William	200 E. Minolta	San Diego	CA	91554-0000	(719)
1002	Williams	Peter	3401 W. Florida Street	Lake Hudson	NY	23412-1311	(201)
1003	Snyder	Patricia	4001 SE Mason	Mission	CA	92144-9243	(798)
1004	Broadman	Frank	301 S. Mineral	Detroit	MI	45812-0000	(355)
1005	Tepley	Joanne	45721 Madison	George Mason	NY	23310-2710	(211)
1006	Mason	Sue	33975 E. Mississippi	Aurora	IL	61645-3412	(312)
1007	Cummings	Bethany	101 E. Remington	Ft. Winchester	CA	98134-6584	(767)

Macros

You create Access macros using the Macro window to specify each action a macro will accomplish when the macro is run. Figure A.12 shows the Macro window.

FIGURE A.12

AddCustomerRecord : Macro

Action	Comment
GoToRecord	Navigate to a New Record

Action Arguments

Object Type — Form
Object Name — Customers
Record — New
Offset —

Makes the specified record the current record in a table, form, or query result set. Press F1 for help on this action.

Using the Office Assistant

As you work with Access 2000, there will be times when you need to look up a feature or a function using the online help system. In every Office 2000 application, including Access, the Office Assistant is available to provide assistance at any time.

To use the Office Assistant in Access, click Help, and choose Show the Office Assistant. You can also press (F1) to get help in Office. When the Office Assistant appears, type a question, as shown in Figure A.13.

FIGURE A.13

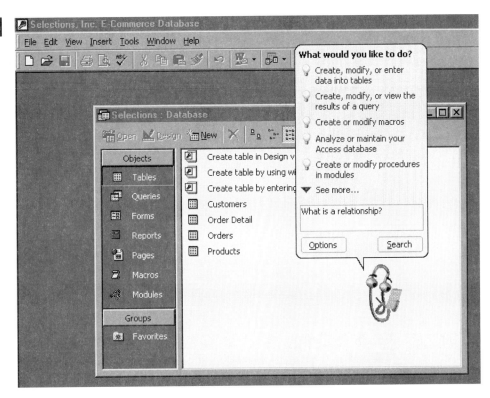

TIP To hide the Office Assistant, right-click over the Assistant and choose Hide. You can also use the Help menu to show and hide the Office Assistant.

Click Search. The Office Assistant will display a list of associated topics, as shown in Figure A.14.

FIGURE A.14

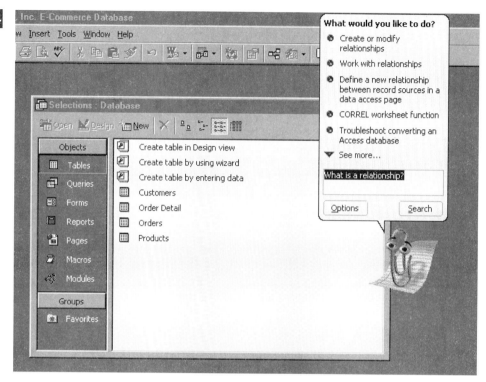

When you click a topic, it is displayed, as shown in Figure A.15, where the *Create or modify relationships* topic was selected from the list of topics.

FIGURE A.15

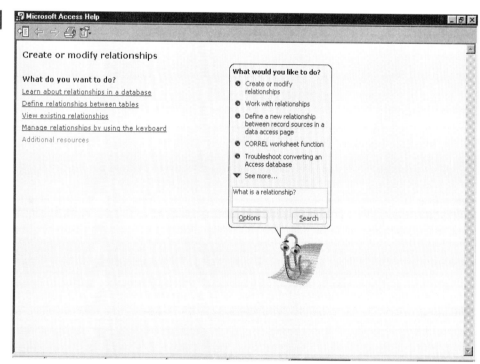

Specific topics that you click are displayed in a list, as shown in Figure A.16. As you click topics in the Office Assistant, the topic links you have visited will appear as purple text.

FIGURE A.16

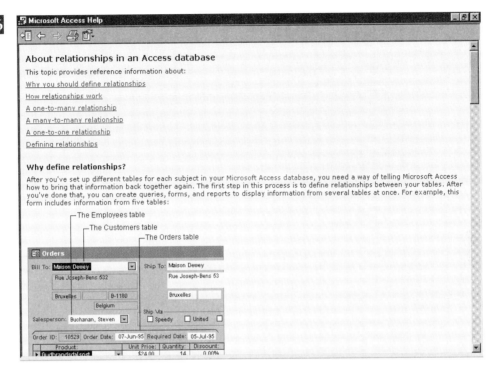

You can use the tools in the various Help Windows to navigate through Help. You can close any visible windows by clicking the window's Close button.

TIP For more information about using the Office Assistant, search for *Getting help in Microsoft Access*.

Access 2000 Function Reference Guide

Function	Mouse Action or Button	Menu	Keyboard Shortcut
Database, close	Click ✖	Choose File, Close	
Database, convert		Choose Tools, Database Utilities, Convert Database, and select the appropriate action	Press (ALT) + T, D, T
Database, create new	Click ▢	Choose File, New Database	Press (CTRL) + N
Database, open existing	Click ☞	Choose File, Open	Press (CTRL) + O
Display page of database window	Click the appropriate button	Choose View, Database Objects, and then choose desired database window page	Press (CTRL) + (TAB) until the database window page appears
Database Password, set		Close Tools, Security, Set Database Password	Press (ALT) + T, T, D
Database Window, hide or unhide		Close Window, Hide or Unhide	Press (ALT) + W, H or U
Exit Access 2000	Click ✖ in the application window	Choose File, Exit	Press (ALT) + F, X
Field, delete	Display table in Design view, click field row, and click ⇥	Display table in Design view, click field row, and choose Edit, Delete Rows	Display table in Design view, click field row, and press (DEL)
Field, insert	Display table in Design view, click field row where new field is desired, and click ⇥ᶜ	Display table in Design view, click field row where new field is desired, and choose Edit, Insert Row	
Field, sort	Select field in data sheet view and click ⬇ or ⬇	Select field in data sheet view (or Form) and choose Records, Sort, Sort Ascending or Sort Descending	

Function	Mouse Action or Button	Menu	Keyboard Shortcut
Filter, apply	Click 🔽	Choose Records, Apply Filter/Sort	Press ALT + R, F, F or S
Filter, remove		Choose Records, Remove Filter	Press ALT + R, R
Form, create new	Click 📇 Forms and click 📇 New	Choose Insert, Form	Press ALT + I, F
Form, design	Select form name in the database window and click Design OR open form and click ⬛▾	Open form and choose View, Design View	
Form, open	Select form name in the database window and click 📂 Open	Select form name in Forms page of database window and press ENTER	
Forms, display	Click 📇 Forms		
Help	Click ❓	Choose Help, Microsoft Access Help	Press F1
Macro, create new	Click 📄 Macros and then click 📄 New		
Open, (table, query, form, page)	Select the object name in the database window and click 📂 Open		
Page, display	Click 📄 Pages		
Page, create new	Click 📄 Pages and click 📄 New	Choose Insert, Page	Press ALT + I, P
Preview	Click 🔍	Choose File, Print Preview	Press ALT + F, V
Primary key, assign	Display table in Design view, click field, and click 🔑	Display table in Design view, select field, and choose Edit, Primary Key	
Print	Click 🖨	Choose File, Print	Press CTRL + P
Query, add fields	Double-click field name		

Function	Mouse Action or Button	Menu	Keyboard Shortcut
Query, add table	Click 🔲	Choose Query, Show Table	Press (ALT) + Q, T
Query, create new	Click 🔲 Queries and click 🔲 New	Choose Insert, Query	Press (ALT) + I, Q
Query, design	Select query name in the database window and click Design OR open query and click 📐▾	Open query and choose View, Design View	
Query, delete		Select the query and choose Edit, Delete	Select the query and press (DEL)
Query, open	Select query name in the database window and click open 🔲 Open		Select query in Forms page of database window and press (ENTER)
Query, run	In Query Design, click ❗	In Query Design, choose Query, Run	
Query, set criteria			Select Criteria row, type operator and symbol
Record, add data		Display Datasheet or Form view and type data into fields	
Record, delete	Click record selection bar or button, and click ✖	Select record and choose Edit, Delete Record	Select record and press (DEL)
Record, insert	Display table to contain record and click ▶✱	Open table to contain record and choose Insert, New Record	
Relationships, create or edit	Click the Relationships button 🔲 to open the Relationships Window	Choose Insert, Query	Press (ALT) + T, R
Report, create new	Click 🔲 Reports and click 🔲 New	Choose Insert, Report	
Reports, display	Click 🔲 Reports		

Function	Mouse Action or Button	Menu	Keyboard Shortcut
Report, design	Select report name in database window and click Design OR open report and click ⬔ ▾	Open report and choose View, Design View	
Report, open	Select report name in Reports page of database window and click 🗂Open		Select report name in Reports page of database window and press (ENTER)
Save	Click 🖫	Choose File, Save	Press (CTRL) + S
Send		Choose File, Send to	Press (ALT) + F, D
Spelling check	Click ✓	Choose Tools, Spelling	Press (F7)
Table or query filter by form	Open the table or query in Datasheet view and click 🔲	Choose Records, Filter, Filter By Form	Press (ALT) + R, F, F
Table or query filter by selection	Open the table or query in Datasheet view and click 🔲	Choose Records, Filter, Filter By Selection	Press (ALT) + R, F, S
Table, copy structure	Click table name in database window, click 🗈, click 🗈 and type new table name and select structure only	Click table name in database window, choose Edit, Copy, choose Edit, Paste and type new table name; select structure only	Click table name in database window, press (CTRL) + C, press (CTRL) + V and type new table name; select structure only
Table, create new	Click 🔲 Tables and click 🔲New	Select Table from the Insert menu	Press (ALT) + I, T
Table, design	Select table name in database window and click Design OR Open table and click ⬔ ▾	Open table and choose View, Design View	Open table and press (ALT) + V, D
Tables, display	Click 🔲 Tables		
Table, link		Choose File, Get External Data, Link Tables	Press (ALT) + F, G, L

Function	Mouse Action or Button	Menu	Keyboard Shortcut
Table, open	Select table name in Tables page of database window and click 🗒 Open		Select table name in Tables page of database window and press (ENTER)
Text, copy	Select the text and click 🗎	Select the text and choose Edit, Copy	Press (CTRL) + C
Text, cut	Select the text and click ✂	Select the text and choose Edit, Cut	Press (CTRL) + X
Text, find	Click 🔍	Choose Edit, Find	Press (CTRL) + F
Text, paste	Select the text and click 📋	Choose Edit, Paste	Press (CTRL) + V
Text, replace		Choose Edit, Replace	Press (CTRL) + H
Text, select	Drag through text		Press (SHIFT) + any cursor movement key, such as (→) or (END)
Toolbars, display or hide	Right-click toolbar and select the toolbar	Choose View, Toolbars and select the toolbar	Press (ALT) + V, T
Undo	Click ↩ ▾	Choose Edit, Undo	Press (CTRL) + Z
View, change	Click 📝 ▾ or 🖿 ▾	Choose View, Type View	

Glossary

A → B Symbolic notation representing a functional dependency.

Access menu bar The menu appearing at the top of the screen when Access is launched.

Access page See *Data access page*

Action query A query that makes changes to many records in just one operation.

AND condition A query expression using different criteria in the same criteria row of the Query Design grid. When Access uses the AND operator, only the records that meet the criteria in all the cells will be returned.

Application title bar The title bar for Microsoft Access that contains the Database window for an open database, and the window controls to minimize, maximize, restore, and close Access.

Ascending order A sort order in which records are arranged alphabetically from A to Z or numerically from smallest to largest.

ASCII (American Standard for Computer Information Interchange) text A format for storing computer data, consisting of the letters *A* to *Z*, the digits 0 to 9, and special characters. ASCII data can be shared among microcomputers using different operating systems.

Attribute One or more characteristics of any entity that distinguishes it from other entity instances. In an address database, last name is an example of an attribute of the addressee entity.

AutoForm A feature used to create forms with the fields and information stored as part of the table or query.

AutoNumber field A field set to automatically enter a sequential number as each record is added to the table.

AutoReport A feature used to create simple report formats by using the fields contained in a table or query.

Bound control A control that is tied to a field in an underlying table or query.

Boyce-Codd normal form (BCNF) A stage in database normalization where every determinant in a relation is a candidate key.

Calculated control A control that uses an expression as its source of data.

Calculated field A field in a query that contains an expression. When the results of a calculation in a field are displayed, the results aren't actually stored in the underlying table. In-

stead, Microsoft Access reruns the calculation each time the query is run so that the results are always based on the most current data in the database.

Candidate key One or more fields in a database that uniquely identify each record.

Cardinality The number of instances of one entity that may or must be associated with instances of a second entity.

Cascade Delete For relationships that enforce referential integrity between tables, cascade delete refers to an action that deletes all related records in the related table or tables when a record in the primary table is deleted.

Cascade Update For relationships that enforce referential integrity between tables, cascade update refers to an action that updates all related records in the related table or tables when a record in the primary table is changed.

Child table The table on the "many" side of a one-to-many relationship, or a main form/subform solution.

Class A category of objects used in an Access database. A specific table is an instance of an object from the table class.

Command button A Visual Basic control placed on a form to run a macro or a Visual Basic sub procedure.

Compound key A candidate key consisting of more than one attribute.

Conceptual data model A conceptual model that displays the overall structure of an organization's data flow and specific data requirements. A conceptual data model is developed independent of any RDBMS.

Control A specific object, such as a text box, that is added to a form or report.

Controls Objects on a form or report that display data, perform actions, or decorate the form or report.

ControlTip A helpful tip that pops up over controls when the mouse pointer moves over a control.

Criteria Conditions set in a query to limit the information displayed in the datasheet.

Criteria expression A text string that defines the prompt that will appear in the text box when a parameter query is run.

Currency A data type useful for calculations involving money and for fixed-point calculations in which accuracy is particularly important.

Data Raw, unevaluated facts and figures that have not been interpreted in any meaningful way for a specific purpose.

Data access page A database object used for creating a special type of Web page for viewing and working with data stored in a Microsoft Access database or Microsoft SQL Server database from an Internet or intranet.

Data control A Visual Basic control that binds other controls on a form to an Access record set.

Data dictionary A document listing the entities and attributes that define the structure of tables in a database.

Data type The characteristic of a field or a variable that determines what kind of data it holds.

Data validation Methods for controlling how data is entered into a database. Validation rules and input masks are two useful methods for data validation.

Database A collection of information related to a particular subject, or organized for a specific purpose.

Database design process A systematic approach to designing a database that includes planning, analysis, design, implementation, and maintenance phases.

Database Management System (DBMS) A computer application used to create and maintain databases.

Database object The tables, queries, forms, pages, reports, macros, or modules that comprise an Access database.

Database password A password assigned in Access that must be entered correctly before a user can open the database.

Database window The database interface in Access that provides a listing of tables, queries, forms, reports, macros, and modules.

Datasheet view The view for a table, query, or form in which a user can see multiple records on-screen at the same time; this view makes data entry more efficient.

Date/time A data type that contains date and time values for the years 100 through 9999.

Delimited text ASCII text listing database fields where each field is bound by one or more characters that differentiate it from other fields.

Delimiting character (delimiter) The character that delimits, or differentiates, fields in a delimited file.

Design time The mode in Visual Basic used to design a user interface and develop sub procedures.

Descending order A sort order in which records are arranged alphabetically from Z to A or numerically from largest to smallest.

Design modifications Any enhancements made to a database object.

Design view A view of a table, query, form, or report object that can modify the object's properties.

Detail section The part of a form or report that holds the field data controls and pulls information from database tables.

Determinant The attribute in a functional dependency that uniquely identifies a second attribute.

Display control The specific database control that appears in a table's field for selecting a lookup value when a lookup list is defined.

Dynamic resource A Web resource that is bound to a database and therefore is updated automatically when the database changes.

Edit To change the field information contained in a record.

Enterprise data model A high-level conceptual model listing an organization's entities and the relationships that exist between them.

Entity A person, place, thing, or event about which an organization collects and keeps data.

Entity-Relationship (E-R) Diagram A diagram displaying entities, attributes, and relationships. E-R diagrams usually include notations indicating the cardinality of relationships.

Event A user, system, or error response that triggers a specific change in a program. An example of a user event is a click of the mouse.

Event-driven A programming environment where specific program routines are run in response to specific events.

Expression A combination of symbols—identifiers, operators, and values—that produces a result.

Expression Builder A graphical workspace for designing expressions for a specific control object or control.

Field Represents a column of data with a common data type and a common set of properties.

Field properties An attribute of a field that defines one of its characteristics. An example is the size property of a text field.

First normal form (1NF) A stage in database normalization in which all multi-valued attributes or repeating groups have been eliminated from a table.

Filter To select only those records in a table that contains the same value in the selected field.

Filter-by-form A technique for filtering data that uses a version of the current form or datasheet with empty fields in which the user enters the criteria in the appropriate fields.

Filter-by-selection A technique for filtering data that's based on data selected in a form, datasheet, or data access page. In a form or datasheet, the user filters for all or part of a value selected. In a data access page, the user can only filter for the entire value in the field.

Find A feature available using the Find dialog box to locate one or more records displayed in a table or form.

Find and replace A technique for locating and replacing all instances of a specified value, either all at once, or verifying each occurrence one at a time.

Form An Access database object used to display data from tables or queries in an aesthetically-pleasing format.

Form view The view for a form that displays the underlying recordset.

Front end An application written in a programming environment, such as Visual Basic, that provides the user interface for a database.

Full functional dependency A dependency where attribute B is completely determined by attribute A.

Grouped data access page A data access page where records are grouped hierarchically based upon a one-to-many relationship.

Groups bar A button on the Database Objects bar to store the names of your groups, which can contain shortcuts to database objects of different types.

Hyperlink Underlined text or graphic used to jump to a location on the Internet or on an intranet, to an object in your database or in another database, or to a document on your computer or on another computer connected by a network.

Hyperlink data type A data type in Access that displays a URL for a file resource formatted as a functioning hyperlink.

Image control A control used to display pictures in an object, such as a form or report.

Information Data that has been interpreted to be meaningful in a given context.

Inner join The default join in Access where a query returns records from associated tables only if the join field is equal in both tables.

Input mask A field property that displays literal display characters in the field with blanks to fill in.

InputMask property The property of a field in a table or query that provides a template consisting of characters to assist with data entry.

Instance A unique database record for a given entity.

Jet database engine That part of the Microsoft Access database system that retrieves data from and stores data in user and system databases. The Microsoft Jet database engine can be thought of as a data manager upon which database systems, such as Microsoft Access, are built.

Join An association between a field in one table or query and a field of the same data type in another table or query. A join tells Microsoft Access how data is related. Access enables a user to create inner joins, outer joins, and self-joins.

Junction table The table in a many-to-many relationship that includes the primary key fields from each of the other two tables to this table.

Label control An unbound control used to display descriptive text such as titles, captions, or brief instructions on a form or report.

Linking The process of attaching an Access table object to an external data source.

Literal expression A literal value and expression, such as >400, that determines which records a query recordset will display.

Lookup field A field that displays a list of data that either looks up data from an existing table or query, or from a list that stores a fixed set of values that won't change.

Macro A set of one or more actions, each performing a particular operation, such as opening a form or printing a report. Macros can automate common tasks.

Macro Builder The tool in Microsoft Access for creating and editing macros.

Main form In a main form/subform solution, the form that displays records on the "one" side of a one-to-many relationship.

Mandatory cardinality A circumstance in which a record that exists in one table must also exist in a related table. For example, in an Orders database, each order record must have a corresponding customer record.

Memo A data type used to store random entries exceeding 255 characters.

Many-to-many relationship An association between two tables in which one record in either table can relate to many records in the other table.

Method In Visual Basic, the predefined actions provided with objects.

Microsoft Graph 2000 A Microsoft Office 2000 application for creating charts in any application in the Office Suite.

Migrate data The process of moving data from the old system to the new system when implementing a new database system.

Module A collection of Visual Basic programming procedures stored together to customize the Access environment.

Navigate To move from one record to another in a table or form.

Normal Form The stages of normalization in Codd's process. As normalization progresses, the database is said to be in a specific normal form, or state of normalization.

Normalization The process of converting complex data structures into simple data structures. In Access, normalization is accomplished by splitting data into multiple tables that are related.

Null value A value that indicates missing or unknown data in a field.

Numeric (number) Data type used to hold numeric data used in mathematical calculations.

Object A table, query, form, page, report, macro, or module in a database.

Object bar A vertical toolbar that contains buttons for viewing the specific database objects in the current database.

Object shortcut Shortcuts in the Database window for creating new objects using Design view, or using a wizard.

Office Assistant The interactive help feature that appears on-screen to offer help on the task a user is performing.

OLE Object Linking and Embedding, a way of automating how information is shared among applications.

One-to-many relationship In a database, a relationship between tables where each record in Table A can have many matching records in Table B, but a record in Table B has only one matching record in Table A.

One-to-one relationship In a database, a relationship between tables where each record in Table A can have only one matching record in Table B, and each record in Table B can have only one matching record in Table A.

Optional cardinality A cardinality where a record is not required in both tables when the two tables are related.

Online help Software specific help accessible from the computer.

OR condition A query result where the records returned meet any of the conditions specified.

Page footer Section at the bottom of a form that contains information pertaining to a form, such as date or file name.

Page header Section at the top of a form that contains information pertaining to a form, such as date or file name.

Parameter query A query that when run displays its own dialog box prompting the user for information, such as criteria for retrieving records or a value inserted in a field.

Parent table The table on the "one" side of the relationship in a one-to-many relationship or a main form sub form solution.

Partial functional dependency Occurs when one or more non-key attributes are not fully functionally dependent upon the entire primary key.

Performance Analyzer An Access add-in that analyzes the optimization of a database and provides recommendations for improvement.

Primary key A field or set of fields that uniquely identifies each record stored in the table.

Property An attribute of an object that defines one of the object's characteristics, such as size, color, or screen location, or an aspect of its behavior, such as whether it is enabled or visible.

Query Used to view, change, and analyze data in different ways; the source of records for forms and reports.

Query datasheet A window that displays the results of a query in a row and column format.

Query design grid The lower pane displayed in the query design window containing columns that defines the fields of data the query displays when the query is run.

Query Design view A view where queries are created or modified.

Record A collection of related field data stored in a table, such as a person's name and address.

Record source A table or query that contains the records the form displays.

Referential integrity Rules to preserve the defined relationships between tables when records are entered or deleted. To enforce referential integrity, Microsoft Access prevents users from adding records to a related table when there is no associated record in the primary table, changing values in the primary table that would result in orphan records in a related table, and deleting records from the primary table when there are matching related records in a related table.

Relation A database table that has been normalized to Codd's First Normal forms (1NF).

Relational database management system (RDBMS) A database management system (DBMS) specifically designed to utilize the relational database model.

Relationships window A window containing a graphical workspace for establishing relationships between tables.

Replace An option available in the Find dialog box to replace field values.

Report An organized format for summarizing and grouping database data to provide meaningful information in a printed format.

Report Design window A graphical workspace displaying the report's bound and unbound controls.

Report footer A report section for specifying necessary information at the bottom of an Access report.

Report header A report section for specifying necessary information at the top of an Access report.

Row source The underlying database object that contains the data a user wants to look up when adding a lookup list to a table.

Run The action of applying query specifications to a table to display specific field and record information.

Run time The Visual Basic mode when an application is running.

Second normal form (2NF) A relation that is in the First Normal form (1NF) and also contains no partial dependencies.

Select query A query that returns record information in a query datasheet without changing the underlying data.

Simple key A candidate or primary key based upon a single attribute.

Sort The action of displaying records in ascending or descending order.

Sort criteria Criteria added to a query or report specifying how the records will be ordered.

Stand-alone application A database front end that is bound to an Access table or query, but that can be run independent of Microsoft Access.

Static resource A Web resource not linked to an Access database, and represents a snapshot of the database at a particular point in time.

Sub procedure A Visual Basic procedure that responds to a specific event and executes a predefined sequence of operations.

Subform A form added to a main form that displays related records on the "many" side of a one-to-many relationship.

Subform/subreport control A control in Access for displaying a subform on a main form or a report.

Switchboard An Access form that is displayed when the database is opened, and contains command buttons or other controls for opening the various parts of the database.

Table The primary object of a database that stores field names, field descriptions, and field data. Tables display multiple records in a row/column format similar to a spreadsheet layout.

Table Datasheet view A table view that displays multiple records on the screen in a row and column format.

Table Design view The view used to create or modify the structure of a table.

Table Design window A window displaying the table design grid.

Table Design Wizard An Access Wizard used for creating tables.

Table structure The field names, data types, and properties defining the physical arrangement of a table.

Text Text, including letters and keyboard symbols, or combinations of text and numbers, as well as numbers that don't require calculations, such as phone numbers.

Textbox control A bound control used primarily on a form to modify or add field data to an underlying field.

Third normal form (3NF) A relation that is in both the 1NF and 2NF and also contains no transitive dependencies.

Transitive dependency A functional dependency existing between two or more non-key attributes.

Unbound control A control on a form or report that is not bound to a specific field.

Update To change the field data contained in a record.

Update anomalies Errors that occur in a database when records are updated.

Update query An action query that makes global changes to a group of records in one or more tables.

Validation rule A property used to specify requirements for data entered into a record, field, or control.

Validation text A property used to specify the message to be displayed to the user when a validation rule is violated.

ValidationRule property A property specifying the requirements for data entered into a record, field, or control.

ValidationText property A property specifying the message to be displayed to the user when a ValidationRule property is violated.

Visual Basic Editor The interface in Visual Basic for Applications for creating procedures and sub procedures.

Visual Basic for Applications (VBA) A subset of the Visual Basic programming environment used to customize Microsoft Access.

Visual Basic window The window in the Visual Basic Editor that displays the code for Visual Basic procedures.

Wizard A step-by-step assistant that helps the user design specific database objects.

Yes/No Yes and No values and fields that contain only one of two values (Yes/No, True/False, or On/Off).

Index